W9-CJP-486

JavaServer® Faces 2.0: Essential Guide for Developers

Deepak Vohra

Cengage Learning PTR

CENGAGE
Learning·

Professional • Technical • Reference

Australia • Brazil • Japan • Korea • Mexico • Singapore • Spain • United Kingdom • United States

CENGAGE
Learning·

Professional · Technical · Reference

JavaServer® Faces 2.0: Essential Guide for Developers
Deepak Vohra

Publisher and General Manager, Cengage Learning PTR: Stacy L. Hiquet

Associate Director of Marketing: Sarah Panella

Manager of Editorial Services: Heather Talbot

Senior Marketing Manager: Mark Hughes

Project Manager: Heather Hurley

Project Editor: Kate Shoup

Technical Reviewer: John Yeary

Copy Editor: Kate Shoup

Interior Layout Tech: MPS Limited

Cover Designer: Luke Fletcher

Indexer: Larry Sweazy

Proofreader: Sam Garvey

For product information and technology assistance, contact us at **Cengage Learning Customer & Sales Support, 1-800-354-9706.**

For permission to use material from this text or product, submit all requests online at **cengage.com/permissions**.

Further permissions questions can be emailed to **permissionrequest@cengage.com**.

Library of Congress Control Number: 2014939194

ISBN-13: 978-1-305-27618-5

ISBN-10: 1-305-27618-3

Cengage Learning PTR
20 Channel Center Street
Boston, MA 02210
USA

Cengage Learning is a leading provider of customized learning solutions with office locations around the globe, including Singapore, the United Kingdom, Australia, Mexico, Brazil, and Japan. Locate your local office at: **international.cengage.com/region**.

Cengage Learning products are represented in Canada by Nelson Education, Ltd.

For your lifelong learning solutions, visit **cengageptr.com**.

Visit our corporate website at **cengage.com**.

Printed in the United States of America
1 2 3 4 5 6 7 16 15 14

About the Author

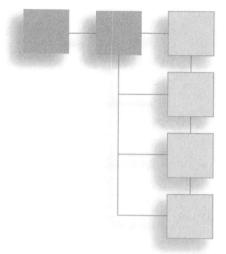

Deepak Vohra is a consultant and a principal member of the NuBean.com software company. Deepak is a Sun Certified Java Programmer and Web Component Developer, and has worked in the fields of XML, Java programming, and Java EE for more than five years. Deepak is the co-author of the Apress book *Pro XML Development with Java Technology* and was the technical reviewer for the O'Reilly book *WebLogic: The Definitive Guide*. Deepak was also the technical reviewer for the Course Technology PTR book *Ruby Programming for the Absolute Beginner*. Deepak is the author of the Packt Publishing books *JDBC 4.0 and Oracle JDeveloper for J2EE Development, Processing XML Documents with Oracle JDeveloper 11g, EJB 3.0 Database Persistence with Oracle Fusion Middleware 11g,* and *Java EE Development with Eclipse*.

CONTENTS

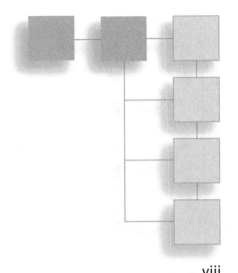

Introduction viii

Chapter 1   **What's New in JSF 2.0** 1

State Saving 2

Facelets 3

Navigation 4

Validation 4

Scopes and Configuration 5

Ajax 5

Resource Handling 5

Composite Components 6

View Parameters 6

Client Behaviors 6

Event Handling and Exception Handling 6

Summary 6

Chapter 2   **Templating with Facelets** 7

Overview of Facelets 8

Setting the Environment 9

Configuring the Integrated WebLogic Server 11

Creating a Facelets Project 15

Creating a Managed Bean 22

Creating a Facelets Template 27

Developing Facelets Composition Pages 30
Creating Navigation 34
Deploying the Facelets Application 34
Running the Facelets Application 44
Summary 46

Chapter 3   **Ajax** **47**
Setting the Environment 47
Creating a Facelets Application 49
Creating a Managed Bean 53
Creating a JSF Page 58
Adding Ajax 60
Deploying and Running the JSF 2.0 Ajax Application 67
Partial Page Rendering: Rendering 73
Grouping Components 76
Summary 82

Chapter 4   **Creating Composite Components** **83**
Setting the Environment 84
Creating a Java EE Web Application 85
Creating a Using Page 86
Creating a Managed Bean 89
Creating Composite Components 94
Running the Composite Components Application 102
Binding Composite Components to Unique Managed Bean Properties 107
Summary 114

Chapter 5   **Enhanced Navigation** **115**
Setting the Environment 115
Creating a Java EE Web Application 116
Implicit Navigation 126
Conditional Navigation 131
Preemptive Navigation and ConfigurableNavigationHandler 140
Summary 150

Chapter 6   **Enhanced Validations** **151**
Setting the Environment 151
Creating a Java EE Application 152
Validation Constraint Annotations 164
New Validators 174
Bean Validation Integration 177

Custom Validators and Null and Empty Values 181
Custom Validators with Bean Validation 185
Summary 191

Chapter 7   View Parameters **193**
Setting the Environment 194
Creating a Java EE Web Application 195
POST Request Parameters in JSF 1.2 205
View Parameters in JSF 2.0 206
Adding Validation with View Parameters 210
PreRenderView Event Handling 214
Preemptive Navigation and Bookmarking 216
Component Parameters with View Parameters 221
View Parameters in Redirects 223
    Redirecting Without View Parameters 225
    Redirecting with View Parameters 226
    Redirecting with View Parameters in <redirect> and from f:viewParam 229
    Overriding View Parameters in f:viewParam 232
Summary 234

Chapter 8   Client Behaviors **235**
Overview of the Behavior API 236
Setting the Environment 238
Creating a Java EE Web Application 239
Creating a Facelets Taglib 249
Configuring the Client Behavior 253
Using a Client Behavior 259
Testing Client Behaviors 262
Summary 264

Chapter 9   Scopes **265**
Overview of Scopes 265
The View Scope 265
    The Flash Scope 266
    The Custom Scope 267
Overview of Simplified Configuration 267
Setting the Environment 269
Creating a Java EE Web Application 270
Simplified Configuration 284
Same View with View Scope 288

Redirecting with Flash Scope 290

Creating a Custom Scoped Managed Bean 294

Summary 301

Chapter 10   **Resource Handling** **303**

Overview of the Resource Handler API 303

Setting the Environment 305

Creating a Java EE Web Application 306

Packaging and Rendering Resources 312

Relocating Resources 323

Ordering of Application Configuration Resources 325

Summary 337

Chapter 11   **Event Handling and Exception Handling** **339**

System Events 339

Setting the Environment 344

Creating a Java EE Web Application 345

Registering an Application-Scoped System Event Listener 356

Registering a Component System Event Listener 365

Declaratively Registering a ComponentSystemEventListener

with the f:event Tag 370

Registering a System Event Listener with the @ListenerFor Annotation 372

Creating an Event Handler for an Ajax Request 375

Creating a Custom Exception Handler 384

Error Handler for an Ajax Request 395

Commented Out JSF 397

Summary 398

Index **399**

INTRODUCTION

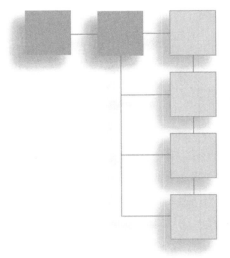

JavaServer® Faces (JSF) is a Java® specification for developing component-based user interfaces for Java EE applications. JSF establishes the standard for building server-side user interfaces. JSF is one of the most commonly used Web frameworks, if not *the* most commonly used. According to a Developer Productivity Report 2012 (http://zeroturn-around.com/rebellabs/developer-productivity-report-2012-java-tools-tech-devs-and-data/), JSF is ranked second of 10 Web frameworks. This book is based on the latest major version, JSF 2.0. One of the main differences from the previous version is that Facelets is the default view definition language in JSF 2.0 instead of JSP.

JSF 2.0 has introduced several new features. These include the following:

- New scopes
- Simplified, annotation-based configuration
- State saving
- Enhanced exception handling
- Enhanced resource handling
- New system events
- Facelets
- Ajax
- Composite components

- Enhanced navigation
- Enhanced validation
- View parameters for GET requests
- Client behaviors

This book discusses the JSF 2.0 new features with examples in Oracle® JDeveloper and the integrated Oracle® WebLogic Server.

The objective of the book is to discuss how a Java EE developer would develop Web applications with JSF 2.0. The book covers all aspects of application development including the following:

- Setting up the environment for an application
- Using the JDeveloper wizards and the Component palette
- Running a sample application

WHAT THIS BOOK COVERS

Chapter 1, "What's New in JSF 2.0," introduces the new features in JSF 2.0 and how they differ from the previous version.

Chapter 2, "Templating with Facelets," discusses Facelets, the default view definition language (VDL) in JSF 2.0. We demonstrate templating with Facelets in a Web application developed in JDeveloper and run on the integrated WebLogic Server. The integrated WebLogic server configuration will be used in subsequent chapters also.

Chapter 3, "Ajax," discusses support for Ajax with the f:ajax tag in the JSF 2.0 component library. It also discusses partial page rendering and grouping of components.

Chapter 4, "Creating Composite Components," introduces composite components. A *composite component* is a composite (integration) of a collection of UI components and simplifies adding reusable collections of components. For example, if an application makes use of the same header, JSF data table, input text field, and Submit command button in several JSF pages, you can create a single composite component from the group of components and add it to a JSF page as a single component.

Chapter 5, "Enhanced Navigation," discusses the enhanced navigation provided by JSF 2.0 with implicit navigation, conditional navigation, and preemptive navigation.

Chapter 6, "Enhanced Validations," discusses the support for enhanced validation in JSF 2.0. It discusses the annotations for validation constraints, the new validators `f:validateRequired` and `f:validateRegex`, integration with bean validation, and support for validation of empty fields.

Chapter 7, "View Parameters," discusses the support for request parameters in a `GET` request with view parameters. It introduces preemptive navigation and bookmarkability of JSF pages made feasible by view parameters. We also discuss how view parameters are used in combination with component parameters and redirection.

Chapter 8, "Client Behaviors," discusses client behaviors. In this chapter, you will develop a Web application in JDeveloper with the integrated WebLogic Server to demonstrate client behaviors.

Chapter 9, "Scopes," discusses the new scopes introduced in JSF 2.0: the view scope, the flash scope, and the custom scope. It also discusses the configuration simplification with annotations. It demonstrates using the new scopes with a Web application.

Chapter 10, "Resource Handling," introduces the new resource-handling feature in JSF 2.0. It discusses how resources such as CSS stylesheets and images are packaged and rendered. It also discusses the ordering of application configuration resources.

Chapter 11, "Event Handling and Exception Handling," discusses the new event-handling and exception-handling features in JSF 2.0. It discusses the support for system events, event handling in `f:ajax`, and custom exception handlers.

WHAT YOU NEED FOR THIS BOOK

You can use JSF 2.0 with any Web server or application server that supports JSF 2.0. In this book, you will use Oracle JDeveloper 12c with the integrated Oracle WebLogic Server 12c, which you can download from www.oracle.com/technetwork/developer-tools/jdev/downloads/index.html. Most of the sample Web applications are database based; for those, you will use Oracle® Database 11g Express Edition, which you can download from www.oracle.com/technetwork/database/database-technologies/express-edition/overview/index.html. For this book, we used the Windows OS, but if you have Linux installed, the book will still prove useful (although the source code and samples have not been tested with Linux). Slight modifications may be required with the Linux install, however—for example, the directory paths on Linux would be different from the Windows directory paths used in the book. Regardless of the OS, you also need to install Java SE 5 or later; Java SE 7 is used in the book.

WHO IS THIS BOOK FOR?

The target audience of the book is Java EE application developers who want to learn about the new features in JSF 2.0. This book is suitable for professional Java EE developers as well as beginners. The book is also suitable for an intermediate/advanced-level course in JSF 2.0. The target audience is expected to have prior, albeit beginner's, knowledge about JavaServer Faces (JSF) and other Web technologies such as Ajax. The book also requires some familiarity with Oracle JDeveloper, Oracle WebLogic Server, and Oracle Database.

COPYRIGHT CREDIT

Some of the content of this book was originally published by Oracle® Technology Network and is republished with permission from Oracle Corporation.

COMPANION WEBSITE DOWNLOADS

You can download the companion files for this book from www.cengageptr.com/downloads.

CHAPTER 1

WHAT'S NEW IN JSF 2.0

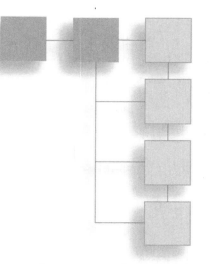

JavaServer Faces (JSF) technology is used for developing server-side user interfaces (UIs) for Java EE applications. JSF 2.0 has introduced several new features, most of which are discussed in this chapter. The salient new features in JSF 2.0 are as follows:

- State saving
- Facelets
- Navigation
- Validations
- Scopes
- Ajax
- Resource handling
- Composite components
- View parameters
- Client behaviors
- Event handling
- Exception handling

STATE SAVING

In JSF 1.2, the full component tree is saved/restored. Attributes are also stored and restored. Saving and restoring the full state has performance and memory ramifications, as the complete state must be saved and restored and the size of the state saved could be large.

In JSF 1.2, each `UIComponent` saves/restores its own state in the component hierarchy using `saveState` and `resoreState` methods in `StateHolder`. If state saving were to be optimized, it would have to be added to each component class in the hierarchy.

JSF 2.0 has introduced partial state saving, in which the initial state of the component tree is marked and only the delta state changes due to modifications are saved. This makes the size of the state saved small. You restore the component tree by re-executing the view and subsequently updating with the saved delta state change. Instead of implementing the `StateHolder` interface, components in JSF 2.0 implement the `PartialStateHolder` interface, which provides the partial state feature. `PartialStateHolder` provides the methods listed in Table 1.1.

Table 1.1 Methods in PartialStateHolder interface

Method	Description
markInitialState()	Invoked to mark the initial state of a component in the view by the runtime.
initialStateMarked()	Returns a Boolean to indicate if delta state changes are being tracked. Returns `true` if delta changes are being marked and `false` otherwise.
clearInitialState()	Clears the initial state to reset to a non-delta tracking state.

To make it easier for `UIComponent`s to implement `PartialSatetHolder`, the `StateHelper`—which is a map-like interface with methods such as `add`, `eval`, `get`, `put`, and `remove`—is provided to store a component's state such as attributes and listeners. Partial state saving makes the size of the state saved about four times smaller. Because you restore the state by re-executing the view, restoring of the component tree could take more time than in JSF 1.2.

By default, JSF 2.0 uses partial state saving. The `javax.faces.PARTIAL_STATE_SAVING` context parameter is provided to turn off/on partial state saving. You can change the partial state saving parameter using the `PARTIAL_STATE_SAVING_PARAM_NAME` parameter.

To implement state saving, JSF 2.0 has introduced tree visiting. In JSF 1.2, only one component could be invoked in a single tree traversal using the `UIComponent.invokeOnComponent()` method. If multiple components must be invoked, as in an Ajax request or state saving, then multiple tree traversals must be applied. With tree visiting, you can invoke multiple components in a single tree traversal. You implement tree visiting using the `visitTree(VisitContext context,VisitCallback callback)` method. `VisitContext` is a context object that holds the state for the component tree visit. `VisitCallback` is an interface to visit a specified `UIComponent` in a tree visit.

FACELETS

JSF 1.2 used the JSP view technology. JSF 2.0 uses the Facelets view definition language (VDL) as the default view rendering technology. Facelets is an extension to JavaServer Faces (JSF) and uses XHTML syntax to define a JSF page. Facelets are XHTML pages and by default use the .xhtml extension. The default Facelets suffix is specified by the `DEFAULT_FACELETS_SUFFIX` context parameter. The Facelets view handler in JSF 1.2 must be specified in `faces-config.xml` with the following configuration:

```
<application>
<view-handler>com.sun.facelets.FaceletViewHandler</view-handler>
</application>
</faces-config>
```

In JSF 2.0, a view handler is not configured, and the default view handler `javax.faces.application.ViewHandler` is used. The default `faces-config.xml` for Facelets in JSF 2.0 is an empty file. The default value of the `DEFAULT_FACELETS_SUFFIX` constant in the `ViewHandler` view handler is .xhtml. Other Facelets suffixes may be specified using the `javax.faces.FACELETS_VIEW_MAPPINGS` context parameter.

```
<context-param>
<param-name>javax.faces.FACELETS_VIEW_MAPPINGS</param-name>
<param-value>.jsf;.jspx</param-value>
</context-param>
```

NAVIGATION

Navigation in JSF 1.2 is configured using navigation rules based on outcomes from a view ID in `faces-config.xml`. For example, to navigate to `output.jsp` if the outcome from `input.jsp` is "success" and to navigate to `error.jsp` if the outcome is "error," specify the following navigation rule in `faces-config.xml`:

```
<navigation-rule>
    <from-view-id>/input.jsp</from-view-id>
    <navigation-case>
      <from-outcome>success</from-outcome>
      <to-view-id>/output.jsp</to-view-id>
    </navigation-case>
    <navigation-case>
      <from-outcome>error</from-outcome>
      <to-view-id>/error.jsp</to-view-id>
    </navigation-case>
  </navigation-rule>
```

JSF 2.0 has simplified navigation with the introduction of implicit navigation. With implicit navigation, the navigation is based on the outcome. Implicitly, the JSF application navigates to a view ID with the same name as the outcome. For example, if the outcome is "output," the navigation handler navigates to `output.xhtml`, if provided.

JSF 2.0 has also introduced conditional navigation, with which the navigation handler navigates to a view ID based on a condition EL expression specified in `faces-config.xml`. JSF 2.0 has also introduced the `ConfigurableNavigationHandler` class for configuring navigation programmatically. Preemptive navigation is another new feature used to determine the destination URL based on outcome. The new components `h:button` and `h:link` support preemptive navigation.

VALIDATION

In JSF 1.2, validation is implemented using built-in validators:

- **`f:validateDoubleRange`.** This is for a `double` value with an optional range.
- **`f:validateLongRange`.** This is a `long` value with an optional range.
- **`f:validateLength`.** This is a `String` value with a minimum and maximum number of characters.

JSF 1.2 also supports custom validators with the `f:validator` tag and the `javax.faces.validator.Validator` interface. JSF 1.2 does not have a built-in provision for empty field validation and validation with regular expressions.

JSF 2.0 has introduced validation of empty fields, which is also available for custom validators. Three new built-in validators have been added:

- `f:validateRegex`. This is for regular expressions.
- `f:validateRequired`. This is for required fields.
- `f:validateBean`. This is for Bean Validation, which is another new feature. Bean Validation is implemented in conjunction with validation constraint annotations, which are defined in the `javax.validation.constraints` package. Validation constraint annotations annotate managed bean properties. For example, the `@Size` annotation constrains size and the `@Pattern` requires conformance with a regular expression. Bean Validation is also supported with annotation custom validators.

SCOPES AND CONFIGURATION

As mentioned, the `faces-config.xml` in JSF 2.0 is an empty file. The JSF 1.2 `faces-config.xml` file has configuration for managed beans, managed bean properties, scopes, validators, converters, and renderers. JSF 2.0 has introduced annotations-based configuration for managed beans, managed bean properties, scopes, validators, converters, and renderers. New scopes—view, flash, and custom—have been added for finer-grained scopes. JSF 2.0 has added a new configuration project stage that indicates the state of a project.

AJAX

JSF 1.2 did not provide built-in support for Ajax. As a result, an Ajax framework such as Ajax4jsf had to be used. Alternatively, you had to implement Ajax via the `XMLHttpRequest` object without any framework. JSF 2.0 has added support for Ajax with the `f:ajax` tag, which includes support for partial page rendering and grouped components.

RESOURCE HANDLING

Resources are files required by a JSF application. Resources might include CSS, JavaScript, or image files. JSF 2.0 has added a `ResourceHandler` API that is based on path-based packaging conventions for serving resources. JSF 2.0 has also added new tags for resource handling: `h:head`, `h:body`, `h:outputScript`, and `h:ouputStylesheet`. Some of the other new resource-handling features include relocating resources and ordering of multiple `faces-config.xml` application configuration resources.

Composite Components

JSF 2.0 has introduced a composite component tag library for creating composite components. A *composite component* is a composite (collection) of other UI components. A composite component consists of a library, which makes use of the new resource-handling feature; a definition page; and a using page. The definition page and using page are based on Facelets. A definition page defines a composite component and a using page makes use of a composite component.

View Parameters

JSF 1.2 includes support for sending parameters only in a POST request. View parameters add the provision to send request parameters in a GET request. View parameters are configured in the f:metadata tag using the f:viewParam tags. View parameters are EditableValueHolder components and may be configured with validators and converters just as other EditableValueHolder components such as h:inputText. View parameters also support component system events using the f:event tag. Preemptive navigation, which was mentioned in the "Navigation" section, and bookmarking are made feasible with view parameters. View parameters may also be used with JavaServer Faces redirects.

Client Behaviors

Client behaviors are scripts that respond to user interaction (events) and may perform an action on the client or trigger a postback response to the JSF lifecycle. Behaviors are objects attached to components to provide additional functionality. Client behaviors are an implementation of behaviors with which scripts may be attached with components to be run from client-side events. A Facelet taglib is required for a client behavior. Client behaviors are added to a Facelets page using tags from the Facelets taglib.

Event Handling and Exception Handling

JSF 2.0 has introduced a new type of events, called system events. System events are of two types: application scoped system events and component system events. System events are similar to—but with more precise granularity than—phase events. For event handling in an Ajax request, the f:ajax tag includes an onevent attribute to register a callback JavaScript function. ExceptionHandler is a new class to handle unexpected exceptions. The f:ajax tag includes an onerror attribute for error-handling callback functions.

Summary

This chapter introduced the new features in JSF 2.0. Subsequent chapters will discuss these new features in more detail.

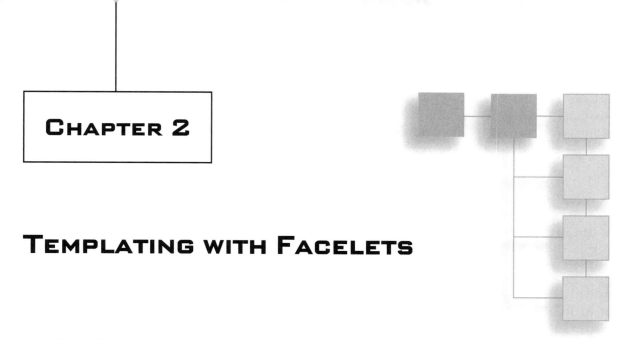

CHAPTER 2

TEMPLATING WITH FACELETS

In JSF 2.0, Facelets is the default View Declaration Language (VDL) instead of JSP. As a result, you don't need to configure a view handler as you did in JSF 1.2. Facelets is a Java-Server Faces–centric view technology.

Facelets is based on compositions. A composition defines a JSF user interface (UI) component structure in a Facelets page. A Facelets application may consist of compositions defined in different Facelets pages and run as an application.

Facelets is a templating framework similar to Tiles. The advantage of Facelets over Tiles is that JSF UIComponents are pre-integrated with Facelets, and Facelets does not require a Facelets configuration file as Tiles does a Tiles configuration file.

JSF validators and converters may be added to Facelets. Facelets provides a complete expression language and JavaServer Pages Standard Tag Library (JSTL) support. Templating, reuse, and ease of development are some of the advantages of using Facelets in a Web application.

In this chapter, you will develop a Facelets Web application in Oracle JDeveloper 12c and deploy the application to Oracle WebLogic Server 12c. In the Facelets application, you will add an input text UIComponent to an input Facelets page. With JSF navigation, the input Facelets page navigates to another Facelets page, which displays the JSF data table generated from the SQL query specified in the input Facelets page. You will use Oracle Database 11g XE as the data source. Templating is demonstrated by including graphics for the header and the footer in the input and the output; the graphics have to be specified only once in the template.

OVERVIEW OF FACELETS

Before you develop the application, let's review the Facelets technology. Facelets provide a set of XML tags in the http://java.sun.com/jsf/facelets namespace. Facelets tags are used with JSF Core and JSF HTML tag libraries to develop a JSF Facelets application. Some of the Facelets tags are discussed in Table 2.1.

Table 2.1 Facelets Tags

Facelets Tag	Description	Attributes
ui:composition	Defines a composition of UIComponents. A composition may consist of multiple UIComponents. Text not within ui:composition tags is not compiled in a Facelets page.	template: This optional attribute specifies the template to use for adding UIComponents within a composition.
ui:define	Used in a Facelets page in conjunction with target template's ui:insert tags to add UIComponents within a composition.	name: This required attribute matches with the name attribute in ui:insert.
ui:decorate	Similar to ui:composition except that text not within the ui:decorate tags is also included in the Facelets page.	template: This required attribute specifies the template to be used for adding UIComponents in ui:decorate tags.
ui:component	Similar to ui:composition except that ui:component adds a new UIComponent as the root component in the UIComponents structure.	id: If id is not specified, Facelets assign an ID. binding: Binds a UIComponent to a property of a JavaBean.
ui:fragment	A non-trimming tag for ui:component, similar to ui:decorate for ui:composition.	id, binding
ui:include	Includes a Facelets page, which defines a composition or a component in a Facelets page or the template page.	src: This required attribute specifies the target Facelet to include with an EL expression or a string literal.

ui:insert	Used in a template to define the layout of a Facelets page that uses the template to define UIComponents. A template client adds UIComponents to a Facelets page with corresponding ui:define tags. If a Facelets page specifies a template and does not specify ui:define tags corresponding to ui:insert tags, the default ui:insert tags are used in the Facelets page.	name: This attribute has a corresponding name attribute in a Facelets page's ui:define tag for matching a template with a Facelets page.
ui:param	Used to specify a variable when a Facelets page is included within a template or a Facelets page.	name: This required attribute specifies a variable name. value: This required attribute specifies a variable's value as an EL expression or literal.

Facelets namespace tags may be used in an XHTML file. A Facelets application consists of the following configuration and templating files:

- A Facelets template page, which is an XHTML page
- Facelets header and footer XHTML pages
- A configuration file, faces-config.xml
- A Facelets composition page, which is also an XHTML page

The template file defines the layout of a Facelets application. A template file consists of `<ui:insert/>` tags to specify the structure of a Facelets application that uses the template for defining UI components. The JSF configuration file is the only configuration file required; a Facelets configuration file is not required. A Facelets page is an XHTML page that includes tags in the Facelets namespace. In the next section you will create a Facelets application in JDeveloper 12c, WebLogic Server 12c, and Oracle Database 11g XE.

SETTING THE ENVIRONMENT

As a first step, download the following software:

- Oracle JDeveloper 12c (12.1.2.0.0) (www.oracle.com/technetwork/developer-tools/ jdev/downloads/index.html)
- Oracle WebLogic Server 12c (included with JDeveloper 12c)

■ Oracle Database Express Edition (XE) 11g (www.oracle.com/technetwork/database/database-technologies/express-edition/downloads/index.html)

To generate a JSF data table, you need a data source. To create a database table in Oracle Database 11g XE, use the SQL script shown in Listing 2.1.

Listing 2.1   SQL Script to Create a Database Table

```
CREATE USER OE IDENTIFIED BY OE;
GRANT CONNECT, RESOURCE to OE;
CREATE TABLE OE.Catalog(CatalogId INTEGER
PRIMARY KEY, Journal VARCHAR(25), Publisher VARCHAR(25),
 Edition VARCHAR(25), Title Varchar(45), Author Varchar(25));
INSERT INTO OE.Catalog VALUES('1', 'Oracle Magazine',
 'Oracle Publishing', 'Nov-Dec 2004', 'Database Resource
Manager', 'Kimberly Floss');
INSERT INTO OE.Catalog VALUES('2', 'Oracle Magazine',
 'Oracle Publishing', 'Nov-Dec 2004', 'From ADF UIX to JSF',
'Jonas Jacobi');
INSERT INTO OE.Catalog VALUES('3', 'Oracle Magazine',
 'Oracle Publishing', 'March-April 2005', 'Starting with
Oracle ADF ', 'Steve Muench');
COMMIT;
```

Run the SQL script in SQL Command Line, as shown in Figure 2.1.

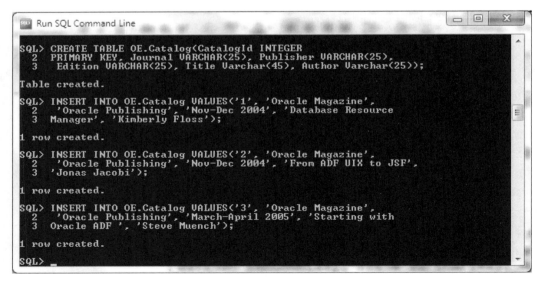

Figure 2.1
Creating a database table in Oracle Database using SQL Command Line.
Source: Oracle Corporation.

CONFIGURING THE INTEGRATED WEBLOGIC SERVER

You will be deploying the Facelets Web application to the WebLogic Server integrated with the JDeveloper 12c. By default, the integrated WebLogic Server does not have a domain associated with it. You should configure the domain before deploying the application to the server. Next, create a domain for the Integrated WebLogic Server. Follow these steps:

1. Select Window > Application Servers, as shown in Figure 2.2.

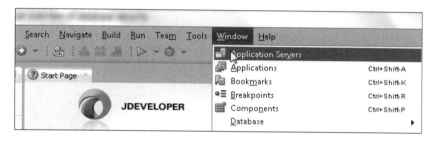

Figure 2.2
Select Window > Application Servers to list the application servers.
Source: Oracle Corporation.

2. In the Application Servers tab, IntegratedWebLogicServer is listed. The domain for the server is not configured, as indicated by the "domain unconfigured" status, as shown in Figure 2.3. Right-click the IntegratedWebLogicServer node and choose Create Default Domain, as shown in Figure 2.4.

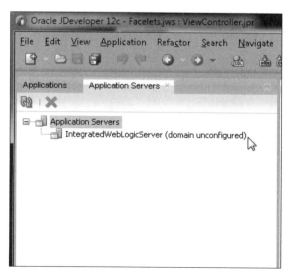

Figure 2.3
IntegratedWebLogicServer is listed in the Application Servers tab.
Source: Oracle Corporation.

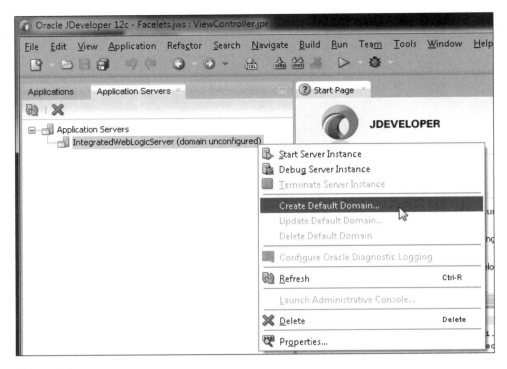

Figure 2.4
Select Create Default Domain for IntegratedWebLogicServer.
Source: Oracle Corporation.

3. In the Create Default Domain dialog box, type `weblogic` in the Administrator ID field and type a password in the Password and Confirm Password fields. In the Listen Address drop-down list, choose 127.0.0.1. The Listen Port and the SSL Listen Port are set to 7101 and 7102 by default; leave those as is. Finally, click OK, as shown in Figure 2.5. The IntegratedWebLogicServer domain is created, as shown in Figure 2.6.

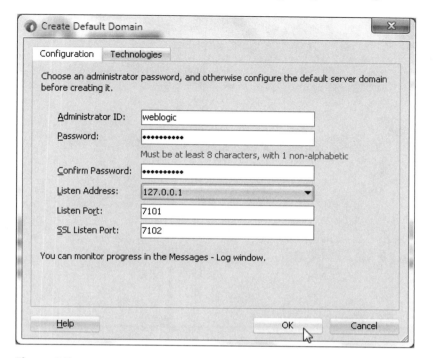

Figure 2.5
Specifying parameters for the default domain for IntegratedWebLogicServer.
Source: Oracle Corporation.

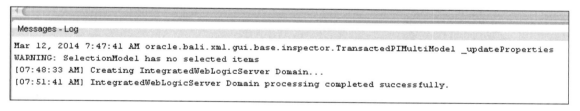

Figure 2.6
Creating the default domain for IntegratedWebLogicServer.
Source: Oracle Corporation.

4. Before an application is deployed to and run on IntegratedWebLogicServer, you must start the server. To do so, right-click the IntegratedWebLogicServer node and select Start Server Instance, as shown in Figure 2.7. IntegratedWebLogicServer starts, as shown in Figure 2.8.

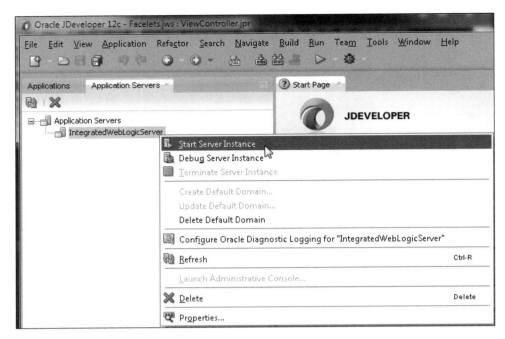

Figure 2.7
Starting IntegratedWebLogicServer Instance.
Source: Oracle Corporation.

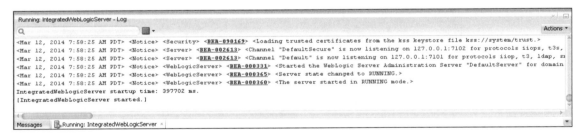

Figure 2.8
IntegratedWebLogicServer is started.
Source: Oracle Corporation.

CREATING A FACELETS PROJECT

In this section, you will create a Java EE Web application in JDeveloper 12c. Follow these steps:

1. Select File > New.

2. In the New Gallery dialog box, in the Categories pane, click General and then click Applications.

3. In the Items pane, click Java EE Web Application. Then click OK, as shown in Figure 2.9.

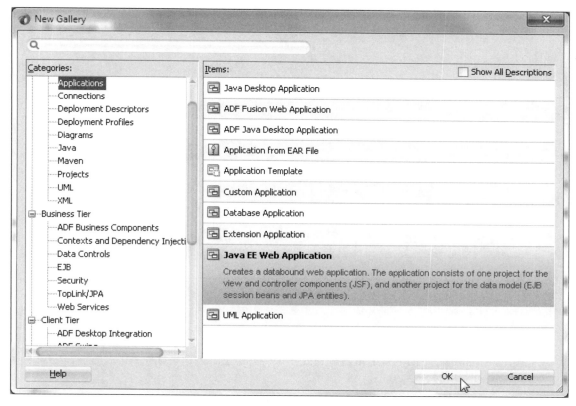

Figure 2.9
Creating a Java EE Web application.
Source: Oracle Corporation.

4. In the Application Name field, type `Facelets`. Then select the default directory in the Directory field or choose a directory by clicking the Browse button. When you're finished, click Next, as shown in Figure 2.10.

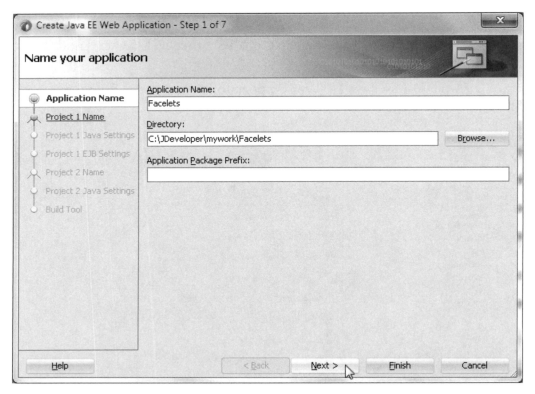

Figure 2.10
Specifying the name of the Java EE Web application.
Source: Oracle Corporation.

5. A Java EE Web application in JDeveloper consists of two projects: a Model project and a ViewController project. Select the default settings for the Model project name (Project 1) and click Next.

6. Select the default Java settings for the Model project and click Next.

7. Select the default EJB settings for the Model project and click Next.

8. Select the default Project 2 Name (ViewController). Then, in the Project Features pane, choose JavaServer Faces (JSF). Then click Next, as shown in Figure 2.11.

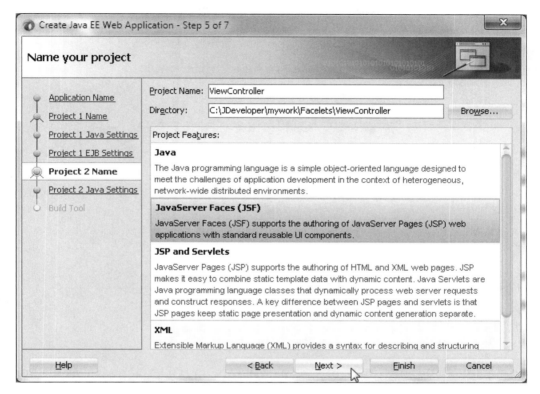

Figure 2.11
Selecting the JavaServer Faces project feature.
Source: Oracle Corporation.

9. Select the default Java settings for the ViewController project and click Next, as shown in Figure 2.12.

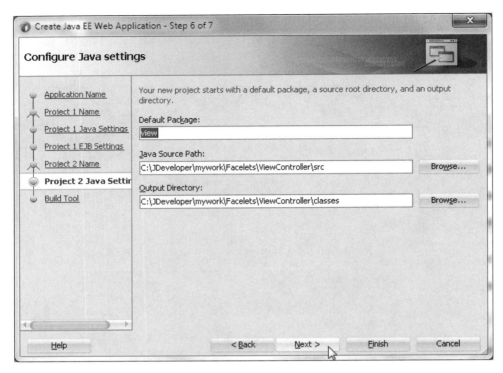

Figure 2.12
Selecting the default Java settings.
Source: Oracle Corporation.

10. In the Select Build Environment screen, select the Use JDeveloper's Default Build Tools option button and click Finish, as shown in Figure 2.13.

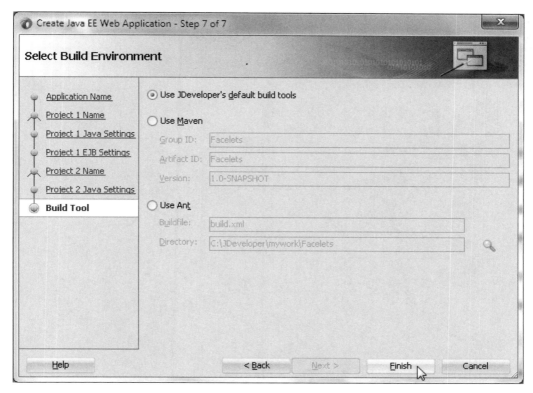

Figure 2.13
Selecting the build environment.
Source: Oracle Corporation.

11. A JDeveloper application consisting of a Model and a ViewController project is created. Right-click the ViewController project in the JDeveloper Applications tab and choose Project Properties, as shown in Figure 2.14.

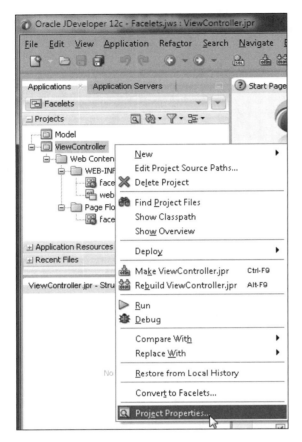

Figure 2.14
Choose Project Properties.
Source: Oracle Corporation.

12. In the pane on the left, select Libraries and Classpath. The JSF 2.1 library should appear in the Classpath Entries pane on the right. The JSP Runtime and the JSTL 1.2 library are also in the classpath. Click OK, as shown in Figure 2.15.

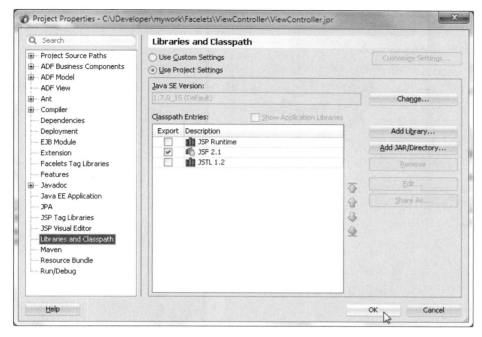

Figure 2.15
Creating a Java EE Web application.
Source: Oracle Corporation.

Because you selected JSF in step 8, the Faces Servlet gets configured in the web.xml deployment descriptor. The servlet mapping for the Faces Servlet is also configured using URL pattern /faces/*. By default, the suffix for a Facelets page is .xhtml. The web.xml deployment descriptor is shown in Figure 2.16.

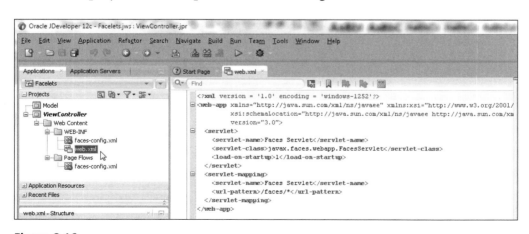

Figure 2.16
The web.xml deployment descriptor.
Source: Oracle Corporation.

The web.xml deployment descriptor is shown in Listing 2.2.

Listing 2.2   The web.xml Configuration File

```
<?xml version = '1.0' encoding = 'windows-1252'?>
<web-app xmlns="http://java.sun.com/xml/ns/javaee" xmlns:xsi="http://www.w3.org/2001/
XMLSchema-instance"
        xsi:schemaLocation="http://java.sun.com/xml/ns/javaee http://java.sun.com/
xml/ns/javaee/web-app_3_0.xsd"
        version="3.0">
  <servlet>
    <servlet-name>Faces Servlet</servlet-name>
    <servlet-class>javax.faces.webapp.FacesServlet</servlet-class>
    <load-on-startup>1</load-on-startup>
  </servlet>
  <servlet-mapping>
    <servlet-name>Faces Servlet</servlet-name>
    <url-pattern>/faces/*</url-pattern>
  </servlet-mapping>
</web-app>
```

CREATING A MANAGED BEAN

JSF pages are connected to server-side components that contain the business logic using a managed bean. A *managed bean* is just a plain old Java object (POJO) that is managed by the JSF framework. In JSF 1.2, managed beans had to be declared in the faces-config.xml deployment descriptor using the managed-bean element. In JSF 2.0 a managed bean may be declared using the @ManagedBean annotation.

To create a managed bean for the JSF application, follow these steps:

1. Right-click the faces-config.xml deployment descriptor and choose Open, as shown in Figure 2.17.

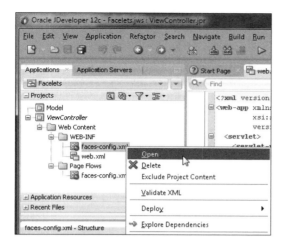

Figure 2.17
Right click the faces-config.xml deployment descriptor and choose Open.
Source: Oracle Corporation.

2. Click the Overview tab and then click the Managed Beans option. Next, click the Add button to add a new managed bean, as shown in Figure 2.18.

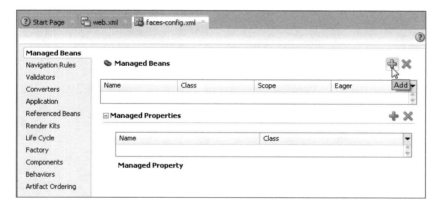

Figure 2.18
Click the Add button on the Managed Beans page to add a new managed bean.
Source: Oracle Corporation.

3. In the Create Managed Bean dialog box, type `catalog` in the Bean Name field; type `Catalog` in the Class Name field; type `view` in the Package field, and choose the desired option from the Scope drop-down list (the default is request). Finally, select the Annotations option button and click OK, as shown in Figure 2.19.

Create Managed Bean

Bean Name:	catalog
Class Name:	Catalog
Package:	view
Extends:	java.lang.Object
Scope:	request

Registration: ○ Configuration File   ◉ Annotations

☑ Generate Class If It Does Not Exist

Help   OK   Cancel

Figure 2.19
Creating a managed bean.
Source: Oracle Corporation.

The `Catalog` Java class is annotated with the `@ManagedBean` annotation to indicate that a managed bean is created. The default scope is `@RequestScoped`. Simplified configuration using the `@ManagedBean` and `@RequestScoped` annotations is a new feature in JSF 2.0.

```
@ManagedBean(name="catalog")
@RequestScoped
public class Catalog {
    public Catalog() {
    }
}
```

The managed bean POJO is shown in the Facelets application in Figure 2.20.

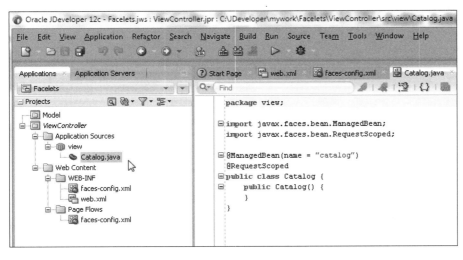

Figure 2.20
The managed bean class `Catalog.java`.
Source: Oracle Corporation.

The Facelets application consists of input.xhtml and ouput.xhtml Facelets pages. The input.xhtml page consists of an input text field and a Submit button. The input.xhtml page also consists of a header and a footer JPEG, which are defined in the BasicTemplate.xhtml template, discussed in the next section. The managed bean consists of bean properties for the input text field and the command button. The managed bean also consists of a `commandButton_action` method that is invoked when the Submit button in the input.xhtml is clicked:

```
public String commandButton1_action() { }
```

In the `action` method, the SQL query specified in the input text field is retrieved and run against the Oracle Database. As shown in the following code, the `createStatement` method specifies a `ResultSet` of type `ResultSet.TYPE_SCROLL_INSENSITIVE`, and result set concurrency of type `ResultSet.CONCUR_READ_ONLY`. The `ResultSet.TYPE_SCROLL_INSENSITIVE` string makes the result set scrollable both forward and backward relative to the current position of the cursor and scrollable to an absolute position. The `ResultSet.CONCUR_READ_ONLY` concurrency makes the result set read only and not updateable.

```
Class.forName("oracle.jdbc.OracleDriver");
String url = "jdbc:oracle:thin:@localhost:1521:XE";
connection = DriverManager.getConnection(url, "OE", "OE");
stmt =
connection.createStatement(ResultSet.TYPE_SCROLL_INSENSITIVE,ResultSet.
CONCUR_READ_ONLY);
resultSet = stmt.executeQuery((String)inputText1.getValue());
```

The `ResultSet` is stored in bean property and bound to an `h:dataTable` element in input.xhtml, as discussed in a later section.

```
if (resultSet != null) {
            this.setResultSet(resultSet);
        }
```

For navigation, you would have returned "success" and "failure" if you were using JSF 1.2 and added corresponding navigation rules in faces-config.xml. JSF 2.0 has added a navigation feature in which navigation rules are not required and the outcome is mapped to an XHTML page. For example, if the outcome is "output" and an output.xhtml page is provided, the JSF application navigates to the output.xhtml page. Return `"output.xhtml"` in the `commandButton_action` method if an error is not generated and return `"error.xhtml"` if an error is generated. You already added the output.xhtml and error.xhtml pages in an earlier section. The managed bean class appears in Listing 2.3.

Listing 2.3   The `Catalog.java` Managed Bean Class

```java
package view;

import javax.faces.component.html.HtmlInputText;
import java.sql.*;
import javax.faces.bean.ManagedBean;
import javax.faces.component.html.HtmlCommandButton;
import javax.faces.component.html.HtmlOutputLabel;

@ManagedBean(name = "catalog")
@RequestScoped
public class Catalog {
    private HtmlInputText inputText1;
    private HtmlOutputLabel outputLabel1;
    private HtmlCommandButton commandButton1;
    private Statement stmt;
    private Connection connection;
    private ResultSet resultSet;
    public void setInputText1(HtmlInputText inputText1) {
        this.inputText1 = inputText1;
    }
    public HtmlInputText getInputText1() {
        return inputText1;
    }
    public void setOutputLabel1(HtmlOutputLabel outputLabel1) {
        this.outputLabel1 = outputLabel1;
    }
    public HtmlOutputLabel getOutputLabel1() {
        return outputLabel1;
    }
    public void setCommandButton1(HtmlCommandButton commandButton1) {
        this.commandButton1 = commandButton1;
    }
    public HtmlCommandButton getCommandButton1() {
        return commandButton1;
    }
    public void setResultSet(ResultSet resultSet) {
        this.resultSet = resultSet;
    }
    public ResultSet getResultSet() {
        return resultSet;
    }
```

```java
    public String commandButton_action() {
        try {
            Class.forName("oracle.jdbc.OracleDriver");
            String url = "jdbc:oracle:thin:@localhost:1521:XE";
            connection = DriverManager.getConnection(url, "OE", "OE");
            stmt = connection.createStatement(ResultSet.TYPE_SCROLL_INSENSITIVE,
ResultSet.CONCUR_READ_ONLY);
            resultSet = stmt.executeQuery((String)inputText1.getValue());
            if (resultSet != null) {
                this.setResultSet(resultSet);
            }
        } catch (SQLException e) {
            System.out.println(e.getMessage());
            return "error";
        } catch (ClassNotFoundException e) {
            System.out.println(e.getMessage());
            return "error";
        } catch (Exception e) {
            System.out.println(e.getMessage());
            return "error";
        } finally {
        }
        return "output";
    }
}
```

CREATING A FACELETS TEMPLATE

A Facelets template serves as a template for the Facelets pages and provides common content to Facelets pages. First, create a templates directory in the WEB-INF directory. Next, add an XHTML page for the Facelets template file to the templates directory. Follow these steps:

1. Select File > New.

2. In the New Gallery dialog box, click Web Tier in the Categories pane, and then click HTML.

3. In the Items pane, select HTML Page, and click OK, as shown in Figure 2.21.

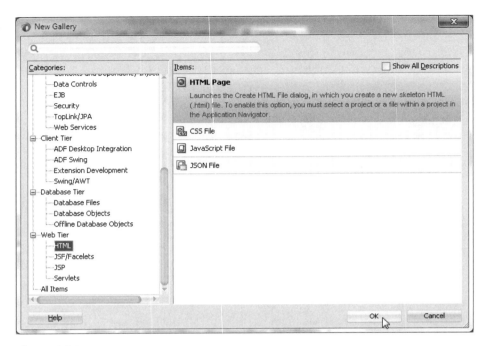

Figure 2.21
Select HTML Page.
Source: Oracle Corporation.

4. In the Create HTML File dialog box, type `BasicTemplate.xhtml` in the File Name field.

5. Click Browse, and then locate and select the templates directory.

6. Select the Create as XML File (*.xhtml) checkbox. Then click OK, as shown in Figure 2.22. The BasicTemplate.xhtml file is added to the WEB-INF/templates directory.

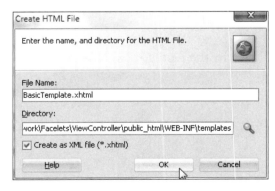

Figure 2.22
Creating an HTML file.
Source: Oracle Corporation.

Similarly, add header.xhtml and footer.xhtml to the templates directory. For the input Facelets page, add the input.xhtml page to the Web Content root directory, which is the public_html directory. For the output Facelets page, add the output.xhtml page to the public_html directory. Also add an error.xhtml page to the public_html directory. Copy the header and footer JPEGSs—in this case, the FaceletsHeader.jpg and FaceletsFooter.jpg files included with the source code ZIP file—to the root directory of the ViewController project, the public_html directory. This is the same directory containing the composition pages input.xhtml and output.xhtml. Some other JPEGs may also be used. The directory structure of the Facelets application is shown in Figure 2.23.

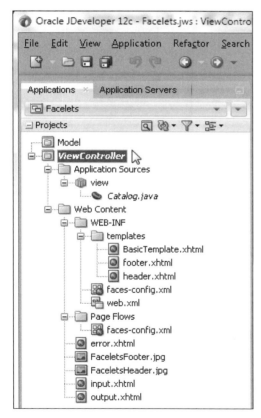

Figure 2.23
Directory structure of the Facelets application.
Source: Oracle Corporation.

The BasicTemplate.xhtml template consists of a header, content, and a footer. The root element of the template is HTML, which includes the namespace declaration for the Facelets namespace and the XHTML namespace. To the template, add `ui:insert` tags enclosed in <div/> tags for the different sections of a Facelets composition: a title, a header, a content section, and a footer. Specify the relative path to the header.xhtml and footer.xhtml Facelets pages using the ui:include tag. The code for BasicTemplate.xhtml appears in Listing 2.4.

Listing 2.4   BasicTemplate.xhtml

```
<?xml version='1.0' encoding='windows-1252'?>
<html xmlns="http://www.w3.org/1999/xhtml"
      xmlns:ui="http://java.sun.com/jsf/facelets">
<head>
<title><ui:insert name="title">JSF Facelets</ui:insert></title>
</head>
<body>
<div id="header">
    <ui:insert name="header">
       <ui:include src="/WEB-INF/templates/header.xhtml" />
    </ui:insert>
</div>
<div id="content">
   <ui:insert name="content">
     <!-- include your content file or uncomment the include below and create
content.xhtml in this directory -->
      <!-- <div> -->
      <!-- <ui:include src="content.xhtml"/> -->
      <!-- </div> -->
   </ui:insert>
</div>
<div id="footer">
   <ui:insert name="footer">
      <ui:include src="/WEB-INF/templates/footer.xhtml" />
   </ui:insert></div>
</body>
</html>
```

DEVELOPING FACELETS COMPOSITION PAGES

Similar to the BasicTemplate.xhtml, you added XHTML pages for header.xhtml and footer.xhtml, an input Facelets page (input.xhtml), and an output Facelets page (output.xhtml). In the header.xhtml page, you specify a JPEG for the header with an h:graphicImage tag. The code for the header.xhtml page appears in Listing 2.5.

Listing 2.5   The header.xhtml Page

```
<?xml version='1.0' encoding='windows-1252'?>
<html xmlns="http://www.w3.org/1999/xhtml"
    xmlns:ui="http://java.sun.com/jsf/facelets"
    xmlns:h="http://java.sun.com/jsf/html"
    xmlns:f="http://java.sun.com/jsf/core">
<f:view>
        <h:form>
            <h:panelGrid columns="1">
                    <h:graphicImage value="FaceletsHeader.jpg" />
    </h:panelGrid>
            </h:form>
    </f:view>
</html>
```

In the footer.xhtml page, specify a JPEG for the footer using the h:graphicImage tag enclosed in an h:panelGrid tag. The code for the footer.xhtml page appears in Listing 2.6.

Listing 2.6   The footer.xhtml Page

```
<?xml version='1.0' encoding='windows-1252'?>
<html xmlns="http://www.w3.org/1999/xhtml"
    xmlns:ui="http://java.sun.com/jsf/facelets"
    xmlns:h="http://java.sun.com/jsf/html"
    xmlns:f="http://java.sun.com/jsf/core">
<f:view>
        <h:form>
            <h:panelGrid columns="1">
            <h:graphicImage value="FaceletsFooter.jpg" />
    </h:panelGrid>
                </h:form>
    </f:view>
</html>
```

Next, define the input.xhtml Facelets composition page, which has an input field (h:inputText component) for input text and an h:commandButton for submitting the input in the content section. The h:commandButton has binding specified to the commandButton1 property in the managed bean catalog. The action attribute of the command button is set to the catalog.commandButton1_action method in the managed bean. The input.xhtml Facelets page consists of a ui:composition tag for defining the composition of the Facelets page, and ui:define tags within the ui:composition tag for defining UIComponents for the different sections of the Facelets composition: header, content, and footer. You specify the template name in the template attribute of the ui:composition tag. The ui:define tags correspond to ui:insert tags in the template. If a ui:define tag that corresponds to a ui:insert tag is not specified, the default ui:insert tag in the BasicTemplate.xhtml page is used in the Facelets composition page. Only the ui:define tag for the content is defined in the input.xhtml page. The header and footer JPEGs specified in the header.xhtml and output.xhtml and included in BasicTemplate.xhtml with ui:insert/ui:include tags are used for the header and footer sections. The code for the input.xhtml file appears in Listing 2.7.

Listing 2.7   The input.xhtml Page

```
<?xml version='1.0' encoding='windows-1252'?>
<html xmlns="http://www.w3.org/1999/xhtml" xmlns:ui="http://java.sun.com/jsf/facelets"
      xmlns:h="http://java.sun.com/jsf/html" xmlns:f="http://java.sun.com/jsf/core">
    <ui:composition template="/WEB-INF/templates/BasicTemplate.xhtml">
        <ui:define name="content">
            <h:form>
                <h:panelGrid columns="2">
                    <h:outputLabel binding="#{catalog.outputLabel1}" value="SQL
Query:"/>
                    <h:inputText binding="#{catalog.inputText1}"/>
                    <h:commandButton value="Submit" binding="#{catalog.commandButton1}"
                                     action="#{catalog.commandButton_action}"/>
                </h:panelGrid>
            </h:form>
        </ui:define>
    </ui:composition>
</html>
```

The output.xhtml Facelets composition page consists of an h:dataTable UI component in the content section to output the JSF data table for the SQL query in the input.xhtml Facelets composition page. The ui:define tag for content defines the composition of the Facelets page. The h:dataTable tag has value binding to the resultSet property in the managed bean. The iteration variable is resultset, which represents a row in the result set. The h:column components have value binding to the columns of a result set row. The code for the output.xhtml Facelets composition page appears in Listing 2.8.

Listing 2.8   The output.xhtml Page

```
<?xml version='1.0' encoding='windows-1252'?>
<html xmlns="http://www.w3.org/1999/xhtml" xmlns:ui="http://java.sun.com/jsf/facelets"
      xmlns:h="http://java.sun.com/jsf/html" xmlns:f="http://java.sun.com/jsf/core">
    <ui:composition template="/WEB-INF/templates/BasicTemplate.xhtml">
```

```
        <ui:define name="content">
            <h:dataTable value="#{catalog.resultSet}" var="resultset" border="1"
rows="4">
                <h:column>
                    <f:facet name="header">
                        <h:outputText value="Catalog Id"/>
                    </f:facet>
                    <h:outputText value="#{resultset.catalogid}"/>
                </h:column>
                <h:column>
                    <f:facet name="header">
                        <h:outputText value="Journal"/>
                    </f:facet>
                    <h:outputText value="#{resultset.journal}"/>
                </h:column>
                <h:column>
                    <f:facet name="header">
                        <h:outputText value="Publisher"/>
                    </f:facet>
                    <h:outputText value="#{resultset.publisher}"/>
                </h:column>
                <h:column>
                    <f:facet name="header">
                        <h:outputText value="Edition"/>
                    </f:facet>
                    <h:outputText value="#{resultset.edition}"/>
                </h:column>
                <h:column>
                    <f:facet name="header">
                        <h:outputText value="Title"/>
                    </f:facet>
                    <h:outputText value="#{resultset.title}"/>
                </h:column>
                <h:column>
                    <f:facet name="header">
                        <h:outputText value="Author"/>
                    </f:facet>
                    <h:outputText value="#{resultset.author}"/>
                </h:column>
            </h:dataTable>
        </ui:define>
    </ui:composition>
</html>
```

CREATING NAVIGATION

Next, you will add navigation to the Facelets application. The navigation section is much shorter than if you were using JSF 1.2. In JSF 1.2, you had to add navigation rules to the faces-config.xml file. JSF 2.0 provides a default navigation between the outcome String value and an XHTML page of the same name as the outcome String value. In the managed bean, you added an outcome value of "output" if no error is generated:

```
return "output";
```

You also added an outcome of "error" if an error is generated:

```
return "error";
```

If no error is generated, the application navigates to output.xhtml. If an error *is* generated, the application navigates to error.xhtml. JSF 2.0 has simplified the managed bean configuration using the @ManagedBean annotation. This simplifies the navigation rules configuration due to default navigation. The faces-config.xml configuration file without any managed bean configuration and without any navigation rules appears in Listing 2.9.

Listing 2.9   The JavaServer Faces Configuration File (faces-config.xml)

```
<?xml version='1.0' encoding='windows-1252'?>
<faces-config
    xmlns="http://java.sun.com/xml/ns/javaee"
    version="2.1">
</faces-config>
```

DEPLOYING THE FACELETS APPLICATION

Your next task is to create a deployment profile for the Facelets application. Follow these steps:

1. In the New Gallery dialog box, in the Categories pane, click General and choose Deployment Profiles.

2. In the Items pane, select WAR File, and click OK, as shown in Figure 2.24.

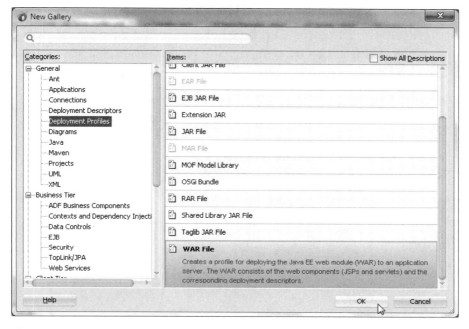

Figure 2.24
Selecting the WAR Deployment Profile.
Source: Oracle Corporation.

3. In the Deployment Profile Name field, type webapp1. Then click OK, as shown in Figure 2.25.

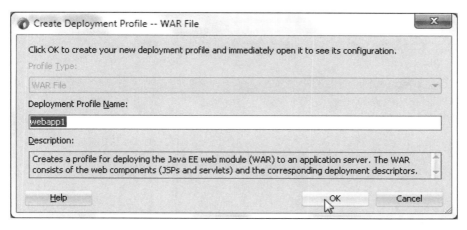

Figure 2.25
Specifying the deployment profile name.
Source: Oracle Corporation.

4. In the Edit WAR Deployment Profile Properties dialog box, select the Specify Java
   EE Web Context Root option button and type webapp1 in the corresponding field, as
   shown in Figure 2.26. Then click OK. The webapp1 Web module is added to the
   deployment, as shown in Figure 2.27. Click OK.

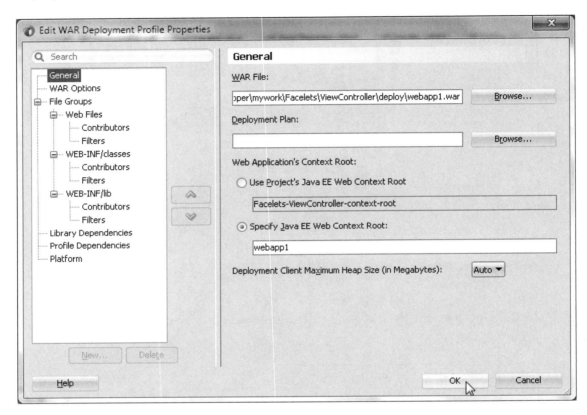

Figure 2.26
Specifying the Web context root.
Source: Oracle Corporation.

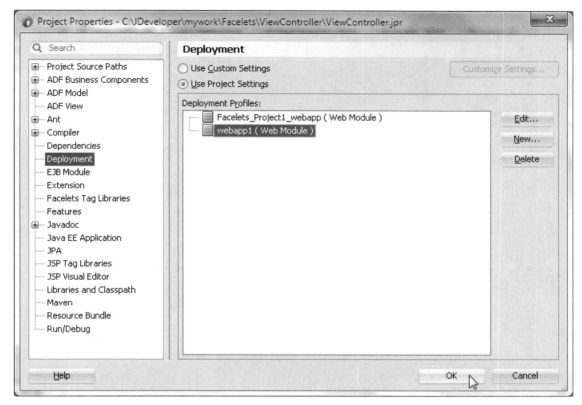

Figure 2.27
Web module webapp1.
Source: Oracle Corporation.

5. If it's not already started, start the WebLogic Server as discussed in the section "Configuring the Integrated WebLogic Server."

6. To run the Facelets application, right-click ViewController and select Deploy > webapp1, as shown in Figure 2.28.

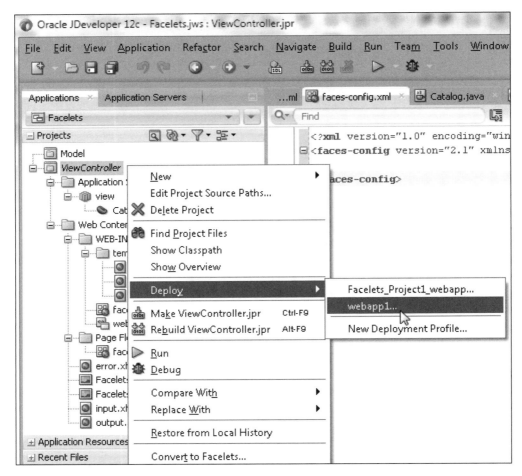

Figure 2.28
Deploying webapp1.
Source: Oracle Corporation.

7. The Deploy webapp1 dialog box opens. In the Deployment Action screen, select Deploy to Application Server, and click Next, as shown in Figure 2.29.

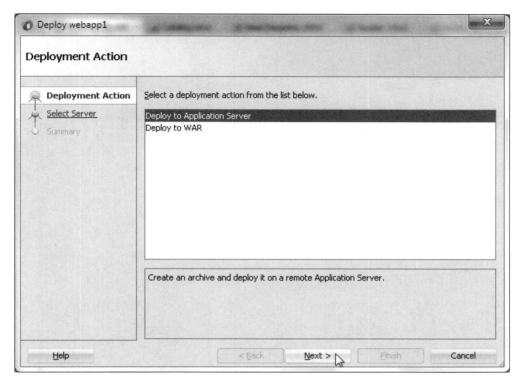

Figure 2.29
Selecting a deployment action.
Source: Oracle Corporation.

8. In the Select Server screen, select IntegratedWebLogicServer, which you configured earlier. Then click Next, as shown in Figure 2.30.

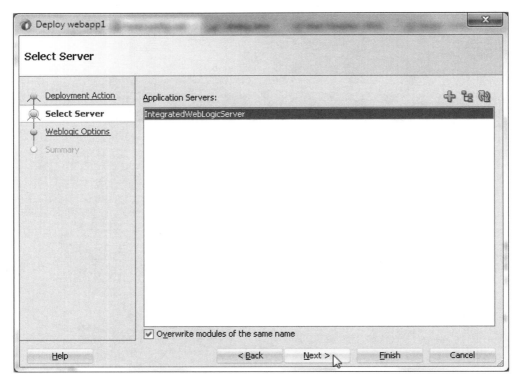

Figure 2.30
Selecting IntegratedWebLogicServer to deploy to.
Source: Oracle Corporation.

9. In the Weblogic Options screen, select one of the option buttons, such as the Deploy to Selected Instances in the Domain option button or the Deploy to All Standalone Servers and Clusters in the Domain option button. Notice that DefaultServer is listed as "RUNNING."

10. Select the Deploy as a Standalone Application option button and click Next, as shown in Figure 2.31.

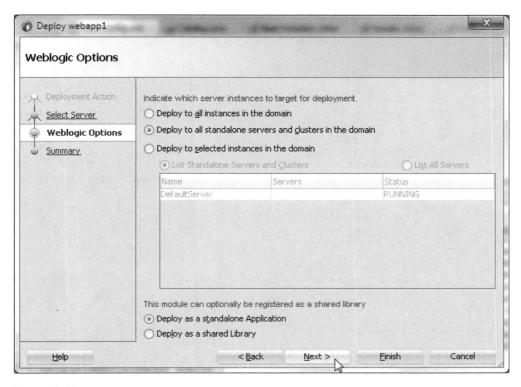

Figure 2.31
Selecting WebLogic options.
Source: Oracle Corporation.

11. In the Deployment Summary screen, click Finish, as shown in Figure 2.32. A WAR application, webapp1.war, is created and deployed to the DefaultServer, which is the integrated WebLogic Server. (See Figure 2.33.)

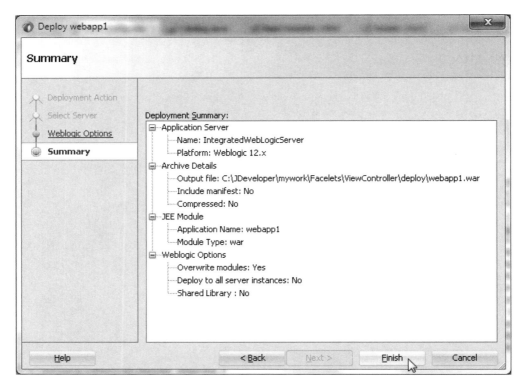

Figure 2.32
The Deployment Summary screen.
Source: Oracle Corporation.

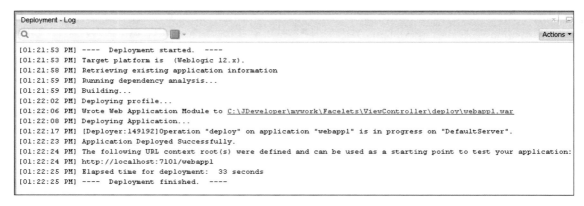

Figure 2.33
The webapp1 application deployed to IntegratedWebLogicServer.
Source: Oracle Corporation.

12. The webapp1 application is deployed on the integrated WebLogic Server and can be found in the WebLogic Server Console. Log in to the WebLogic Server Admin Console with the URL http://localhost:7101/webapp1 and click Deployments. The JSF 2.1 library and the JSTL 1.2 library are deployed by default, as shown in Figure 2.34. The Facelets application webapp1 is also listed as deployed, as shown in Figure 2.35.

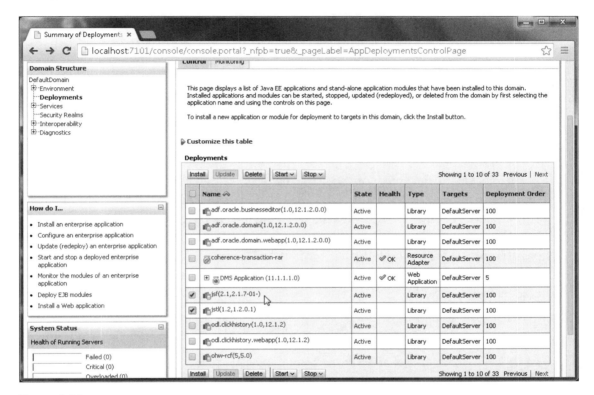

Figure 2.34
The JSF 2.1 library for the Facelets application is deployed by default.
Source: Oracle Corporation.

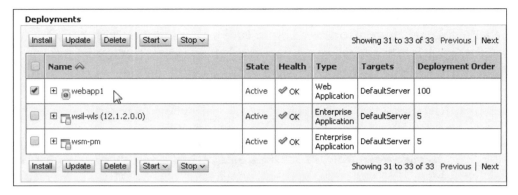

Figure 2.35
The webapp1 Facelets application is listed as deployed.
Source: Oracle Corporation.

RUNNING THE FACELETS APPLICATION

Run the input.xhtml Facelets composition page on the WebLogic Server that you config-ured earlier for JSF 2.0 with the URL http://localhost:7101/webapp1/faces/input.xhtml. The three sections of the input Facelets page are the header, content, and footer, as shown in Figure 2.36. The different sections of the Facelets composition page correspond to the different ui:define tags in the input.xhtml Facelets composition. The header.xhtml and footer.xhtml files from the BasicTemplate.xhtml template get included in the compo-sition. (See Figure 2.36.)

Figure 2.36
The input.xhtml Facelets page.
Google and the Google logo are registered trademarks of Google Inc., used with permission.

Specify the SQL query, `SELECT * FROM OE.CATALOG`, and click Submit, as shown in Figure 2.37. The output.xhtml Facelets composition page is displayed with a JSF data table generated for the SQL query. Templating is demonstrated by including the same header.xhtml and footer.xhtml in the composition page; the same header and footer JPEGs get displayed, as shown in Figure 2.38.

Figure 2.37
Specifying the SQL query for the JSF data table.
Google and the Google logo are registered trademarks of Google Inc., used with permission.

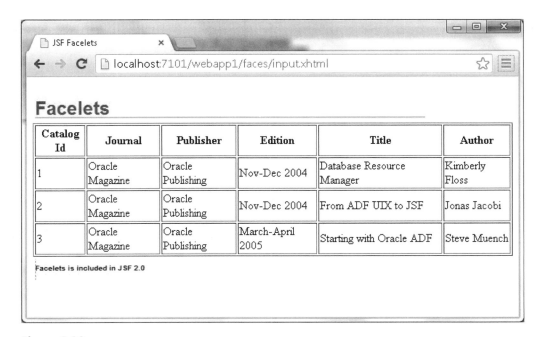

Figure 2.38
The JSF data table with the templated header and footer.
Google and the Google logo are registered trademarks of Google Inc., used with permission.

After an application has been deployed to the IntegratedWebLogicServer, the Integerated-WebLogicServer gets listed when deploying an application from the JDeveloper Applications navigator with right-click > Deploy, as shown in Figure 2.39.

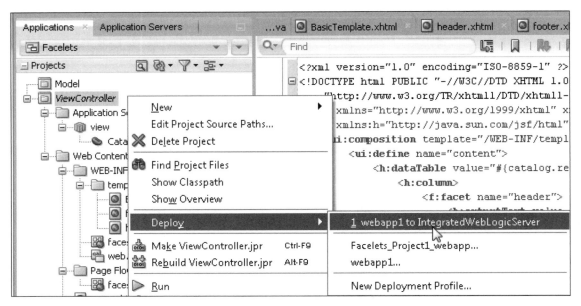

Figure 2.39
Right-click and choose Deploy > webapp1 to IntegratedWebLogicServer.
Source: Oracle Corporation.

SUMMARY

In this chapter, you developed a Facelets application consisting of a Facelets template page, Facelets header and footer pages, the faces-config.xml configuration file, and a Facelets composition page. You deployed the Facelets application to a WebLogic Server and ran the application to generate a data table from an SQL query. The next chapter discusses the Ajax functionality added to JSF 2.0.

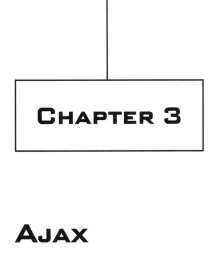

CHAPTER 3

AJAX

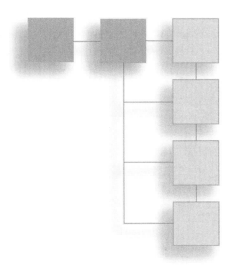

Chapter 2, "Templating with Facelets," discussed Facelets, which is the default view definition language in JSF 2.0. This chapter discusses another new feature in JSF 2.0: support for Ajax in UI components.

JSF 2.0 has introduced a provision for adding Ajax functionality to any JSF component. Ajax provides asynchronous transfer of data between a client and a server. Ajax features in JSF 2.0 include support for partial page rendering, partial page processing, and grouping of components. You can add support of Ajax in JSF 2.0 by using the f:ajax tag. In this chapter, you will add Ajax support to a JSF 2.0 data table.

SETTING THE ENVIRONMENT

As a first step, if you haven't done so already, download and install the following software:

- Oracle JDeveloper 12c (12.1.2.0.0) (www.oracle.com/technetwork/developer-tools/jdev/downloads/index.html)
- Oracle WebLogic Server 12c (included with JDeveloper 12c)
- Oracle Database Express Edition (XE) 11g (www.oracle.com/technetwork/database/database-technologies/express-edition/downloads/index.html)

To generate a JSF data table, you need a data source from which to create a database table in Oracle Database 11g XE if you haven't done so already. See the SQL script in Listing 3.1 to specify one.

Listing 3.1   SQL Script to Create a Database Table

```
CREATE USER OE IDENTIFIED BY OE;
GRANT CONNECT, RESOURCE to OE;
CREATE TABLE OE.Catalog(CatalogId INTEGER
PRIMARY KEY, Journal VARCHAR(25), Publisher VARCHAR(25),
 Edition VARCHAR(25), Title Varchar(45), Author Varchar(25));
INSERT INTO OE.Catalog VALUES('1', 'Oracle Magazine',
 'Oracle Publishing', 'Nov-Dec 2004', 'Database Resource
Manager', 'Kimberly Floss');
INSERT INTO OE.Catalog VALUES('2', 'Oracle Magazine',
 'Oracle Publishing', 'Nov-Dec 2004', 'From ADF UIX to JSF',
'Jonas Jacobi');
INSERT INTO OE.Catalog VALUES('3', 'Oracle Magazine',
 'Oracle Publishing', 'March-April 2005', 'Starting with
Oracle ADF ', 'Steve Muench');
COMMIT;
```

Run the SQL script in SQL Command Line, as shown in Figure 3.1.

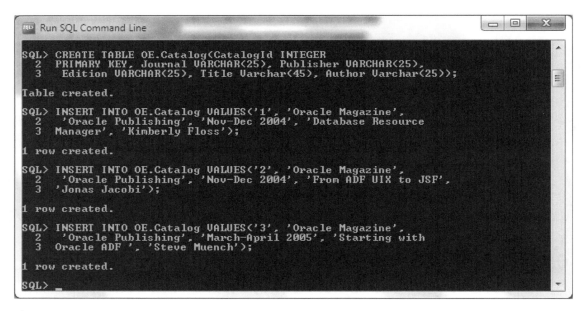

Figure 3.1
Creating a database table in Oracle Database using SQL Command Line.
Source: Oracle Corporation.

Finally, configure and start the IntegratedWebLogicServer, as explained in Chapter 2.

CREATING A FACELETS APPLICATION

Next, you will create a JDeveloper application. Follow these steps:

1. Choose File > New > From Gallery.

2. In the New Gallery dialog box, choose General > Applications in the Categories pane. Then select Java EE Web Application in the Items pane. Finally, click OK.

3. In the Create Java EE Web Application wizard, type AjaxJSF2.0 in the Application Name field and click Next, as shown in Figure 3.2.

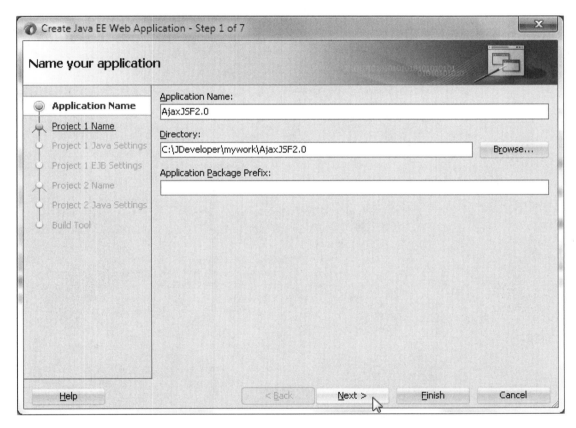

Figure 3.2
Specifying an application name.
Source: Oracle Corporation.

4. Project 1 is the Model project. For Project 1, select the default settings for Project Name and Directory and click Next.

5. Select the default Java settings for Project 1 and click Next.

6. Select the default EJB settings for Project 1 and click Next.

7. For Project 2, which is the ViewController project, select JavaServer Faces (JSF) in the Project Features list and click Next, as shown in Figure 3.3.

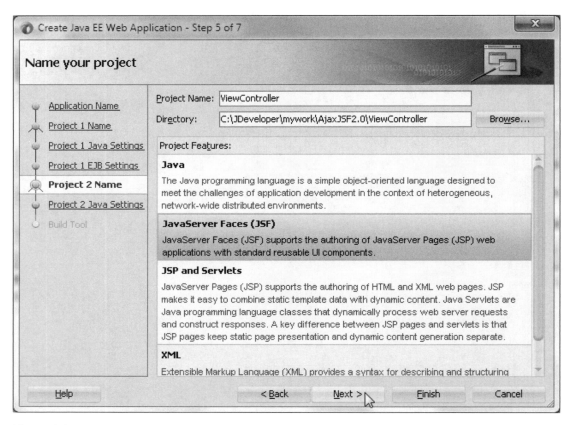

Figure 3.3
Selecting JavaServer Faces in the Project Features list.
Source: Oracle Corporation.

8. Select the default Java settings for the ViewController project and click Next.

9. Select the default Build Environment settings for the ViewController project and click Finish. A JDeveloper application consisting of a Model project and a ViewController project is created, as shown in Figure 3.4.

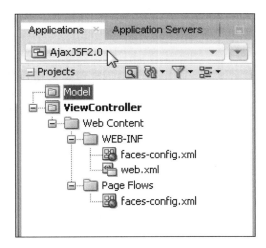

Figure 3.4
The AjaxJSF2.0 Java EE Web application.
Source: Oracle Corporation.

10. Right-click the ViewController project and select Project Properties.

11. In the pane on the left, select Libraries and Classpath. The JSF 2.1 library should be selected in the Classpath Entries pane. The JSP Runtime and JSTL 1.2 libraries should also be selected. (See Figure 3.5.) Because you selected the JSF Project technology, the web.xml consists of the Faces Servlet servlet and its mapping to a URL pattern, as shown in Figure 3.6.

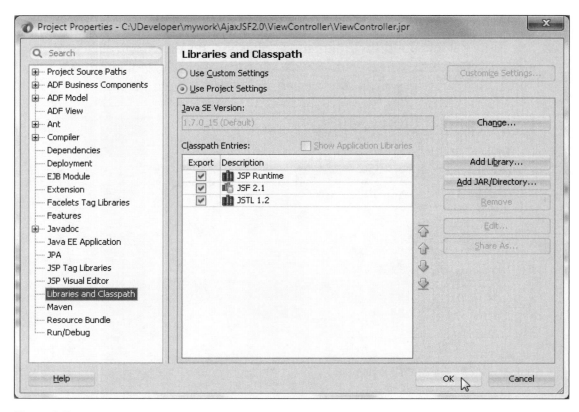

Figure 3.5
The required libraries for the AjaxJSF2.0 application.
Source: Oracle Corporation.

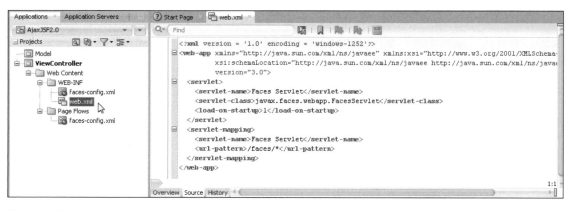

Figure 3.6
The web.xml deployment descriptor.
Source: Oracle Corporation.

The `javax.faces.application.ViewHandler` class provides the mechanism to handle JSF views (user interface pages). The `DEFAULT_SUFFIX` field specifies the file extension for a JSF page. The default setting is "`.xhtml, .jsp`", which implies that .xhtml and .jsp suffixed pages are JSF pages. The JSF pages you will create in this chapter are XHTML pages. The web.xml page appears in Listing 3.2.

Listing 3.2   The web.xml Page

```
<?xml version = '1.0' encoding = 'windows-1252'?>
<web-app xmlns="http://java.sun.com/xml/ns/javaee" xmlns:xsi="http://www.w3.org/2001/
XMLSchema-instance"
         xsi:schemaLocation="http://java.sun.com/xml/ns/javaee http://java.sun.com/
xml/ns/javaee/web-app_3_0.xsd"
         version="3.0">
    <servlet>
        <servlet-name>Faces Servlet</servlet-name>
        <servlet-class>javax.faces.webapp.FacesServlet</servlet-class>
        <load-on-startup>1</load-on-startup>
    </servlet>
    <servlet-mapping>
        <servlet-name>Faces Servlet</servlet-name>
        <url-pattern>/faces/*</url-pattern>
    </servlet-mapping>
</web-app>
```

CREATING A MANAGED BEAN

For the JSF pages, you must create a managed bean, which is just a POJO class. Follow these steps:

1. In the Applications navigator, right-click faces-config.xml and select Open, as shown in Figure 3.7.

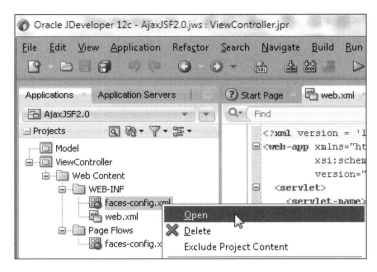

Figure 3.7
Right-click faces-config.xml and choose Open.
Source: Oracle Corporation.

2. Click the Overview tab and the Managed Beans node. Then click the Add button to add a new managed bean, as shown in Figure 3.8.

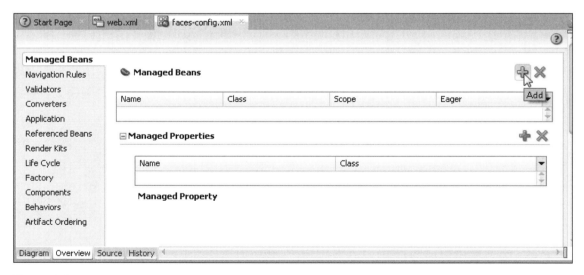

Figure 3.8
Adding a new managed bean.
Source: Oracle Corporation.

3. In the Create Managed Bean dialog box, type `catalog` in the Bean Name field, type `Catalog` in the Class Name field, type `view` in the Package field, and select an option from the Scope field (the default is request). Finally, select the Annotations option button and click OK, as shown in Figure 3.9.

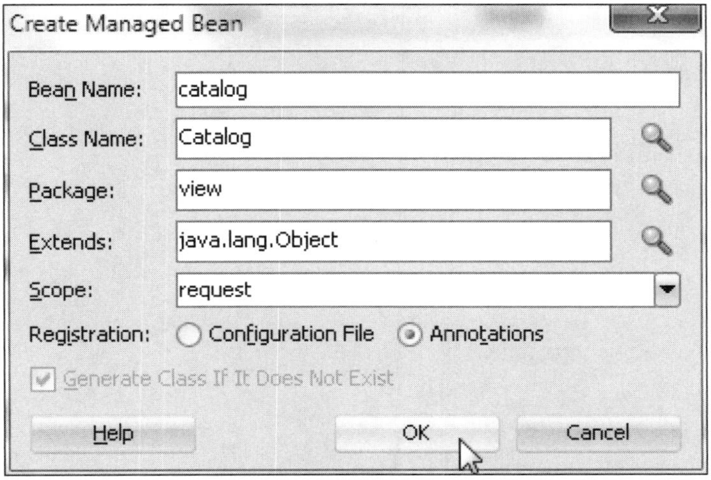

Figure 3.9
Configuring a managed bean.
Source: Oracle Corporation.

The `Catalog` Java class with the `@ManagedBean` annotation to indicate a managed bean is created. The default scope is `@RequestScoped`. Simplified configuration using the `@ManagedBean` and `@RequestScoped` annotations is a new feature in JSF 2.0. (See Listing 3.3.)

Listing 3.3   Managed Bean Annotations

```
@ManagedBean(name="catalog")
@RequestScoped
public class Catalog {
    public Catalog() {
    }
}
```

In the managed bean, specify the properties `inputText1`, `commandButton1`, and `resultSet`. Add accessor methods for the managed bean properties. Add a value change listener method `inputTextListener`. This is where the SQL query specified in an input text field is retrieved and run in the Oracle Database to generate a result set, whose value is set on the `resultSet` managed bean property. Add a listener method that is invoked in an Ajax request initiated from a `f:ajax` tag. The Ajax listener method takes an `AjaxBehaviorEvent` object, which represents the component behavior to Ajax, as a parameter:

```
public void inputTextListener(AjaxBehaviorEvent event) {
}
```

The managed bean class `Catalog.java` appears in Listing 3.4.

Listing 3.4   `Catalog.java` Managed Bean Class

```
package view;
import javax.faces.component.html.HtmlInputText;
import javax.faces.event.AjaxBehaviorEvent;
import java.sql.*;
import javax.faces.bean.ManagedBean;
import javax.faces.bean.RequestScoped;
import javax.faces.bean.SessionScoped;
import javax.faces.component.html.HtmlCommandButton;
@ManagedBean(name="catalog")
@RequestScoped
public class Catalog {
    private HtmlInputText inputText1;
    private HtmlCommandButton commandButton1;
    private Statement stmt;
    private Connection connection;
    private ResultSet resultSet;
    public void setInputText1(HtmlInputText inputText1) {
        this.inputText1 = inputText1;
    }
    public HtmlInputText getInputText1() {
        return inputText1;
    }
  public void setCommandButton1(HtmlCommandButton commandButton1) {
      this.commandButton1 = commandButton1;
  }
  public HtmlCommandButton getCommandButton1() {
      return commandButton1;
  }
    public void setResultSet(ResultSet resultSet) {
        this.resultSet = resultSet;
    }
    public ResultSet getResultSet() {
        return resultSet;
    }
```

```java
    public void inputTextListener(AjaxBehaviorEvent event) {
        try {
            Class.forName("oracle.jdbc.OracleDriver");
            String url = "jdbc:oracle:thin:@localhost:1521:XE";
            connection = DriverManager.getConnection(url, "OE", "OE");
            stmt =
connection.createStatement(ResultSet.TYPE_SCROLL_INSENSITIVE,
                        ResultSet.CONCUR_READ_ONLY);
            resultSet = stmt.executeQuery((String)inputText1.getValue());
            if (resultSet != null) {
                this.setResultSet(resultSet);
            }
        } catch (SQLException e) {
            System.out.println(e.getMessage());
        } catch (ClassNotFoundException e) {
            System.out.println(e.getMessage());
        } catch (Exception e) {
            System.out.println(e.getMessage());
        } finally {
        }
    }
  public void inputTextListener() {
      try {
          Class.forName("oracle.jdbc.OracleDriver");
          String url = "jdbc:oracle:thin:@localhost:1521:XE";
          connection = DriverManager.getConnection(url, "OE", "OE");
          stmt =
  connection.createStatement(ResultSet.TYPE_SCROLL_INSENSITIVE,
                      ResultSet.CONCUR_READ_ONLY);
          resultSet = stmt.executeQuery((String)inputText1.getValue());
          if (resultSet != null) {
              this.setResultSet(resultSet);
          }
      } catch (SQLException e) {
          System.out.println(e.getMessage());
      } catch (ClassNotFoundException e) {
          System.out.println(e.getMessage());
      } catch (Exception e) {
          System.out.println(e.getMessage());
      } finally {
      }
  }
}
```

The `Catalog.java` managed bean is shown in Figure 3.10.

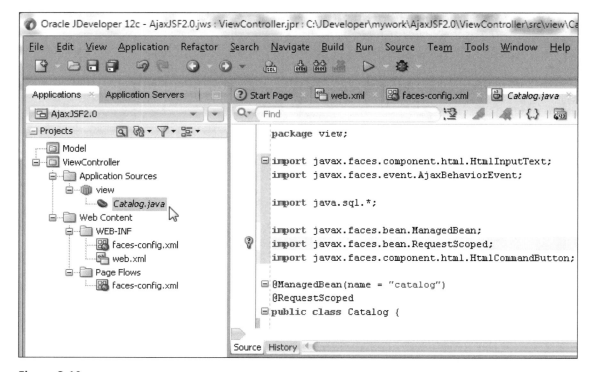

Figure 3.10
Managed bean class `Catalog.java`.
Source: Oracle Corporation.

If you were using JSF 1.2, you would have configured the managed beans in faces-config.xml. But because you are using the `@ManagedBean` annotation, new in JSF 2.0, to specify a managed bean, faces-config.xml is an empty file.

```
<?xml version="1.0" encoding="windows-1252"?>
<faces-config version="2.1" xmlns="http://java.sun.com/xml/ns/javaee">
</faces-config>
```

CREATING A JSF PAGE

Because we are using the default view definition language in JSF 2.0, Facelets, you will create XHTML pages for the JSF pages. Follow these steps:

1. In the New Gallery dialog box, select Web Tier > HTML and Items > HTML Page.

2. Type `catalog.xhtml` in the File Name field, select the Create as XML File checkbox, and click OK, as shown in Figure 3.11.

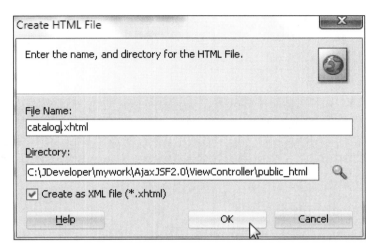

Figure 3.11
Creating a JSF (XHTML) page.
Source: Oracle Corporation.

3. Add another XHTML page, catalog2.xhtml, to demonstrate the different features of the Ajax support in JSF 2.0. The directory structure of the AjaxJSF2.0 application is shown in Figure 3.12.

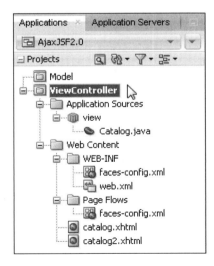

Figure 3.12
The directory structure of the AjaxJSF2.0 application.
Source: Oracle Corporation.

ADDING AJAX

Next, you will add Ajax functionality to a JSF data table in catalog.xhtml. The `h:head` tag is required in the JSF page for the JSF page to run:

```
<h:head>
  <title></title>
</h:head>
```

For JSF components, add six columns to the data table and add a header and an `h:outputText` tag to each column. Then specify the `ResultSet` values as value expressions in `h:outputText`. For example, specify a header of "Catalog Id" for the first column and specify the `h:outputText` value expression as the `CatalogId` column value in the `ResultSet`.

To see all this in action, follow these steps:

1. Add a JSF data table to catalog.xhtml.

2. Specify a JDBC `ResultSet` that you will obtain in the managed bean in the `value` attribute and specify the iteration variable with the `var` attribute, as shown here:

```
<h:dataTable id="dataTable1" value="#{catalog.resultSet}" var="resultset"
             border="1" rows="4">
</h:dataTable>
<h:column id="column1">
    <f:facet name="header">
     <h:outputText value="Catalog Id"/>
    </f:facet>
    <h:outputText id="outputText1" value="#{resultset.catalogid}"/>
    </h:column>
```

3. Add an `h:inputText` component to specify an SQL query from which to create the data table.

4. Position the cursor in the `<h:inputText></h:inputText>` tags and add an `f:ajax` tag in the `h:inputText` component from the JSF > Core Components palette, as shown in Figure 3.13.

Figure 3.13
Adding Ajax from the JSF > Core Components palette.
Source: Oracle Corporation.

5. Add attributes for the `f:ajax` tag. To do so, position the cursor in the `<f:ajax />` tag and select the `render` attribute from the drop-down list, as shown in Figure 3.14.

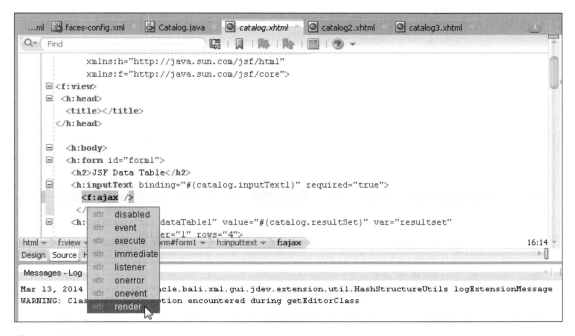

Figure 3.14
Adding the `render` attribute to `f:ajax`.
Source: Oracle Corporation.

6. Set the `render` attribute value to `"dataTable1"`.

7. Add an `event` attribute, as shown in Figure 3.15.

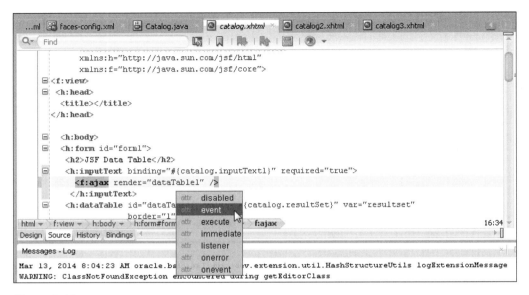

Figure 3.15
Adding the event attribute to f:ajax.
Source: Oracle Corporation.

8. Set the event attribute to "keyup".

9. Position the cursor within the <f:ajax /> tag and add the execute attribute from the list of attributes, as shown in Figure 3.16.

Figure 3.16
Adding the execute attribute to f:ajax.
Source: Oracle Corporation.

10. Set the `execute` attribute to `"@form"`.

11. Add the `listener` attribute, as shown in Figure 3.17.

Figure 3.17
Adding the `listener` attribute to `f:ajax`.
Source: Oracle Corporation.

12. Set the `listener` attribute to the EL expression for the `inputTextListener` method in the managed bean catalog. The `f:ajax` tag renders the `dataTable1` data table and binds to a listener `inputTextListener(AjaxBehaviorEvent)` in the managed bean:

```
<h:inputText binding="#{catalog.inputText1}" required="true">
    <f:ajax execute="@form" event="keyup" render="dataTable1"
            listener="#{catalog.inputTextListener}"/>
</h:inputText>
```

The `execute` attribute specifies which components (space delimited, if multiple components are specified) of the JSF page participate in the execute portion of the request. The values in Table 3.1 may be specified.

Table 3.1 execute Attribute Values

execute Attribute Value	Description
@this	This component. The default value.
@all	All components.
@form	The form component
@none	No components
clientId1 clientId2...	Specified components. Components are identified by their ID—for example, form1:dataTable1 to specify a dataTable1 in a form1. If the specified component is at the same level as the component for which the f:ajax tag is specified, the preceding component ID may be omitted.

The event attribute specifies which Document Object Model (DOM) event initiates an Ajax request. The event attribute value may be one of the following.

■ Supported DOM events for the component, such as click, change, dblclick; the on prefix is omitted.

■ The action event may be specified, and is the default, for Faces ActionSource components such as command buttons or command links.

■ The valueChange event may be specified for, and is the default for, Faces Editable ValueHolder components, which are editable components, such as an input text component.

The event specified should be supported by the component. For example, the valueChange event is not supported by a command button. We have specified the keyup event to indicate that an Ajax request is sent with each keyup event in the input text. The render attribute specifies the components to be rendered in the render response phase of the request. Because the dataTable1 component is at the same hierarchical level as the inputText component, the form1: prefix is omitted; only dataTable1 is specified in the render attribute. The same values as those for the execute attribute may be specified, except the default value is @none. The listener attribute specifies the method to invoke when an AjaxBehaviorEvent is broadcast. We have specified the listener with a method expression as listener="#{catalog.inputTextListener}", which invokes the inputTextListener (AjaxBehaviorEvent event) method in the managed bean.

Note

The different attributes that may be specified in the `f:ajax` tag are discussed in the `f:ajax` reference, available here: http://download.oracle.com/javaee/6/javaserverfaces/2.1/docs/vdldocs/facelets/f/ajax.html.

The catalog.xhtml consists of two JSF data tables: `dataTable1` and `dataTable2`. In the first run, the XHTML page is run with one data table and in the second run with two data tables to demonstrate rendering of multiple components. For the first run, comment out the second data table `dataTable2`, and uncomment the `dataTable2` for the second run. (See Listing 3.5)

Listing 3.5   The catalog.xhtml Page

```
<!DOCTYPE html PUBLIC "-//W3C//DTD XHTML 1.0 Transitional//EN"
    "http://www.w3.org/TR/xhtml1/DTD/xhtml1-transitional.dtd">
<html xmlns="http://www.w3.org/1999/xhtml"
      xmlns:ui="http://java.sun.com/jsf/facelets"
      xmlns:h="http://java.sun.com/jsf/html"
      xmlns:f="http://java.sun.com/jsf/core">
<f:view>
 <h:head>
  <title></title>
</h:head>
  <h:body>
  <h:form id="form1">
   <h2>JSF Data Table</h2>
   <h:inputText binding="#{catalog.inputText1}" required="true">
    <f:ajax execute="@form" event="keyup" render="dataTable1"
            listener="#{catalog.inputTextListener}"/>
   </h:inputText>
   <h:dataTable id="dataTable1" value="#{catalog.resultSet}" var="resultset"
                border="1" rows="4">
    <h:column id="column1">
     <f:facet name="header">
      <h:outputText value="Catalog Id"/>
     </f:facet>
     <h:outputText id="outputText1" value="#{resultset.catalogid}"/>
    </h:column>
    <h:column id="column2">
     <f:facet name="header">
      <h:outputText value="Journal"/>
     </f:facet>
     <h:outputText id="outputText2" value="#{resultset.journal}"/>
    </h:column>
```

```
<h:column id="column3">
 <f:facet name="header">
  <h:outputText value="Publisher"/>
 </f:facet>
 <h:outputText id="outputText3" value="#{resultset.publisher}"/>
</h:column>
<h:column id="column4">
 <f:facet name="header">
  <h:outputText value="Edition"/>
 </f:facet>
 <h:outputText id="outputText4" value="#{resultset.edition}"/>
</h:column>
<h:column id="column5">
 <f:facet name="header">
  <h:outputText value="Title"/>
 </f:facet>
 <h:outputText id="outputText5" value="#{resultset.title}"/>
</h:column>
<h:column id="column6">
 <f:facet name="header">
  <h:outputText value="Author"/>
 </f:facet>
 <h:outputText id="outputText6" value="#{resultset.author}"/>
</h:column>
</h:dataTable>
<!-- <h:dataTable id="dataTable2" value="#{catalog.resultSet}" var="resultset"
              border="1" rows="4">
<h:column id="column4">
 <f:facet name="header">
  <h:outputText value="Edition"/>
 </f:facet>
 <h:outputText value="#{resultset.edition}"/>
</h:column>
<h:column id="column5">
 <f:facet name="header">
  <h:outputText value="Title"/>
 </f:facet>
 <h:outputText  value="#{resultset.title}"/>
</h:column>
```

```
  <h:column id="column6">
   <f:facet name="header">
    <h:outputText value="Author"/>
   </f:facet>
   <h:outputText value="#{resultset.author}"/>
  </h:column>
 </h:dataTable>
 </h:form>
</h:body>
</f:view>
</html>
```

DEPLOYING AND RUNNING THE JSF 2.0 AJAX APPLICATION

Next, you will run the JSF page catalog.xhtml to demonstrate Ajax functionality. In the first run, include only one data table. Follow these steps:

1. Create a deployment profile. To do so, select Deployment Profiles > WAR File in the New Gallery dialog box. (Creating a WAR deployment profile is discussed in more detail in Chapter 2.)

2. Specify the deployment profile name as webapp1 and click OK.

3. Specify the Java EE Web Context root as webapp1.

4. Deploy the webapp1 deployment profile to a WebLogic Server. To begin, right-click the ViewController project and select Deploy > webapp1.

5. In the Deployment Action screen, select Deploy to Application Server and click Next.

6. In the Select Server screen, select IntegeratedWebLogicServer and click Next.

7. In the WebLogic Options screen, select Deploy to Selected Instances in the Domain. Then select DefaultServer from the List Standalone Servers and Clusters list, as shown in Figure 3.18. Finally, select Deploy as a Standalone Application, and click Next.

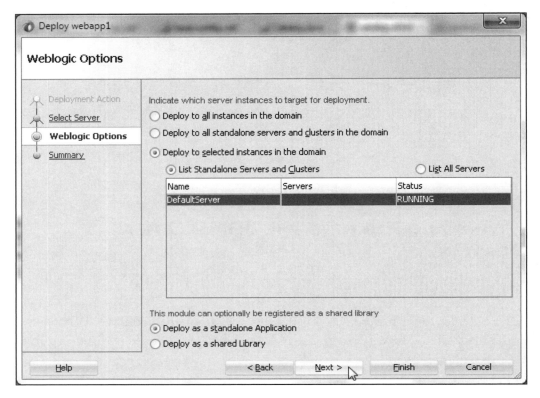

Figure 3.18
Selecting WebLogic options.
Source: Oracle Corporation.

8. In the Summary screen, click Finish.

If the application was previously deployed to the IntegratedWebLogicServer, the option to deploy to the IntegratedWebLogicServer will be listed, as shown in Figure 3.19. (Deploying a Web application to the IntegratedWebLogicServer is discussed in more detail in Chapter 2.) The JSF 2.0 application gets deployed to the WebLogic Server, as shown in Figure 3.20.

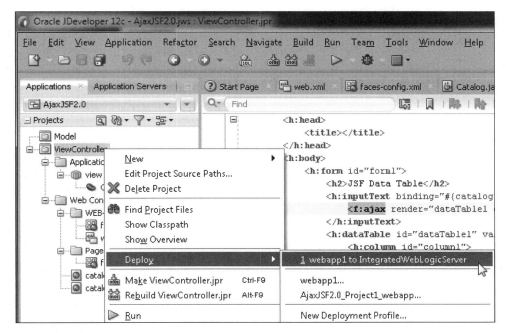

Figure 3.19
Deploying to the IntegeratedWebLogicServer from the Applications navigator.

Source: Oracle Corporation.

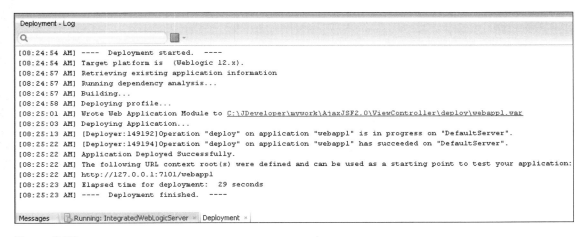

Figure 3.20
The output from deploying the AjaxJSF2.0 application.

Source: Oracle Corporation.

To find out if webapp1 has been deployed and to run catalog.xhtml, follow these steps:

1. Log in to the Administration Console for DefaultServer using the following URL: http://localhost:7101/console.

2. Select Deployments. As you can see, webapp1 is listed.

3. Start the IntegratedWebLogicServer if it's not already started.

4. Run the catalog.xhtml page with the following URL: http://localhost:7101/webapp1/faces/catalog.xhtml. The catalog.xhtml is rendered, as shown in Figure 3.21.

Figure 3.21
The catalog.xhtml JSF page.
Google and the Google logo are registered trademarks of Google Inc., used with permission.

5. Start to specify an SQL query in the input text field, as shown in Figure 3.22. An Ajax request is sent with each modification. When the SQL query generates a JDBC result set (for example, SELECT * FROM OE.CATALOG), a data table is generated, as shown in Figure 3.23. You need not click a button to send a request to the server.

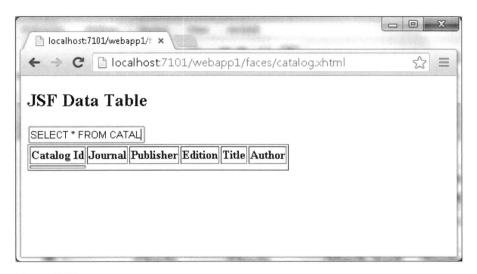

Figure 3.22
Partial SQL queries also send an Ajax request.
Google and the Google logo are registered trademarks of Google Inc., used with permission.

Figure 3.23
A data table rendered with the SQL query sent with Ajax.
Google and the Google logo are registered trademarks of Google Inc., used with permission.

6. You can modify the SQL query—for example, by specifying a WHERE clause (SELECT * FROM OE.CATALOG WHERE CATALOGID=1) for a modified result set, as shown in Figure 3.24.

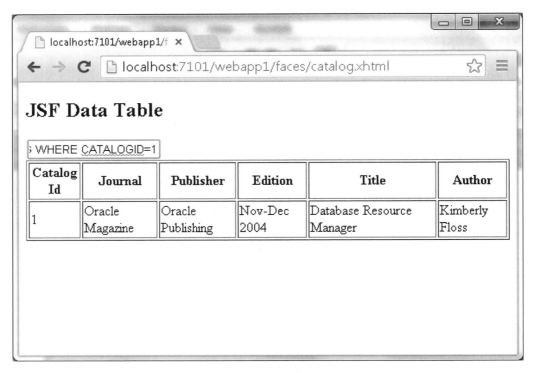

Figure 3.24
A JSF data table generated from an Ajax request for a filtered SQL query.
Google and the Google logo are registered trademarks of Google Inc., used with permission.

7. As another example of a filtered SQL query, specify SELECT * FROM OE.CATALOG WHERE EDITION='Nov-Dec 2004', as shown in Figure 3.25.

Figure 3.25
Another example of a filtered SQL query.

Google and the Google logo are registered trademarks of Google Inc., used with permission.

PARTIAL PAGE RENDERING: RENDERING

You can specify multiple components in the `render` attribute of the `f:ajax` tag to render multiple components simultaneously. To see how, follow these steps:

1. Add the second data table to catalog.xhtml by uncommenting the `h:dataTable` with the id `dataTable2`.

2. Specify the `render` attribute as `render="dataTable1 dataTable2"` if both data tables are to be rendered. Specify `render="dataTable1"` if only one `dataTable1` (for example) of the data tables is to be rendered.

3. Let's explore partial page rendering by setting render="dataTable1". First, redeploy and rerun the catalog.xhtml page. Headers for two data tables are displayed, as shown in Figure 3.26.

Figure 3.26
Headers for two JSF data tables.
Google and the Google logo are registered trademarks of Google Inc., used with permission.

4. Specify an SQL query. Because only one of the data tables is specified in the render attribute, only one data table is rendered. This demonstrates partial page rendering. (See Figure 3.27.)

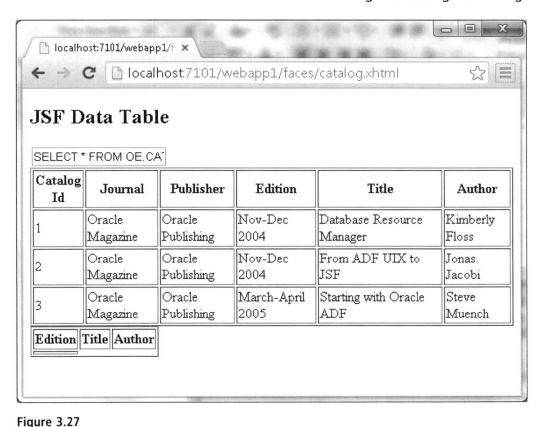

Figure 3.27
Partial page rendering.

5. You can render both the data tables by specifying `render="dataTable1 dataTable2"`, as shown in Figure 3.28.

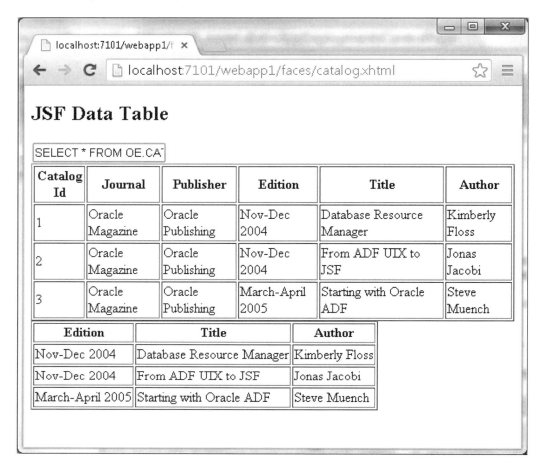

Figure 3.28
Rendering both JSF data tables.

Google and the Google logo are registered trademarks of Google Inc., used with permission.

GROUPING COMPONENTS

In this section, you will group components within the f:ajax tag. Grouping components invokes an Ajax request when a specified/default event is invoked for any of the components. If an event is specified in the enclosing f:ajax tag, it applies to all the components within the tag (assuming the component supports the event). You can specify an additional event using another f:ajax tag for a specific component within the outer f:ajax tag. In catalog2.xhtml, add an f:ajax tag enclosing two components:

```
<f:ajax execute="@form" event="valueChange" render="form1:dataTable1 form1:dataTable2"
        listener="#{catalog.inputTextListener}">
```

```
<h:inputText binding="#{catalog.inputText1}" required="true"/>
<h:commandButton binding="#{catalog.commandButton1}" value="Submit">
<f:ajax event="click"/>
</h:commandButton>
</f:ajax>
```

The `h:commandButton` does not support the `valueChange` event. You have added a `click` event for the command button. When the catalog2.xhtml page is run, the `valueChange` event is added to the input text component and the `click` event to the command button component, as shown in Figure 3.29.

Figure 3.29
The `valueChange` event.
Google and the Google logo are registered trademarks of Google Inc., used with permission.

As an example, do not add any event handlers, as in the following grouping of components:

```
<f:ajax execute="@form" render="form1:dataTable1 form1:dataTable2"
        listener="#{catalog.inputTextListener}">
  <h:inputText binding="#{catalog.inputText1}" required="true"/>
  <h:commandButton binding="#{catalog.commandButton1}" value="Submit">
  </h:commandButton>
</f:ajax>
```

The `valueChange` event gets added to the input text component and the `action` event gets added to the command button component when catalog2.xhtml is run, as shown in Figure 3.30.

Figure 3.30
The `action` event in the command button.

Google and the Google logo are registered trademarks of Google Inc., used with permission.

The catalog2.xhtml page appears in Listing 3.6.

Listing 3.6   The catalog2.xhtml Page

```
<!DOCTYPE html PUBLIC "-//W3C//DTD XHTML 1.0 Transitional//EN"
    "http://www.w3.org/TR/xhtml1/DTD/xhtml1-transitional.dtd">
<html xmlns="http://www.w3.org/1999/xhtml"
       xmlns:ui="http://java.sun.com/jsf/facelets"
       xmlns:h="http://java.sun.com/jsf/html"
       xmlns:f="http://java.sun.com/jsf/core">
<f:view>
 <h:head>
  <title></title>
</h:head>
  <h:body>
  <h:form id="form1">
   <h2>JSF Data Table</h2>
   <f:ajax execute="@form" event="valueChange" render="form1:dataTable1 form1:
dataTable2"
            listener="#{catalog.inputTextListener}">
   <h:inputText binding="#{catalog.inputText1}" required="true"/>
   <h:commandButton binding="#{catalog.commandButton1}" value="Submit">
```

```
<f:ajax event="click"/>
</h:commandButton>
</f:ajax>
<h:dataTable id="dataTable1" value="#{catalog.resultSet}" var="resultset"
             border="1" rows="4">
 <h:column id="column1">
  <f:facet name="header">
   <h:outputText value="Catalog Id"/>
  </f:facet>
  <h:outputText id="outputText1" value="#{resultset.catalogid}"/>
 </h:column>
 <h:column id="column2">
  <f:facet name="header">
   <h:outputText value="Journal"/>
  </f:facet>
  <h:outputText id="outputText2" value="#{resultset.journal}"/>
 </h:column>
 <h:column id="column3">
  <f:facet name="header">
   <h:outputText value="Publisher"/>
  </f:facet>
  <h:outputText id="outputText3" value="#{resultset.publisher}"/>
 </h:column>
 <h:column id="column4">
  <f:facet name="header">
   <h:outputText value="Edition"/>
  </f:facet>
  <h:outputText id="outputText4" value="#{resultset.edition}"/>
 </h:column>
 <h:column id="column5">
  <f:facet name="header">
   <h:outputText value="Title"/>
  </f:facet>
  <h:outputText id="outputText5" value="#{resultset.title}"/>
 </h:column>
 <h:column id="column6">
  <f:facet name="header">
   <h:outputText value="Author"/>
  </f:facet>
  <h:outputText id="outputText6" value="#{resultset.author}"/>
 </h:column>
</h:dataTable>
```

```
<h:dataTable id="dataTable2" value="#{catalog.resultSet}" var="resultset"
             border="1" rows="4">
  <h:column id="column4">
   <f:facet name="header">
    <h:outputText value="Edition"/>
   </f:facet>
   <h:outputText value="#{resultset.edition}"/>
  </h:column>
  <h:column id="column5">
   <f:facet name="header">
    <h:outputText value="Title"/>
   </f:facet>
   <h:outputText value="#{resultset.title}"/>
  </h:column>
  <h:column id="column6">
   <f:facet name="header">
    <h:outputText value="Author"/>
   </f:facet>
   <h:outputText value="#{resultset.author}"/>
  </h:column>
 </h:dataTable>
</h:form>
</h:body>
</f:view>
</html>
```

Deploy the AjaxJSF2.0 application to the IntegeratedWebLogicServer and run the catalog2.xhtml with the following URL: http://localhost:7101/webapp1/faces/catalog2 .xhtml. Specify an SQL query and click outside the input text field to invoke the valueChange event. Two data tables are displayed, as shown in Figure 3.31.

Figure 3.31
Grouping two JSF data tables with a `valueChange` event.
Google and the Google logo are registered trademarks of Google Inc., used with permission.

In the second run, specify an SQL query and click the Submit button to invoke the `click` event. The two data tables are displayed for the specified query, as shown in Figure 3.32.

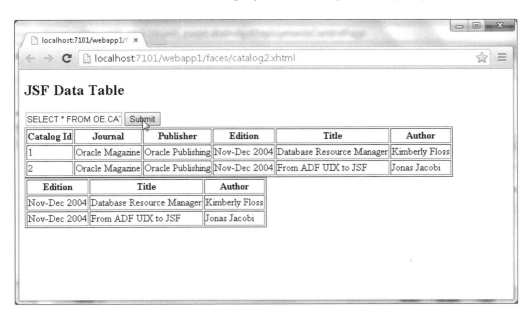

Figure 3.32
Grouping two JSF data tables with the `click` event.
Google and the Google logo are registered trademarks of Google Inc., used with permission.

Summary

This chapter discussed Ajax support in JSF 2.0 using the `f:ajax` tag and the Ajax JSF Java-Script library. It also discussed partial page rendering, demonstrating how to render one or more components. It also discussed adding Ajax support to multiple components by grouping components. The next chapter discusses composite components.

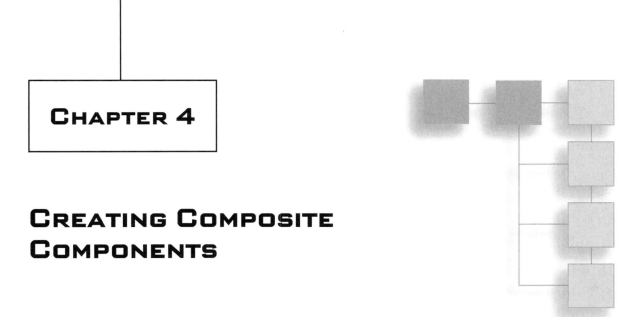

CHAPTER 4

CREATING COMPOSITE COMPONENTS

JSF 2.0 has introduced a new feature, composite components. These are reusable JSF UI components that can be developed from a collection of other JSF UI components. Composite components do not require any Java code or XML configuration file. A composite component consists of a top-level `UIComponent` and a tree (hierarchical structure) of `UIComponents` within the top-level component.

Composite components are built using two other new features in JSF 2.0: Facelets and resources. A composite component is a Facelet markup file, which may include templating tags from the Facelets templating tag library in a resource library. The metadata for a composite component is defined using the composite component tag library (http://docs.oracle.com/javaee/6/javaserverfaces/2.1/docs/vdldocs/facelets/composite/tld-summary.html), which consists of tags in the http://java.sun.com/jsf/composite namespace. The `composite:interface` and the `composite:implementation` tags are the required tags for defining the metadata for a composite component.

A composite components application consists of the following artifacts:

- **Definition page.** This Facelets markup page contains the composite component declaration and definition. The composite component declaration is specified within the `composite:interface` tag, and the composite component definition is specified within the `composite:implementation` tag. Each definition page defines one composite component.

- **Composite component library.** This resource library contains the definition pages for the different composite components in the library.

■ **A "using page."** This is a view definition language (VDL) page, a Facelets XHTML page in which the composite component is used using a composite component tag. The `HTML_BASIC` render kit contains a new renderer called `javax.faces.Composite` for composite components.

In this chapter, you will create two composite components, each for a JSF data table, in two separate resource libraries, using the composite components in a using page. Each of the composite components consists of the following JSF UI components:

■ An output label for an input text field

■ An input text field for an SQL query from which a data table is to be created

■ A Submit button

■ A data table created when a user submits an SQL query

SETTING THE ENVIRONMENT

As a first step, download and install the following software:

■ Oracle JDeveloper 12c (12.1.2.0.0) (www.oracle.com/technetwork/developer-tools/jdev/downloads/index.html)

■ Oracle WebLogic Server 12c (included with JDeveloper 12c)

■ Oracle Database Express Edition (XE) 11g (www.oracle.com/technetwork/database/database-technologies/express-edition/downloads/index.html)

To generate a JSF data table, you need a data source from which to create a database table in Oracle Database 11g XE. Use the SQL script in Listing 4.1 to specify one. (The database table is the same as the one used in the previous chapter. If you've already created it, you don't have to create it again.)

Listing 4.1   SQL Script to Create an Oracle Database Table

```
CREATE USER OE IDENTIFIED BY OE;
GRANT CONNECT, RESOURCE to OE;
CREATE TABLE OE.Catalog(CatalogId INTEGER
PRIMARY KEY, Journal VARCHAR(25), Publisher VARCHAR(25),
 Edition VARCHAR(25), Title Varchar(45), Author Varchar(25));
INSERT INTO OE.Catalog VALUES('1', 'Oracle Magazine',
 'Oracle Publishing', 'Nov-Dec 2004', 'Database Resource
Manager', 'Kimberly Floss');
INSERT INTO OE.Catalog VALUES('2', 'Oracle Magazine',
 'Oracle Publishing', 'Nov-Dec 2004', 'From ADF UIX to JSF',
```

```
'Jonas Jacobi');
INSERT INTO OE.Catalog VALUES('3', 'Oracle Magazine',
 'Oracle Publishing', 'March-April 2005', 'Starting with
Oracle ADF ', 'Steve Muench');
```

Run the SQL script in SQL Command Line to create a database table OE.CATALOG. As in the previous chapter, configure and start the IntegratedWebLogicServer.

CREATING A JAVA EE WEB APPLICATION

First, you need to create a Java EE application in which to develop the composite components. Follow these steps:

1. Select File > New > From Gallery.

2. In the New Gallery dialog box, select General > Applications in the Categories pane and Java EE Web Application in the Items pane. Then click OK.

3. The Create Java EE Web Application wizard starts. Type Composite in the Application Name field and click Next.

4. Select the default settings for the Model project name and click Next.

5. Select the default Java settings for the Model project and click Next.

6. Select the default EJB settings for the Model project and click Next.

7. In the ViewController Project Features screen, select JavaServer Faces and click Next.

8. Select the default Java settings for the ViewController project and click Next.

9. Select the default Build Environment settings and click Finish. A Java EE Web application is created, as shown in Figure 4.1.

Figure 4.1
A Java EE Web application called "Composite."
Source: Oracle Corporation.

CREATING A USING PAGE

A using page is a view definition language (VDL) page, a Facelets markup XHTML page, on which a composite component is used. To create a using page, follow these steps:

1. Select the ViewController project and choose File > New > From Gallery.

2. Select Web Tier > HTML in the Categories pane and choose HTML Page in the Items pane. Then click OK, as shown in Figure 4.2.

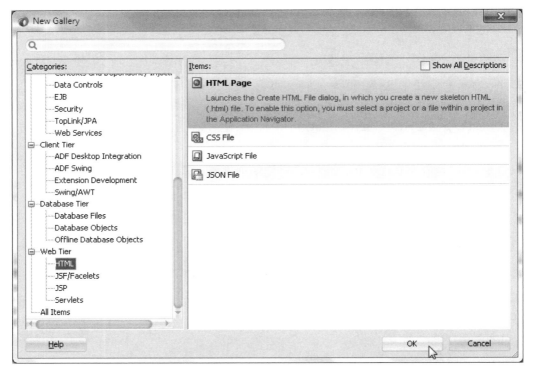

Figure 4.2
Selecting HTML Page in the New Gallery dialog box.
Source: Oracle Corporation.

3. In the Create HTML File screen, select the Create as XML File checkbox, type catalog.xhtml in the File Name field, and click OK, as shown in Figure 4.3.

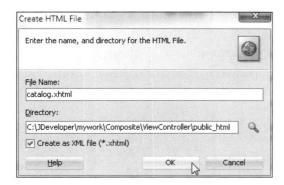

Figure 4.3
Creating an HTML file.
Source: Oracle Corporation.

4. In the using page, declare the namespace for the resource libraries `dataTable1` and `dataTable2`, in which the composite components are defined. (Creating the resource libraries is discussed in a later section.) The choice of the namespace prefixes `dt1` and `dt2` is arbitrary.

```
xmlns:dt1="http://java.sun.com/jsf/composite/dataTable1"
xmlns:dt2="http://java.sun.com/jsf/composite/dataTable2"
```

5. Add composite components from the `dataTable1` and `dataTable2` resource libraries to the using page. The `dataTable1` resource library defines a composite component `compositeDataTable1`, and the `dataTable2` resource library defines a composite component `compositeDataTable2`.

The EL expressions used for the composite component tag attributes are the same for the two composite component tags. This implies that the UI component tags in the two data tables in the composite view constructed from the two composite components bind to the same managed bean properties in the `catalog` managed bean. The effect of binding the UI component tags in different composite components to the same managed bean properties will become apparent later.

```
<dt1:compositeDataTable1 bindingSQLQuery="#{catalog.inputText1}"
bindingCommandButton="#{catalog.commandButton1}"
valueDataTable="#{catalog.resultSet}"
submitAction="#{catalog.commandButton_action}" />

 <dt2:compositeDataTable2 bindingSQLQuery="#{catalog.inputText1}"
bindingCommandButton="#{catalog.commandButton1}"
valueDataTable="#{catalog.resultSet}"
submitAction="#{catalog.commandButton_action}" sqlQueryLabel="SQL Query:"/>
```

`dt1:compositeDataTable1` and `dt2:compositeDataTable2` are called composite component tags. They refer to the composite components defined in the definition page, to be discussed later in this chapter. The composite component tags contain the attributes discussed in Table 4.1 to specify the EL expressions to bind to the actual `h:dataTable` elements in the data tables.

Table 4.1 Composite Component Tag Attributes

Attribute	Description
`bindingSQLQuery`	The EL expression for the `binding` attribute of the `h:inputText` element in the composite component
`bindingCommandButton`	The EL expression for the `binding` attribute of the `h:commandButton` element in the composite component
`valueDataTable`	The value expression for the `value` attribute of the `h:dataTable` element in the composite component
`submitAction`	The EL expression for the `action` attribute of the `h:commandButton` element in the composite component

The using page catalog.xhtml appears in Listing 4.2.

Listing 4.2   Using Page catalog.xhtml

```
<!DOCTYPE html PUBLIC "-//W3C//DTD XHTML 1.0 Transitional//EN"
     "http://www.w3.org/TR/xhtml1/DTD/xhtml1-transitional.dtd">
<html xmlns="http://www.w3.org/1999/xhtml"
      xmlns:h="http://java.sun.com/jsf/html"
      xmlns:f="http://java.sun.com/jsf/core"
      xmlns:dt1="http://java.sun.com/jsf/composite/dataTable1"
      xmlns:dt2="http://java.sun.com/jsf/composite/dataTable2">
<f:view>
 <h:head>
  <title>Composite DataTable</title>
</h:head>
  <h:body>
  <h:form>
   <h2>Composite DataTable(Request Scope)</h2>
   <dt1:compositeDataTable1 bindingSQLQuery="#{catalog.inputText1}"
bindingCommandButton="#{catalog.commandButton1}"
valueDataTable="#{catalog.resultSet}"
submitAction="#{catalog.commandButton_action}" />
```

```
<dt2:compositeDataTable2 bindingSQLQuery="#{catalog.inputText1}"
bindingCommandButton="#{catalog.commandButton1}"
valueDataTable="#{catalog.resultSet}" submitAction="#{catalog.commandButton_action}"
sqlQueryLabel="SQL Query:"/>
  </h:form>
</h:body>
</f:view>
</html>
```

Figure 4.4 shows the using page in the JDeveloper.

Figure 4.4
The catalog.xhtml using page.
Source: Oracle Corporation.

We have yet to add the resource libraries `dataTable1` and `dataTable2`, which consist of the compositeDataTable1.xhtml and compositeDataTable2.xhtml definition pages. These are discussed in subsequent sections.

CREATING A MANAGED BEAN

In this section, you will create the managed bean for the composite components. Follow these steps:

1. In the Applications navigator, right-click faces-config.xml and select Open, as shown in Figure 4.5.

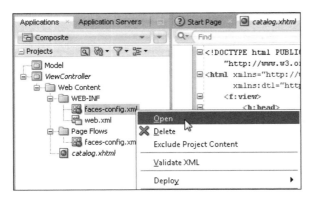

Figure 4.5
Right-click faces-config.xml and choose Open.
Source: Oracle Corporation.

2. Click the Overview tab and the Managed Beans node. Then click the Add button to add a new managed bean, as shown in Figure 4.6.

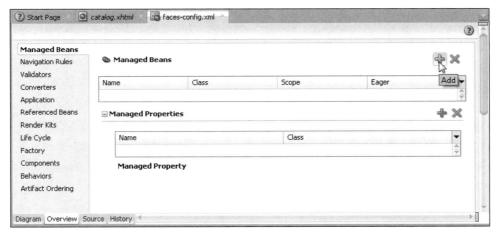

Figure 4.6
Adding a new managed bean.
Source: Oracle Corporation.

3. In the Create Managed Bean dialog box, type `catalog` in the Bean Name field, type `Catalog` in the Class Name field, type `view` in the Package field, and select an option from the Scope drop-down list (the default is request). Finally, select the Annotations option button and click OK, as shown in Figure 4.7.

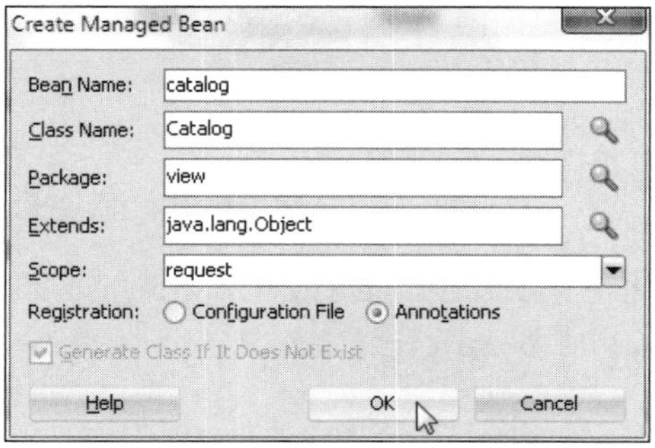

Figure 4.7
Creating a managed bean.
Source: Oracle Corporation.

A managed bean is added to the Composite application. The managed bean `Catalog` class is annotated with `@ManagedBean` annotation.

```
@ManagedBean(name = "catalog")
public class Catalog {
}
```

4. Specify bean properties for an input text field, a command button, and an SQL result set as follows:

```
private HtmlInputText inputText1;
private HtmlCommandButton commandButton1;
private ResultSet resultSet;
```

5. Add accessor methods (getter and setter) for the bean properties.

6. Add a `commandButton_action()` method to be invoked when the Submit button in the composite components is clicked:

```
public void commandButton_action() {
}
```

7. In the `action` method, obtain a connection with the Oracle Database 11g XE:

```
Class.forName("oracle.jdbc.OracleDriver");
String url = "jdbc:oracle:thin:@localhost:1521:XE";
connection = DriverManager.getConnection(url, "OE", "OE");
```

8. Create a `Statement` object and run the SQL query specified in the input text field:

```
stmt =
connection.createStatement(ResultSet.TYPE_SCROLL_INSENSITIVE,
ResultSet.CONCUR_READ_ONLY);
resultSet = stmt.executeQuery((String)inputText1.getValue());
```

If the result set is not null set the bean property resultSet to the result set returned.

```
if (resultSet != null) {
                this.setResultSet(resultSet);
            }
```

In this way, the resultSet property is bound to the value expression in the h:dataTable elements in the composite components. The managed bean class Catalog.java appears in Listing 4.3.

Listing 4.3   Managed Bean Class Catalog.java

```
package view;

import javax.faces.component.html.HtmlInputText;
import java.sql.*;
import javax.faces.bean.ManagedBean;
import javax.faces.bean.RequestScoped;
import javax.faces.component.html.HtmlCommandButton;

@ManagedBean(name="catalog")
@RequestScoped
public class Catalog {
    public Catalog() {
    }
    private HtmlInputText inputText1;
    private HtmlCommandButton commandButton1;
    private Statement stmt;
    private Connection connection;
    private ResultSet resultSet;
    public void setInputText1(HtmlInputText inputText1) {
        this.inputText1 = inputText1;
    }
    public HtmlInputText getInputText1() {
        return inputText1;
    }
    public void setCommandButton1(HtmlCommandButton commandButton1) {
        this.commandButton1 = commandButton1;
    }
    public HtmlCommandButton getCommandButton1() {
        return commandButton1;
    }
```

```java
        public void setResultSet(ResultSet resultSet) {
            this.resultSet = resultSet;
        }
        public ResultSet getResultSet() {
            return resultSet;
        }
        public void commandButton_action() {
            try {
                Class.forName("oracle.jdbc.OracleDriver");
                String url = "jdbc:oracle:thin:@localhost:1521:XE";
                connection = DriverManager.getConnection(url, "OE", "OE");
                stmt =
connection.createStatement(ResultSet.TYPE_SCROLL_INSENSITIVE,
                            ResultSet.CONCUR_READ_ONLY);
                resultSet = stmt.executeQuery((String)inputText1.getValue());
                if (resultSet != null) {
                    this.setResultSet(resultSet);
                }
            } catch (SQLException e) {
                System.out.println("SQLException" + e.getMessage());
            } catch (ClassNotFoundException e) {
                System.out.println("ClassNotFoundException" + e.getMessage());
            } catch (Exception e) {
                e.printStackTrace();
            } finally {
            }
        }
}
```

The managed bean class `Catalog.java` is shown in Figure 4.8.

Figure 4.8
Managed bean class `Catalog.java`.
Source: Oracle Corporation.

CREATING COMPOSITE COMPONENTS

A composite component consists of a definition page, which is a Facelets markup page, and a resource library. Resource handling is a new feature in JSF 2.0. The default implementation for a Web application consists of packaging resources in the resources folder in the Web application root folder.

In this section, you will create two composite components in two different resource libraries. You could create the composite components in the same resource library, but this section demonstrates the use of multiple resource libraries. Follow these steps:

1. Create a resources folder in the public_html folder.

2. In the resources folder, create two folders, dataTable1 and dataTable2, for the two resource libraries. (See Figure 4.9.)

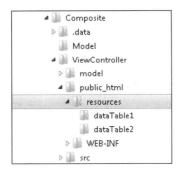

Figure 4.9
Folders for composite component libraries.
Source: Oracle Corporation.

3. In the dataTable1 folder, create a Facelets markup file, compositeDataTable1.xhtml. To do so, choose File > New > From Gallery. Then, in the New Gallery dialog box, select Web Tier > HTML in the Categories pane and choose HTML Page in the Items pane. Finally, click OK.

4. In the Create HTML File dialog box, select the Create as XML File checkbox, type `compositeDataTable1.xhtml` in the File Name field, and type `public_html/resources/dataTable1` in the Directory field. Finally, click OK, as shown in Figure 4.10.

Figure 4.10
Creating a composite component definition page.

Source: Oracle Corporation.

5. Similarly, create a Facelets markup file, compositeDataTable2.xhtml, in the dataTable2 folder. Figure 4.11 shows the directory structure of the Composite application after the addition of the markup files.

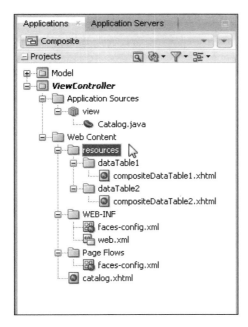

Figure 4.11
Directory structure with composite component definition pages.

Source: Oracle Corporation.

6. In the `compositeDataTable1.xhtml` Facelets markup file, add the namespace declaration for the Composite Tag Library:

```
<html xmlns:cc=http://java.sun.com/jsf/composite
>
```

7. The composite component declaration with the `<cc:interface>` tag and the composite component definition with the `<cc:implementation>` tag are the only two required tags to define the metadata for a composite tag. Add a `<cc:interface>` tag and, in the tag, add `<cc:attribute>` tags. A `<cc:attribute>` tag specifies an attribute that may be given to an instance of a composite component tag in a using page. A composite component's attributes are declared in the `<cc:interface>` tag and implemented or used in the `<cc:implementation>` tag, and values for the attributes are specified in the using page.

8. For a data table, add the attributes discussed in Table 4.2 using the `<cc:attribute>` tag. The attribute names are arbitrary.

Table 4.2 Composite Component Definition Page Attributes

Attribute	Description
bindingSQLQuery	Specifies the binding for `h:inputText`
bindingCommandButton	Specifies the binding for `h:commandButton`
valueCommandButton	Specifies the value expression for `h:commandButton`
valueDataTable	Specifies the value expression for `h:dataTable`
submitAction	Specifies the action method for `h:commandButton`
sqlQueryLabel	Specifies the value expression for `h:outputLabel`

9. Required attributes, for which a value must be supplied, are specified using `required`. Because a binding EL expression for an `h:inputText` element is needed, specify `bindingSQLQuery` as required:

```
<cc:attribute name="bindingSQLQuery" required="true"/>
```

10. You specify default values using `default`. Set the default value for the Submit button to `"Submit"`:

```
<cc:attribute name="valueCommandButton" default="Submit"/>
```

11. The `action` attribute of an `h:commandButton` element requires a method expression. The `method-signature` attribute of the `<cc:attribute>` tag specifies that the attribute value must be a `MethodExpression` with the specified method signature. The Submit button (`h:commandButton`) requires a `MethodExpression` in the `action` attribute.

```
<cc:attribute name="submitAction" method-signature="void f()" required="true"/>
```

12. Add facets using the `<cc:facet>` tag for a header and a footer.

13. Because we are using an `h:inputText` element in the composite component, add a `<cc:editableValueHolder>` tag within the `<cc:interface>` tag to specify a `UIComponent` of type `editableValueHolder`. `HtmlInputText` implements the interface. The UI component tags in a definition page are bound to UI component properties in a managed bean. The `"targets"` attribute of the `<cc:editableValueHolder>` tag specifies space-delimited client IDs, which are relative to the ID of the top-level element, of the target elements within the `<cc:implementation>` tag.

```
<cc:editableValueHolder name="sqlquery1" targets="sqlquery1"/>
```

14. For the `h:commandButton` tag in the composite component, add a `<cc:actionSource>` tag in the `<cc:interface>` tag to indicate a `UIComponent` of type `ActionSource2`. `HtmlCommandButton` implements the interface. The `"targets"` attribute specifies the space-delimited client IDs of the target elements within the `<cc:implementation>` tag.

```
<cc:actionSource name="submit1" targets="submit1"/>
```

15. Specify the implementation for the composite component in the `<cc:implementation>` tag. Then render the header and footer facets using the `renderFacet` tag.

```
<cc:renderFacet name="header"/>
```

16. Add an `<h:outputLabel>` element for an output label. The `for` attribute specifies the client ID of the UI component for which the label is created. The value expression for `h:outputLabel` is specified using the `cc:attrs` map, which provides the encapsulation of the component attributes.

```
<h:outputLabel for="#{cc.clientId}:sqlquery1"
value="#{cc.attrs.sqlQueryLabel}"/>
```

17. The value expression `"#{cc.attrs.sqlQueryLabel}"` maps to the `sqlQueryLabel` attribute declared in the `<cc:interface>` tag. The value for the attribute that a user specifies in the component declaration tag in a using page gets applied to the `h:outputLabel` UI component tag. In the `<cc:implementation>` tag, specify an `h:inputText` UI component tag.

```
<h:inputText id="sqlquery1" binding="#{cc.attrs.bindingSQLQuery}"/>
```

18. The EL expression for the binding is mapped to the `bindingSQLQuery` `<cc:attribute>`, which implies that the value for the `bindingSQLQuery` attribute specified in the component declaration tag in a using page gets applied to the binding attribute of the `h:inputText` UI component tag. Add an `<h:commandButton>` UI component for a Submit button. The `id` of the Submit button matches the client ID specified in the `targets` attribute of the `<cc:actionSource>` tag within the `<cc:interface>` tag. The value expression for the `h:commandButton` is mapped to the `valueCommandButton` `<cc:attribute>` in the `<cc:interface>` tag. The value for the `valueCommandButton` attribute specified in the composite component tag in a using page is applied to the `h:commandButton`'s `value` attribute. Similarly, the EL expression for the `binding` attribute maps to the `bindingCommandButton` `<cc:attribute>`, and the EL expression for the `action` attribute maps to the `submitAction` `<cc:attribute>` in the `<cc:interface>` tag.

```
<h:commandButton id="submit1" value="#{cc.attrs.valueCommandButton}"
binding="#{cc.attrs.bindingCommandButton}"
action="#{cc.attrs.submitAction}"/>
```

19. Add an `<h:dataTable>` UI component tag for a JSF data table. The `value` expression for the data table is mapped to the `valueDataTable` `<cc:attribute>`. The value for the composite component attribute specified in the composite component tag in a using page is applied to the `value` attribute of the `h:dataTable` UI component tag.

```
<h:dataTable id="dataTable1" value="#{cc.attrs.valueDataTable}"
var="resultset" border="1" rows="5">
```

The definition page for the composite component compositeDataTable1.xhtml appears in Listing 4.4.

Listing 4.4   Definition Page compositeDataTable1.xhtml

```
<!DOCTYPE html PUBLIC "-//W3C//DTD XHTML 1.0 Transitional//EN"
"http://www.w3.org/TR/xhtml1/DTD/xhtml1-transitional.dtd">
<html xmlns="http://www.w3.org/1999/xhtml"
    xmlns:h="http://java.sun.com/jsf/html"
    xmlns:f="http://java.sun.com/jsf/core"
    xmlns:ui="http://java.sun.com/jsf/facelets"
    xmlns:cc="http://java.sun.com/jsf/composite">
  <head>
    <title>Composite DataTable</title>
  </head>
```

```
<body>
  <cc:interface>
    <!-- start top level attributes -->
    <cc:attribute name="bindingSQLQuery" required="true"/>
    <cc:attribute name="bindingCommandButton"/>
    <cc:attribute name="valueCommandButton" default="Submit"/>
    <cc:attribute name="valueDataTable" required="true"/>
    <cc:attribute name="submitAction" method-signature="void f()"
                  required="true"/>
    <cc:attribute name="sqlQueryLabel"/>
    <!-- end top level attributes -->
    <!-- start facets -->
    <cc:facet name="header"/>
    <cc:facet name="footer"/>
    <!-- end facets -->
    <!-- start attached objects -->
    <cc:editableValueHolder name="sqlquery1" targets="sqlquery1"/>
    <cc:actionSource name="submit1" targets="submit1"/>
    <!-- end attached objects -->
  </cc:interface>
  <cc:implementation>
    <cc:renderFacet name="header"/>
    <p>
      <h:outputLabel for="#{cc.clientId}:sqlquery1"
                     value="#{cc.attrs.sqlQueryLabel}"/>
      <h:inputText id="sqlquery1" binding="#{cc.attrs.bindingSQLQuery}"/>
    </p>
    <p>
      <h:commandButton id="submit1" value="#{cc.attrs.valueCommandButton}"
                       binding="#{cc.attrs.bindingCommandButton}"
                       action="#{cc.attrs.submitAction}"/>
    </p>
    <p>
      <h:dataTable id="dataTable1" value="#{cc.attrs.valueDataTable}"
var="resultset" border="1" rows="5">
        <h:column>
          <f:facet name="header">
            <h:outputText value="Catalog Id"/>
          </f:facet>
          <h:outputText value="#{resultset.catalogid}"/>
        </h:column>
```

```
          <h:column>
            <f:facet name="header">
              <h:outputText value="Journal"/>
            </f:facet>
            <h:outputText value="#{resultset.journal}"/>
          </h:column>
          <h:column>
            <f:facet name="header">
              <h:outputText value="Publisher"/>
            </f:facet>
            <h:outputText value="#{resultset.publisher}"/>
          </h:column>
          <h:column>
            <f:facet name="header">
              <h:outputText value="Edition"/>
            </f:facet>
            <h:outputText value="#{resultset.edition}"/>
          </h:column>
          <h:column>
            <f:facet name="header">
              <h:outputText value="Title"/>
            </f:facet>
            <h:outputText value="#{resultset.title}"/>
          </h:column>
          <h:column>
            <f:facet name="header">
              <h:outputText value="Author"/>
            </f:facet>
            <h:outputText value="#{resultset.author}"/>
          </h:column>
        </h:dataTable>
      </p>
      <cc:renderFacet name="footer"/>
    </cc:implementation>
  </body>
</html>
```

20. Add a definition page for composite component compositeDataTable2.xhtml in resource library dataTable2. The definition page is exactly the same as the first definition page except that the UI component IDs are different. (See Listing 4.5.)

Listing 4.5   Definition Page compositeDataTable2.xhtml

```xhtml
<!DOCTYPE html PUBLIC "-//W3C//DTD XHTML 1.0 Transitional//EN"
"http://www.w3.org/TR/xhtml1/DTD/xhtml1-transitional.dtd">
<html xmlns="http://www.w3.org/1999/xhtml"
      xmlns:h="http://java.sun.com/jsf/html"
      xmlns:f="http://java.sun.com/jsf/core"
      xmlns:ui="http://java.sun.com/jsf/facelets"
       xmlns:cc="http://java.sun.com/jsf/composite">
  <head>
    <title>Composite DataTable1</title>
  </head>
  <body>
    <cc:interface>
      <!-- start top level attributes -->
      <cc:attribute name="sqlquery"/>
      <cc:attribute name="bindingSQLQuery" required="true"/>
      <cc:attribute name="bindingCommandButton"/>
      <cc:attribute name="valueCommandButton" default="Submit"/>
      <cc:attribute name="valueDataTable" required="true"/>
      <cc:attribute name="submitAction" method-signature="void f()"
                            required="true"/>
      <cc:attribute name="sqlQueryLabel"/>
      <!-- end top level attributes -->
      <!-- start facets -->
      <cc:facet name="header"/>
      <cc:facet name="footer"/>
      <!-- end facets -->
      <!-- start attached objects -->
      <cc:editableValueHolder name="sqlquery2" targets="sqlquery2"/>
      <cc:actionSource name="submit2" targets="submit2"/>
      <!-- end attached objects -->
    </cc:interface>
    <cc:implementation>
      <cc:renderFacet name="header"/>
      <p>
        <h:outputLabel for="#{cc.clientId}:sqlquery2"
                       value="#{cc.attrs.sqlQueryLabel}"/>
      <h:inputText id="sqlquery2" binding="#{cc.attrs.bindingSQLQuery}"/>
      </p>
      <p>
        <h:commandButton id="submit2" value="#{cc.attrs.valueCommandButton}"
binding="#{cc.attrs.bindingCommandButton}"
                         action="#{cc.attrs.submitAction}"/>
      </p>
```

```
      <p>
       <h:dataTable id="dataTable2" value="#{cc.attrs.valueDataTable}" var="resultset"
border="1" rows="5">
    <h:column>
     <f:facet name="header">
      <h:outputText value="Catalog Id"/>
     </f:facet>
     <h:outputText value="#{resultset.catalogid}"/>
    </h:column>
    <h:column>
     <f:facet name="header">
      <h:outputText value="Edition"/>
     </f:facet>
     <h:outputText value="#{resultset.edition}"/>
    </h:column>
    <h:column>
     <f:facet name="header">
      <h:outputText value="Title"/>
     </f:facet>
     <h:outputText value="#{resultset.title}"/>
    </h:column>
    <h:column>
     <f:facet name="header">
      <h:outputText value="Author"/>
     </f:facet>
     <h:outputText value="#{resultset.author}"/>
    </h:column>
   </h:dataTable>
      </p>
      <cc:renderFacet name="footer"/>
    </cc:implementation>
  </body>
</html>
```

RUNNING THE COMPOSITE COMPONENTS APPLICATION

Next, you will deploy and run the composite components application. Follow these steps:

1. Create a deployment profile for the ViewController project. To begin, select File > New > From Gallery.

2. In the New Gallery dialog box, choose General > Deployment Profiles.

3. Select WAR File in the Items pane and click OK.

4. In the Create Deployment Profile wizard, select the default Deployment Profile Name setting (webapp1) and click OK.

5. In the Edit WAR Deployment Profile Properties screen, select the Specify Java EE Web Context Root option button, specify webapp1, and click OK. A webapp1 deployment profile is created.

6. Click OK in Project Properties. This adds the webapp1 deployment profile to the Deployment node.

7. Start the IntegratedWebLogicServer if it's not already started.

8. Right-click the ViewController project and select Deploy > webapp1, as shown in Figure 4.12.

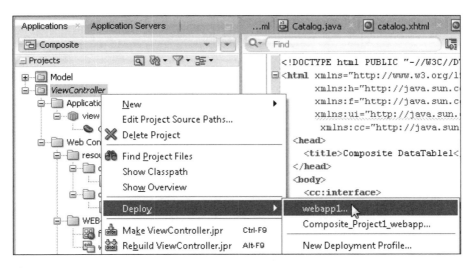

Figure 4.12
Select ViewController > Deploy > webapp1.
Source: Oracle Corporation.

9. In the Deployment Action screen, select Deploy to Application Server and click Next.

10. In the Select Server screen, select IntegratedWebLogicServer and click Next.

11. In the WebLogic Options screen, select DefaultServer, which should be in the RUNNING state, to deploy to and click Next.

12. In the Summary screen, click Finish. The composite components application is deployed to the IntegratedWebLogicServer, as shown in Figure 4.13.

```
Deployment - Log                                                                                            ⊠  ⊟
🔍                               ▣ ▾                                                                      Actions ▾
[08:43:35 AM] ---- Deployment started.  ----
[08:43:35 AM] Target platform is  (Weblogic 12.x).
[08:43:38 AM] Retrieving existing application information
[08:43:39 AM] Running dependency analysis...
[08:43:39 AM] Building...
[08:43:43 AM] Deploying profile...
[08:43:44 AM] Wrote Web Application Module to C:\JDeveloper\mywork\Composite\ViewController\deploy\webapp1.war
[08:43:46 AM] Redeploying Application...
[08:43:49 AM] [Deployer:149192]Operation "deploy" on application "webapp1" is in progress on "DefaultServer".
[08:43:51 AM] [Deployer:149194]Operation "deploy" on application "webapp1" has succeeded on "DefaultServer".
[08:43:51 AM] Application Redeployed Successfully.
[08:43:52 AM] The following URL context root(s) were defined and can be used as a starting point to test your application:
[08:43:52 AM] http://127.0.0.1:7101/webapp1
[08:43:52 AM] Elapsed time for deployment:  17 seconds
[08:43:52 AM] ---- Deployment finished.  ----
```

Figure 4.13
The composite application webapp1, deployed to IntegratedWebLogicServer.
Source: Oracle Corporation.

13. Run the catalog.xhtml using page with the following URL: http://localhost:7101/webapp1/faces/catalog.xhtml. The two composite components are displayed, as shown in Figure 4.14.

Figure 4.14
Running the catalog.xhtml using page.
Google and the Google logo are registered trademarks of Google Inc., used with permission.

Each composite component consists of a data table. Because you have used the same EL expressions for the UI component tags in the two data tables, the data tables are bound to the same managed bean properties. In the composite view consisting of two composite components, the input text field and the Submit button are rendered only once and are associated with both the composite components. When the catalog.xhtml page is run, first the top level component is rendered. The VDL processes the definition page, including a facet named UIComponent.COMPOSITE_FACET_NAME. Because the component identifiers in the composite page are required to be unique, UI component tags bound to the same managed bean property in the managed bean are rendered only once. For example, h:inputText and h:commandButton are defined in each of the definition pages (compositeDataTable1.xhtml and compositeDataTable2.xhtml), but are rendered only once in the using page.

In the page source for the catalog.xhtml using page, the component hierarchical structure for the two composite components is shown with the input text field and Submit button rendered only once (see Figure 4.15). The enclosing form component for both of the composite components is the same, as indicated by the common form ID j_idt5.

Figure 4.15
The component hierarchy in the using page's Source view.
Google and the Google logo are registered trademarks of Google Inc., used with permission.

Specify an SQL query (SELECT * FROM CATALOG) in the input text field and click Submit, as shown in Figure 4.16. Because the two data tables—one each in the two composite components—are bound to the same SQL result set, the two data tables are rendered, as shown in Figure 4.17. Unlike with the h:inputText and h:commandButton components tags, you did not bind the h:dataTable component tags in the definition pages to the same managed bean property. As a result, the component identifiers for the facets generated for the data tables are unique. The next section discusses how to generate the two data tables separately by binding them to unique input text and command button managed bean properties.

Figure 4.16
Submitting an SQL query.
Google and the Google logo are registered trademarks of Google Inc., used with permission.

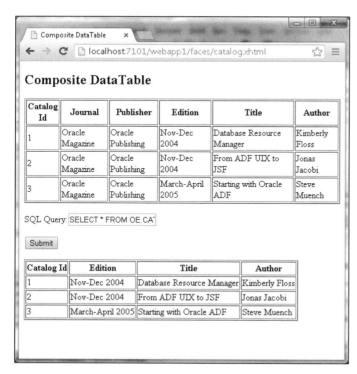

Figure 4.17
Data tables from two different composite components, rendered on the same page.
Google and the Google logo are registered trademarks of Google Inc., used with permission.

BINDING COMPOSITE COMPONENTS TO UNIQUE MANAGED BEAN PROPERTIES

In the using page example in the previous section, you specified the same EL expressions for the attributes in the two composite component tags. As a result, the input text field and command button were rendered only once in the composite view. You can modify the catalog.xhtml using page to specify unique EL expressions for the composite component tag attributes `bindingSQLQuery` and `bindingCommandButton`. The modified catalog.xhtml using page appears in Listing 4.6.

Listing 4.6   Using Page catalog.xhtml

```
<!DOCTYPE html PUBLIC "-//W3C//DTD XHTML 1.0 Transitional//EN"
    "http://www.w3.org/TR/xhtml1/DTD/xhtml1-transitional.dtd">
 <html xmlns="http://www.w3.org/1999/xhtml"
      xmlns:h="http://java.sun.com/jsf/html"
      xmlns:f="http://java.sun.com/jsf/core"
      xmlns:dt1="http://java.sun.com/jsf/composite/dataTable1"
      xmlns:dt2="http://java.sun.com/jsf/composite/dataTable2">
<f:view>
 <h:head>
  <title>Composite DataTable</title>
</h:head>
  <h:body>
  <h:form>
   <h2>Composite DataTable</h2>

    <dt1:compositeDataTable1 bindingSQLQuery="#{catalog.inputText1}"
bindingCommandButton="#{catalog.commandButton1}"
valueDataTable="#{catalog.resultSet1}"
submitAction="#{catalog.commandButton_action1}" />

    <dt2:compositeDataTable2 bindingSQLQuery="#{catalog.inputText2}"
bindingCommandButton="#{catalog.commandButton2}"
valueDataTable="#{catalog.resultSet2}"
submitAction="#{catalog.commandButton_action2}" sqlQueryLabel="SQL Query:"/>
   </h:form>
</h:body>
</f:view></html>
```

Modify the managed bean class `Catalog.java` to add managed bean properties for two input text fields, two command buttons, two result sets, and two action methods instead of one for each. The modified managed bean class appears in Listing 4.7.

Listing 4.7   Modified Managed Bean Catalog.java

```java
package view;
import javax.faces.component.html.HtmlInputText;
import java.sql.*;
import javax.faces.bean.ManagedBean;
import javax.faces.bean.RequestScoped;
import javax.faces.component.html.HtmlCommandButton;

@ManagedBean(name = "catalog")
@RequestScoped
public class Catalog {
    public Catalog() {
    }
    private HtmlInputText inputText1;
    private HtmlInputText inputText2;
    private HtmlCommandButton commandButton1;
    private HtmlCommandButton commandButton2;
    private Statement stmt1;
    private Connection connection1;
    private Statement stmt2;
    private Connection connection2;
    private ResultSet resultSet1;
    private ResultSet resultSet2;
    public void setInputText1(HtmlInputText inputText1) {
        this.inputText1 = inputText1;
    }
    public HtmlInputText getInputText1() {
        return inputText1;
    }
    public void setInputText2(HtmlInputText inputText2) {
        this.inputText2 = inputText2;
    }
    public HtmlInputText getInputText2() {
        return inputText2;
    }
    public void setCommandButton1(HtmlCommandButton commandButton1) {
        this.commandButton1 = commandButton1;
    }
    public HtmlCommandButton getCommandButton1() {
        return commandButton1;
    }
    public void setCommandButton2(HtmlCommandButton commandButton2) {
        this.commandButton2 = commandButton2;
    }
}
```

```java
    public HtmlCommandButton getCommandButton2() {
        return commandButton2;
    }
    public void setResultSet1(ResultSet resultSet1) {
        this.resultSet1 = resultSet1;
    }
    public ResultSet getResultSet1() {
        return resultSet1;
    }
    public void setResultSet2(ResultSet resultSet2) {
        this.resultSet2 = resultSet2;
    }
    public ResultSet getResultSet2() {
        return resultSet2;
    }
    public void commandButton_action1() {
        try {
            Class.forName("oracle.jdbc.OracleDriver");
            String url = "jdbc:oracle:thin:@localhost:1521:XE";
            connection1 = DriverManager.getConnection(url, "OE", "OE");
            stmt1 =
connection1.createStatement(ResultSet.TYPE_SCROLL_INSENSITIVE,
                                        ResultSet.CONCUR_READ_ONLY);
            resultSet1 = stmt1.executeQuery((String)inputText1.getValue());
            if (resultSet1 != null) {
                this.setResultSet1(resultSet1);
            }
        } catch (SQLException e) {
            System.out.println("SQLException" + e.getMessage());
        } catch (ClassNotFoundException e) {
            System.out.println("ClassNotFoundException" + e.getMessage());
        } catch (Exception e) {
            e.printStackTrace();
        } finally {
        }
    }
    public void commandButton_action2() {
        try {
            Class.forName("oracle.jdbc.OracleDriver");
            String url = "jdbc:oracle:thin:@localhost:1521:XE";
            connection2 = DriverManager.getConnection(url, "OE", "OE");

            stmt2 =
connection2.createStatement(ResultSet.TYPE_SCROLL_INSENSITIVE,
                                        ResultSet.CONCUR_READ_ONLY);
```

```
            resultSet2 = stmt2.executeQuery((String)inputText2.getValue());
            if (resultSet2 != null) {
                this.setResultSet2(resultSet2);
            }
        } catch (SQLException e) {
            System.out.println("SQLException" + e.getMessage());
        } catch (ClassNotFoundException e) {
            System.out.println("ClassNotFoundException" + e.getMessage());
        } catch (Exception e) {
            e.printStackTrace();
        } finally {
        }
    }
}
```

The resource libraries and the definition pages that define the composite components within the resource libraries are the same. You have just bound them to unique managed bean properties to generate unique facet component identifiers in the composite view rendered by the using page.

Right-click the ViewController project in the Applications navigator and select Deploy to redeploy the ViewController project. If the application was previously deployed to IntegratedWebLogicServer, it is listed as one of the options to deploy to, as shown in Figure 4.18.

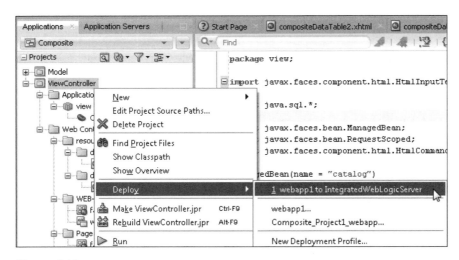

Figure 4.18
Redeploying to IntegratedWebLogicServer.
Source: Oracle Corporation.

Rerun the catalog.xhtml using page with the same URL (http://localhost:7101/webapp1/faces/catalog.xhtml). With the UI component tags bound to unique managed bean properties, two input text fields and two Submit buttons are rendered, as shown in Figure 4.19.

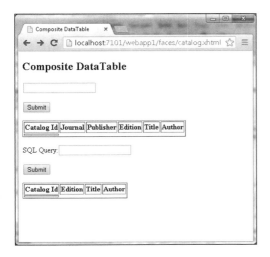

Figure 4.19
Two composite components with separate input text fields and command buttons.

Google and the Google logo are registered trademarks of Google Inc., used with permission.

The UIComponent hierarchical structure displays unique IDs for the UI component tags for input text and command button components, as shown in Figure 4.20. This is because the UI component tags were bound to different managed bean properties.

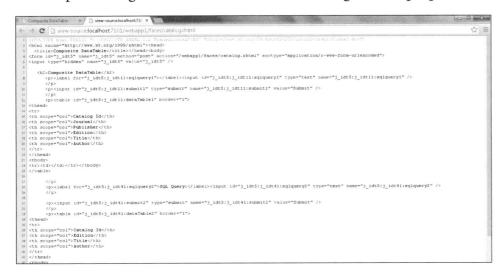

Figure 4.20
Component hierarchy with unique managed bean properties.

Google and the Google logo are registered trademarks of Google Inc., used with permission.

Specify an SQL query (SELECT * FROM CATALOG) for the first data table and click Submit, as shown in Figure 4.21. A data table is generated (see Figure 4.22). Because unique resultSet managed bean properties are used, only one of the data tables is rendered.

Figure 4.21
Submitting an SQL query for one of the composite components.
Google and the Google logo are registered trademarks of Google Inc., used with permission.

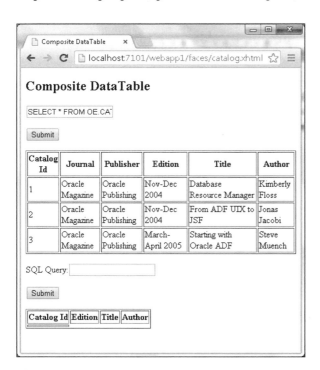

Figure 4.22
Rendering one of the composite component data tables.
Google and the Google logo are registered trademarks of Google Inc., used with permission.

Specify an SQL Query (SELECT * FROM CATALOG) in the second input text field and click Submit, as shown in Figure 4.23. A data table is generated for the specified SQL query, as shown in Figure 4.24. Because the using page is rendered again after the second SQL query is submitted, the data table generated from the first SQL query is not rendered. Only one data table is generated at a time.

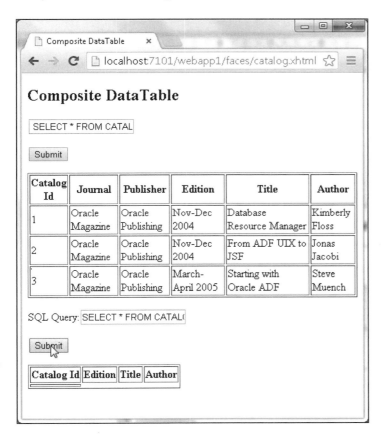

Figure 4.23
Submitting an SQL query for the second composite component data table.

Google and the Google logo are registered trademarks of Google Inc., used with permission.

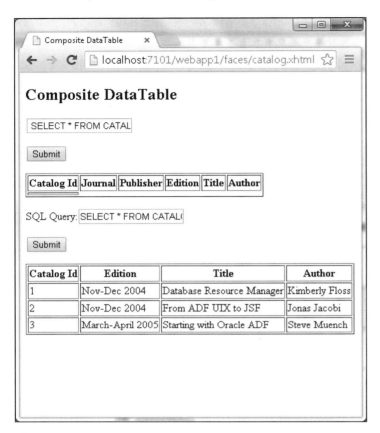

Figure 4.24
Rendering the second composite component data table.

Google and the Google logo are registered trademarks of Google Inc., used with permission.

SUMMARY

In this chapter, you developed a JSF 2.0 application using composite components. First, you defined the composite components in the definition pages. You created a composite library from the composite components. Subsequently, you used the composite components in a using page. This chapter also discussed binding composite components to unique managed bean properties. The next chapter discusses the enhanced navigation in JSF 2.0.

CHAPTER 5

ENHANCED NAVIGATION

Navigation is an important aspect of JSF. Version 1.2 is limited to navigation rules specified in the faces-config.xml configuration file. JSF 2.0, however, provides new features to facilitate navigation, which are discussed in this chapter. The new navigation features are as follows:

- **Implicit navigation.** Implicit navigation is implemented if a navigation rule or navigation case is not specified for an action or outcome from a JSF page.

- **Conditional navigation.** Conditional navigation is specified in the faces-config.xml using an EL expression that evaluates to a Boolean.

- **Preemptive navigation.** JSF 2.0 has introduced a new type of navigation handler called a configurable navigation handler. Using this, the navigation cases for a from-view-id may be retrieved and modified programmatically.

SETTING THE ENVIRONMENT

As a first step, download and install the following software:

- Oracle JDeveloper 12c (12.1.2.0.0) (www.oracle.com/technetwork/developer-tools/jdev/downloads/index.html)

- Oracle WebLogic Server 12c (included with JDeveloper 12c)

- Oracle Database Express Edition (XE) 11g (www.oracle.com/technetwork/database/database-technologies/express-edition/downloads/index.html)

To generate a JSF data table, you need a data source from which to create a database table in Oracle Database 11g XE. Use the SQL script in Listing 5.1 to specify one. (The database table is the same as the one used in the previous chapter. If you've already created it, you don't have to create it again.)

Listing 5.1   SQL Script to Create an Oracle Database Table

```
CREATE USER OE IDENTIFIED BY OE;
GRANT CONNECT, RESOURCE to OE;
CREATE TABLE OE.Catalog(CatalogId INTEGER
PRIMARY KEY, Journal VARCHAR(25), Publisher VARCHAR(25),
 Edition VARCHAR(25), Title Varchar(45), Author Varchar(25));
INSERT INTO OE.Catalog VALUES('1', 'Oracle Magazine',
 'Oracle Publishing', 'Nov-Dec 2004', 'Database Resource
Manager', 'Kimberly Floss');
INSERT INTO OE.Catalog VALUES('2', 'Oracle Magazine',
 'Oracle Publishing', 'Nov-Dec 2004', 'From ADF UIX to JSF',
'Jonas Jacobi');
INSERT INTO OE.Catalog VALUES('3', 'Oracle Magazine',
 'Oracle Publishing', 'March-April 2005', 'Starting with
Oracle ADF ', 'Steve Muench');
```

Run the SQL script in SQL Command Line to create a database table OE.CATALOG. As in the previous chapter, configure and start the IntegratedWebLogicServer.

CREATING A JAVA EE WEB APPLICATION

To demonstrate the new navigation features in JSF 2.0, create a Java EE Web application consisting of an input.xhtml page and an output.xhtml page. The input.xhtml page has an input field for an SQL query and a Submit button to submit the SQL query. The output.xhtml Facelets page consists of a JSF data table generated from the SQL query specified in input.xhtml. An error.xhtml page is also included for navigating to if an error is generated.

To create the JDeveloper application, follow these steps:

1. Select File > New > From Gallery. Select General > Applications in the Categories pane and Java EE Web Application in the Items pane. Then click Next.

2. Type Navigation in the Application Name field and click Next.

3. Select the default settings for the Model project name and directory and click Next.

4. Select the default Java settings for the Model project and click Next.

5. Select the default EJB settings for the Model project and click Next.

6. For the ViewController project, select JavaServer Faces in Project Features and click Next.

7. Select the default Java settings for the ViewController project and click Next.

8. Select the default Build Environment settings and click Finish. A Java EE Web application called "Navigation," consisting of a Model and a ViewController project, is created (see Figure 5.1). You will be using only the ViewController project.

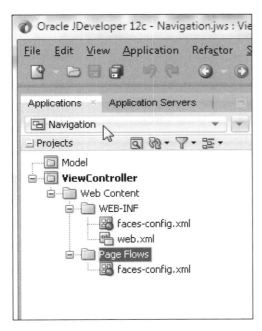

Figure 5.1
A Java EE Web application called "Navigation."
Source: Oracle Corporation.

9. Because you are using the default view definition language in JSF 2.0, which is Facelets, you will create XHTML pages for the JSF pages. To begin, select the ViewController project in Application navigator.

10. Choose File > New > From Gallery.

11. In the New Gallery dialog box, choose Web Tier > HTML in the Categories pane and HTML Page in the Items pane.

12. In the Create HTML File dialog box, select the Create as XML File checkbox, type `input.xhtml` in the File Name field, and click OK.

13. Similarly, add output.xhtml and error.xhtml JSF pages. The XHTML pages are shown in Figure 5.2.

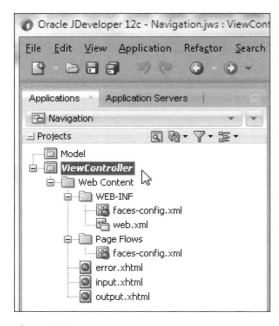

Figure 5.2
XHTML pages.
Source: Oracle Corporation.

14. Next, you will create a managed bean, which is just a POJO. Right-click faces-config.xml and select Open, as shown in Figure 5.3.

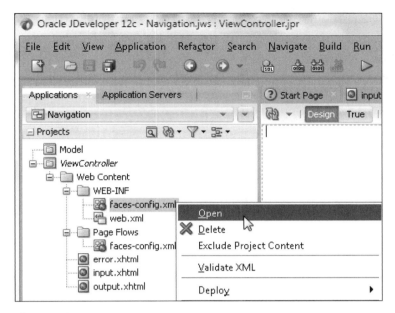

Figure 5.3
Select faces-config.xml > Open.
Source: Oracle Corporation.

15. Click the Overview tab and the Managed Beans node. Then click Add to add a new managed bean, as shown in Figure 5.4.

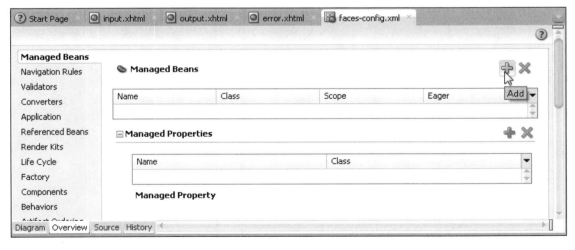

Figure 5.4
Click Add to add a managed bean.
Source: Oracle Corporation.

16. In the Create Managed Bean dialog box, type `catalog` in the Bean Name field, type `Catalog` in the Class Name field, type `view` in the Package field, select request from the Scope drop-down list, and select the Annotations option button. Then click OK. (See Figure 5.5.) A managed bean class `Catalog.java` is added to the Navigation application. The directory structure of the Navigation application is shown in Figure 5.6.

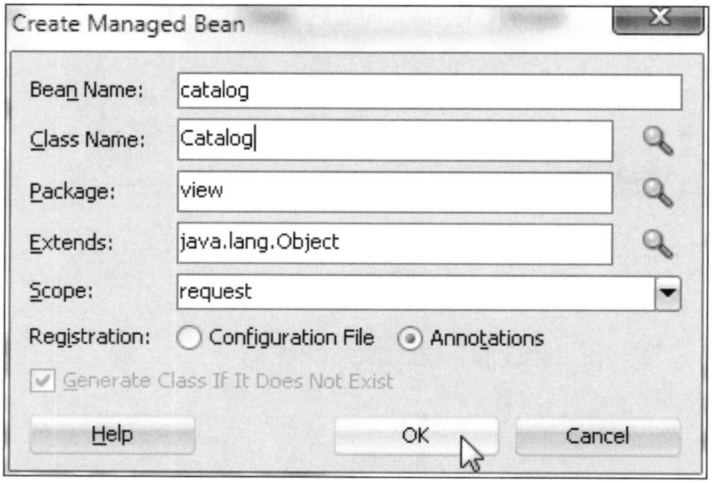

Figure 5.5
Creating a managed bean.
Source: Oracle Corporation.

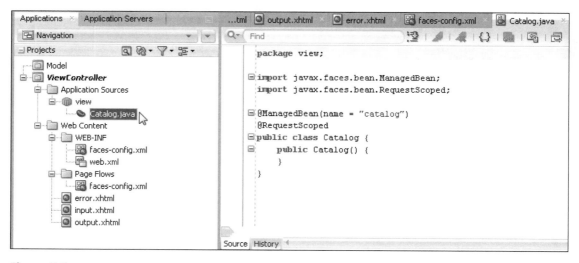

Figure 5.6
The managed bean class `Catalog.java`.
Source: Oracle Corporation.

The managed bean class is annotated with `@ManagedBean` to indicate that the class is a managed bean. The managed bean class is annotated with `@RequestScoped` to indicate that the managed bean is in `request` scope. Because you selected the JSF Project technology, web.xml consists of the `Facelets Servlet` servlet and is mapped to the URL pattern `/faces/*`. Web.xml appears in Listing 5.2.

Listing 5.2   Configuration File web.xml

```xml
<?xml version = '1.0' encoding = 'windows-1252'?>
<web-app xmlns="http://java.sun.com/xml/ns/javaee" xmlns:xsi="http://www.w3.org/2001/
XMLSchema-instance"
        xsi:schemaLocation="http://java.sun.com/xml/ns/javaee
http://java.sun.com/xml/ns/javaee/web-app_3_0.xsd"
        version="3.0">
  <servlet>
    <servlet-name>Faces Servlet</servlet-name>
    <servlet-class>javax.faces.webapp.FacesServlet</servlet-class>
    <load-on-startup>1</load-on-startup>
  </servlet>
  <servlet-mapping>
    <servlet-name>Faces Servlet</servlet-name>
    <url-pattern>/faces/*</url-pattern>
  </servlet-mapping>
</web-app>
```

The enhanced navigation features in JSF 2.0 have much simplified the JSF configuration file faces-config.xml. If you were using JSF 1.2, you would have configured the navigation in faces-config.xml. But, because you are using the navigation features in JSF 2.0, faces-config.xml is an empty file.

```xml
<?xml version="1.0" encoding="windows-1252"?>
<faces-config version="2.1" xmlns="http://java.sun.com/xml/ns/javaee">
</faces-config>
```

The input.xhtml Facelets page consists of an `h:outputLabel` for a label for the input field, an `h:inputText` for an input text field to specify an SQL query, and an `h:commandButton` to submit the SQL query. `h:inputText` binds to a managed bean property `inputText1`. The `h:commandButton` binds to a managed bean property `commandButton1`, and has action binding to a managed bean method `commandButton_action`. Input.xhtml appears in Listing 5.3.

Listing 5.3   The input.xhtml Page

```
<!DOCTYPE html PUBLIC "-//W3C//DTD XHTML 1.0 Transitional//EN"
    "http://www.w3.org/TR/xhtml1/DTD/xhtml1-transitional.dtd">
<html xmlns="http://www.w3.org/1999/xhtml"
      xmlns:ui="http://java.sun.com/jsf/facelets"
      xmlns:h="http://java.sun.com/jsf/html"
      xmlns:f="http://java.sun.com/jsf/core">
<f:view>
 <h:head>
  <title></title>
</h:head>
  <h:body>
  <h:form id="form1">
   <h2>JSF Data Table</h2>
    <h:panelGrid columns="2">
        <h:outputLabel for="inputText1"
                        value="SQL Query: "/>
   <h:inputText id="inputText1" binding="#{catalog.inputText1}" required="true"/>
   <h:commandButton binding="#{catalog.commandButton1}"
action="#{catalog.commandButton_action}" value="Submit"/>
   </h:panelGrid>
   </h:form>
</h:body>
</f:view>
</html>
```

The output.xhtml page consists of an h:dataTable element with a value binding to a managed bean property resultSet, which is the JDBC ResultSet for an SQL query specified in the input field and submitted using the Submit button. The var attribute of h:dataTable specifies the iteration variable to be used to iterate over the data model and is set to resultset. The h:column elements within the h:dataTable have a value binding to the ResultSet columns accessed using the iteration variable specified in the var attribute. The output.xhtml Facelets page appears in Listing 5.4.

Listing 5.4   The output.xhtml Page

```
<!DOCTYPE html PUBLIC "-//W3C//DTD XHTML 1.0 Transitional//EN"
    "http://www.w3.org/TR/xhtml1/DTD/xhtml1-transitional.dtd">
<html xmlns="http://www.w3.org/1999/xhtml"
    xmlns:ui="http://java.sun.com/jsf/facelets"
    xmlns:h="http://java.sun.com/jsf/html"
    xmlns:f="http://java.sun.com/jsf/core">
```

```
<f:view>
 <h:head>
  <title></title>
</h:head>
  <h:body>
   <h:form id="form1">
    <h2>JSF Data Table</h2>
    <h:dataTable id="dataTable1" value="#{catalog.resultSet}" var="resultset"
                 border="1" rows="4">
     <h:column id="column1">
      <f:facet name="header">
       <h:outputText value="Catalog Id"/>
      </f:facet>
      <h:outputText id="outputText1" value="#{resultset.catalogid}"/>
     </h:column>
     <h:column id="column2">
      <f:facet name="header">
       <h:outputText value="Journal"/>
      </f:facet>
      <h:outputText id="outputText2" value="#{resultset.journal}"/>
     </h:column>
     <h:column id="column3">
      <f:facet name="header">
       <h:outputText value="Publisher"/>
      </f:facet>
      <h:outputText id="outputText3" value="#{resultset.publisher}"/>
     </h:column>
     <h:column id="column4">
      <f:facet name="header">
       <h:outputText value="Edition"/>
      </f:facet>
      <h:outputText id="outputText4" value="#{resultset.edition}"/>
     </h:column>
     <h:column id="column5">
      <f:facet name="header">
       <h:outputText value="Title"/>
      </f:facet>
      <h:outputText id="outputText5" value="#{resultset.title}"/>
     </h:column>
     <h:column id="column6">
      <f:facet name="header">
       <h:outputText value="Author"/>
```

```
      </f:facet>
      <h:outputText id="outputText6" value="#{resultset.author}"/>
    </h:column>
  </h:dataTable>
 </h:form>
</h:body>
</f:view>
</html>
```

The error.xhtml page consists of an error message and appears in Listing 5.5.

Listing 5.5   The error.xhtml Page

```
<!DOCTYPE html PUBLIC "-//W3C//DTD XHTML 1.0 Transitional//EN"
    "http://www.w3.org/TR/xhtml1/DTD/xhtml1-transitional.dtd">
<html xmlns="http://www.w3.org/1999/xhtml"
      xmlns:ui="http://java.sun.com/jsf/facelets"
      xmlns:h="http://java.sun.com/jsf/html"
      xmlns:f="http://java.sun.com/jsf/core">
<f:view>
 <h:head>
  <title></title>
</h:head>
  <h:body>Error Page</h:body>
</f:view>
</html>
```

In the managed bean, which is a POJO, do the following:

1. Specify the properties `inputText1`, `commandButton1`, and `resultSet`.

2. Add accessor methods for the managed bean properties.

3. Add an action method, `commandButton_action`, which has action binding to the Submit button in input.xhtml.

In the action method, the SQL query specified in the input text field is retrieved and run in the Oracle Database to generate a `ResultSet`, whose value is set on the `ResultSet` managed bean property. The action method has a return value of `"output"` or a return value of `"error"` if an error is generated. We will discuss the implicit navigation that is implemented using the return value (outcome). `Catalog.java` appears in Listing 5.6.

Listing 5.6   Managed Bean Catalog.java

```java
package view;

import javax.faces.bean.ManagedBean;
import javax.faces.bean.RequestScoped;
import javax.faces.component.html.HtmlInputText;
import java.sql.*;
import javax.faces.component.html.HtmlCommandButton;
@ManagedBean(name = "catalog")
@RequestScoped
public class Catalog {
    public Catalog() {
    }
    private HtmlInputText inputText1;
    private HtmlCommandButton commandButton1;
    private Statement stmt;
    private Connection connection;
    private ResultSet resultSet;
    private boolean navigate;
    public void setInputText1(HtmlInputText inputText1) {
        this.inputText1 = inputText1;
    }
    public HtmlInputText getInputText1() {
        return inputText1;
    }
    public void setNavigate(boolean navigate) {
        this.navigate = navigate;
    }
    public boolean getNavigate() {
        return navigate;
    }
    public void setCommandButton1(HtmlCommandButton commandButton1) {
        this.commandButton1 = commandButton1;
    }
    public HtmlCommandButton getCommandButton1() {
        return commandButton1;
    }
    public void setResultSet(ResultSet resultSet) {
        this.resultSet = resultSet;
    }
```

```
    public ResultSet getResultSet() {
        return resultSet;
    }
    public String commandButton_action() {
        try {
            Class.forName("oracle.jdbc.OracleDriver");
            String url = "jdbc:oracle:thin:@localhost:1521:XE";
            connection = DriverManager.getConnection(url, "OE", "OE");

            stmt =
connection.createStatement(ResultSet.TYPE_SCROLL_INSENSITIVE,
ResultSet.CONCUR_READ_ONLY);
            resultSet = stmt.executeQuery((String) inputText1.getValue());
            if (resultSet != null) {
                this.setResultSet(resultSet);
            }
        }
        catch (SQLException e) {
            System.out.println(e.getMessage());
            return "error";
        } catch (ClassNotFoundException e) {
            System.out.println(e.getMessage());
            return "error";
        } catch (Exception e) {
            System.out.println(e.getMessage());
            return "error";
        } finally {
        }
        return "output";
    }
}
```

The next section discusses the implicit navigation used in the managed bean class.

Implicit Navigation

Implicit navigation is navigation that does not have to be specified. If navigation for a JSF page is not specified in faces-config.xml, implicit navigation is implemented if feasible.

For an outcome value of "output", the JSF application navigates to output.xhtml if the Facelets page output.xhtml is provided in the same directory as the Facelets page from which a request is initiated. In the managed bean class in the previous section, you specified a return value of "output" (see Figure 5.7) and included an output.xhtml file. If an error is returned, an outcome of "error" is returned (also shown in Figure 5.7) from the catch block of the try-catch exception handler. No navigation rules are specified in faces-config.xml.

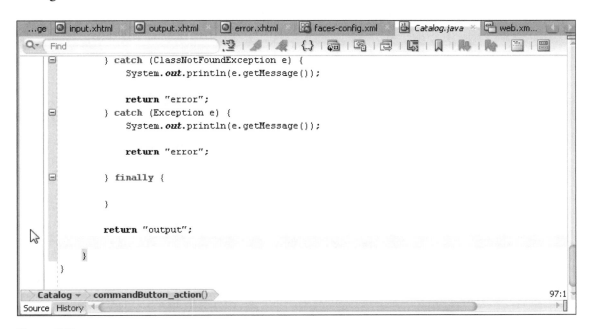

Figure 5.7

An outcome of "output" from the action method in the managed bean class.

Source: Oracle Corporation.

Let's test the implicit navigation. Follow these steps:

1. Create a deployment profile for the Navigation application. To do so, select File > New > From Gallery.

2. In the New Gallery dialog box, choose General > Deployment Profiles in the Categories pane and WAR File in the Items pane. Then click OK.

3. In the Create Deployment Profile screen, specify a deployment profile name of webapp1 and click OK.

4. In the Edit WAR Deployment Profile Properties screen, select the Java EE Web Context Root option button, specify webapp1, and click OK. The webapp1 deployment profile is created.

5. Click OK in the Project Properties dialog box.

6. Right-click ViewController in the Applications navigator and choose Deploy > webapp1, as shown in Figure 5.8.

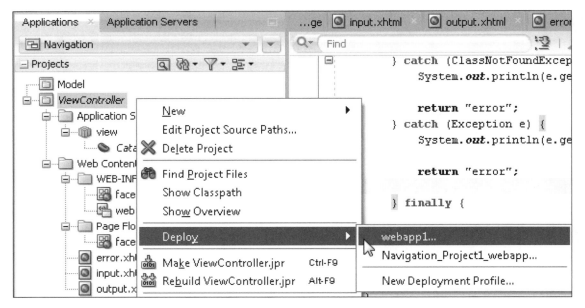

Figure 5.8
Deploying webapp1.
Source: Oracle Corporation.

7. In the Deploy webapp1 wizard, select Deploy to Application Server for Deployment Action and click Next.

8. In the Select Server screen, select IntegratedWebLogicServer and click Next.

9. In the WebLogic Options screen, select DefaultServer, which should be set to RUNNING, and click Next. (See Figure 5.9.)

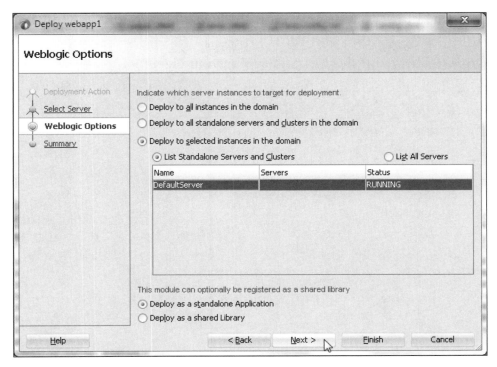

Figure 5.9
Deploying to DefaultServer.
Source: Oracle Corporation.

10. In the Summary screen, click Finish. The Navigation Web application packaged as webapp1 is deployed to IntegratedWebLogicServer, as shown in Figure 5.10.

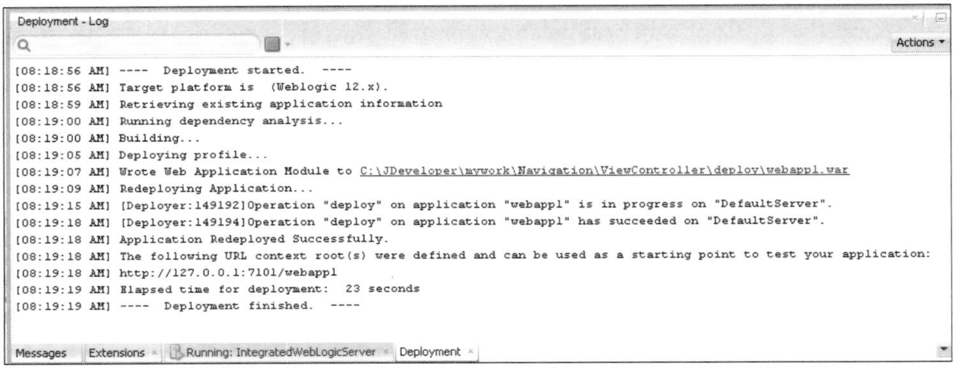

Figure 5.10
Webapp1 deployed to IntegratedWebLogicServer.
Source: Oracle Corporation.

11. Run the input.xhtml Facelets page with the following URL: http://localhost:7101/webapp1/faces/input.xhtml.

12. Specify an SQL query and click Submit, as shown in Figure 5.11.

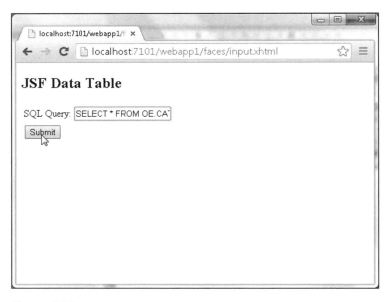

Figure 5.11
Submitting an SQL query.

Google and the Google logo are registered trademarks of Google Inc., used with permission.

Because the default navigation handler does not find a navigation rule or navigation case corresponding to the view ID input.xhtml in faces-config.xml, the JSF application navigates to output.xhtml because the outcome from the Submit action is "output"—the value returned from the action method commandButton_action. The output.xhtml page is rendered and a JSF data table is created from the SQL query specified in input.xtml, as shown in Figure 5.12.

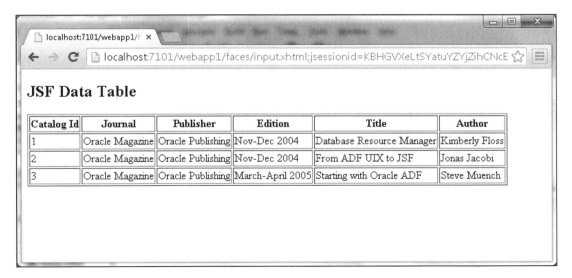

Figure 5.12
Implicit navigation to output.xhtml.
Google and the Google logo are registered trademarks of Google Inc., used with permission.

For implicit navigation to output.xhtml, the outcome from the action method may be specified as "output", "output.xhtml", or "/output.xhtml". If output.xhtml is in the /output folder, then the outcome may be specified as "/output/output.xhtml" or "/output/output".

Implicit navigation is implemented from the following outcome values:

- The return value of an action method.
- The action attribute of a UICommand component such as h:commandButton or h:commandLink.
- The outcome attribute of a UIOutcomeTarget component such as h:link or h:button.
- The handleNavigation() method of the NavigationHandler API.

CONDITIONAL NAVIGATION

JSF 2.0 has introduced a new type of navigation: conditional navigation. You implement conditional navigation using the <if></if> tag in a <navigation-case/> tag in faces-config .xml. A single contiguous EL value expression specified in the <if></if> tag must evaluate to true for the navigation case in which it is defined to be matched. Using the existing match criteria (action method and outcome), navigation is implemented only if the EL expression in the <if></if> evaluates to true.

Another new feature in JSF 2.0 navigation is the provision to match `null` outcomes. For a `null` outcome, the `NavigationHandler` will match or try to match navigation cases that do not specify a `<from-outcome>` and that include a condition expression with the `<if></if>` tag. If none of the navigation cases contain a non-`null` condition expression, the same view ID is re-displayed. If a non-`null` outcome is specified and the condition expression evaluates to `false`, the implicit navigation is implemented. This is discussed in the previous section.

To gain a better understanding of conditional navigation, follow these steps:

1. Add a managed bean property of type `boolean` called `navigate` to the managed bean class `Catalog.java` and set its value as discussed in the subsequent examples.

    ```
    private boolean navigate;
    ```

2. To see conditional navigation in action, set `navigate` to `false` and set the action method outcome to `"output"`. These settings replace the return `"output"` value in the action method, as shown in Figure 5.13.

    ```
    navigate=false;
    return "output"
    ```

Figure 5.13
Setting a Boolean to determine conditional navigation.
Source: Oracle Corporation.

3. Specify the following navigation rule in faces-config.xml. Because `navigate` is set to `false`, the condition expression would evaluate to `false`. Faces-config.xml with the condition expression is shown in Figure 5.14.

```xml
<navigation-rule>
    <from-view-id>/input.xhtml</from-view-id>
    <navigation-case>
      <from-outcome>output</from-outcome>
       <if>#{catalog.navigate}</if>
      <to-view-id>/error.xhtml</to-view-id>
    </navigation-case>
</navigation-rule>
```

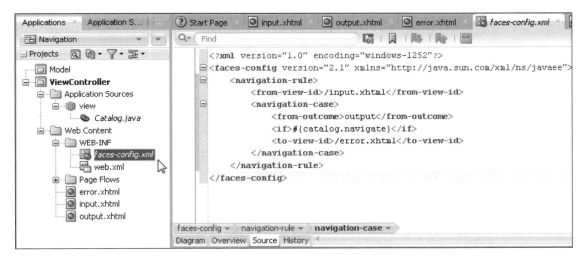

Figure 5.14
Faces-config.xml with the conditional expression.
Source: Oracle Corporation.

4. Right-click the ViewController project and select Deploy > webapp1 to IntegratedWebLogicServer, as shown in Figure 5.15. The JSF 2.0 application is deployed.

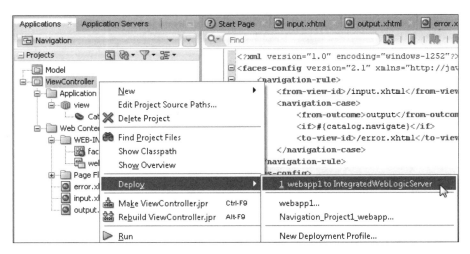

Figure 5.15
Deploying webapp1 to IntegratedWebLogicServer.
Source: Oracle Corporation.

5. Run input.xhtml with the following URL: http://localhost:7101/webapp1/faces/input .xhtml.

6. Specify the SQL query in the input.xhtml Facelets page, as shown in Figure 5.16. Because the condition expression evaluates to `false`, the application does not navigate to the `to-view-id` error.xhtml following the condition expression. As a result, implicit navigation is implemented. The application navigates to output.xhtml and a JSF data table is rendered, as shown in Figure 5.17.

Figure 5.16
Submitting an SQL query to demonstrate conditional navigation.
Google and the Google logo are registered trademarks of Google Inc., used with permission.

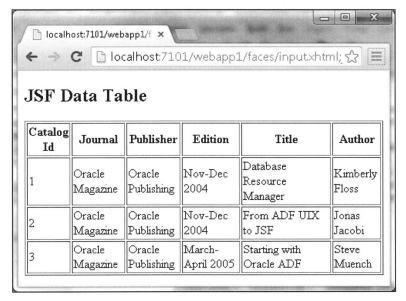

Figure 5.17
Rendering output.xhtml using conditional navigation.

Google and the Google logo are registered trademarks of Google Inc., used with permission.

7. The `<if></if>` tag must be specified before the `<to-view-id>` tag. The EL expression in the condition expression may be specified as `<if>#{false}</if>`. For example, in the managed bean action method, specify the following for the outcome and boolean property:

```
navigate=true;
return "output"
```

8. Specify the following navigation rule in faces-config.xml:

```
<navigation-rule>
    <from-view-id>/input.xhtml</from-view-id>
    <navigation-case>
      <from-outcome>output</from-outcome>
      <if>#{false}</if>
      <to-view-id>/error.xhtml</to-view-id>
    </navigation-case>
  </navigation-rule>
```

When the modified application is deployed and run and an SQL query is submitted from input.xhtml, the application navigates to output.xhtml and the JSF data table is rendered.

9. As another example of conditional navigation, specify the `boolean` property to `true` and outcome to `"output"`:

```
navigate=true;
return "output";
```

10. In faces-config.xml, specify the condition expression that evaluates to `true`:

```
<navigation-rule>
    <from-view-id>/input.xhtml</from-view-id>
    <navigation-case>
      <from-outcome>output</from-outcome>
      <if>#{catalog.navigate}</if>
      <to-view-id>/error.xhtml</to-view-id>
    </navigation-case>
</navigation-rule>
```

11. Redeploy the ViewController project to the IntegeratedWebLogicServer.

12. Run the input.xhtml Facelets page with the following URL: http://localhost:7101 /webapp1/faces/input.xhtml.

13. Specify an SQL query and click Submit, as shown in Figure 5.18. Because the condition expression evaluates to `true` and the `to-view-id` is error.xhtml, the application navigates to the error.xhtml Facelets page, as shown in Figure 5.19.

Figure 5.18
Submitting an SQL query.
Google and the Google logo are registered trademarks of Google Inc., used with permission.

Figure 5.19
Conditional navigation renders error.xhtml.

Google and the Google logo are registered trademarks of Google Inc., used with permission.

The condition expression may be specified as `<if>#{true}</if>`, as in the following faces-config.xml navigation case:

```
<navigation-rule>
    <from-view-id>/input.xhtml</from-view-id>
    <navigation-case>
      <from-outcome>output</from-outcome>
      <if>#{true}</if>
      <to-view-id>/error.xhtml</to-view-id>
    </navigation-case>
</navigation-rule>
```

For non-`null` outcomes, first the `from-outcome` has to match the outcome. For example, if the `navigate` property and the outcome are specified as follows:

```
navigate=true;
return "output";
```

and the navigation rule is specified as follows:

```
<navigation-rule>
    <from-view-id>/input.xhtml</from-view-id>
    <navigation-case>
      <from-outcome>output2</from-outcome>
      <if>#{catalog.navigate}</if>
      <to-view-id>/error.xhtml</to-view-id>
    </navigation-case>
  </navigation-rule>
```

then the `from-outcome` in the navigation case does not match the outcome. The result is that implicit navigation is implemented, and the application navigates to output.xhtml. If the outcome is `null`, and if the `from-outcome` is not specified in the navigation case, and if the `<if/>` condition that evaluates to `true` *is* specified, then the navigation case is matched and the application navigates to the `to-view-id`. For example, specify the following outcome and `boolean` property:

```
navigate = true;
return null;
```

The managed bean class `Catalog.java` with the `null` return value (`null` outcome) from the action method is shown in Figure 5.20.

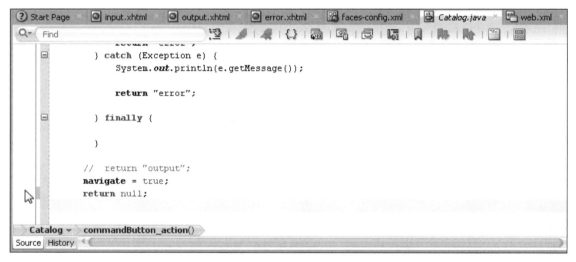

Figure 5.20
Specifying a `null` outcome.
Source: Oracle Corporation.

For an example, follow these steps:

1. Specify the following navigation rule and navigation case, which does not include a `from-outcome` and includes an `<if/>` condition, in faces-config.xml:

```
<navigation-rule>
    <from-view-id>/input.xhtml</from-view-id>
    <navigation-case>
```

```
      <if>#{catalog.navigate}</if>
      <to-view-id>/output2.xhtml</to-view-id>
    </navigation-case>
</navigation-rule>
```

2. Add an output2.xhtml JSF page, which is a copy of output.xhtml, as shown in Figure 5.21.

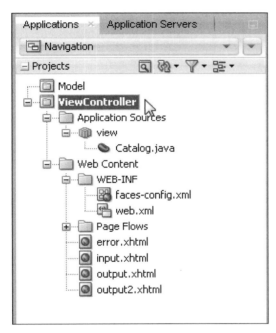

Figure 5.21
The directory structure with output2.xhtml added.
Source: Oracle Corporation.

3. Redeploy the application.

4. Run the input.xhtml JSF page, specify the SQL query in input.xhtml, and click Submit. Even with a null outcome, the navigation case that does not include a from-outcome and does include an if condition that evaluates to true gets matched, and the to-view-id output2.xhtml is rendered, as shown in Figure 5.22.

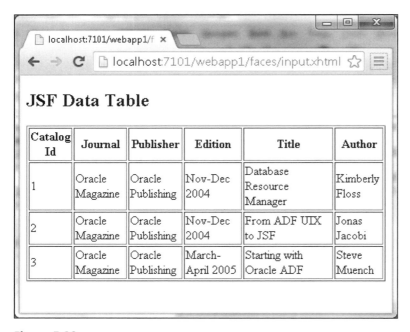

Figure 5.22
Navigation with a `null` outcome.

PREEMPTIVE NAVIGATION AND
ConfigurableNavigationHandler

Preemptive navigation is determining the destination URL of an `h:link` or `h:button` component prior to the `h:link`/`h:button` being activated or selected. The `h:link` and `h:button` components are new components in JSF 2.0. Preemptive navigation is made feasible with the new navigation handler in JSF 2.0. Support for bookmarking and `GET`-based navigation is based on preemptive navigation.

Prior to JSF 2.0, the `NavigationHandler` only implemented the navigation for a Faces request using `handleNavigation()`, as specified in faces-config.xml, after the invoke application phase to navigate to the next view in a `POST` request. The invoke application phase is the phase during which the root component broadcasts events to invoke action listeners and action methods. The main limitations of JSF prior to version 2.0 are as follows:

- Navigation rules are handled only during the invoke application phase while handling a `POST`.

- The navigation target is available only during the invoke application phase.

JSF 2.0 has introduced the `UIOutcomeTarget` component, which has an outcome associated with it. The two subclasses of `UIOutcomeTarget` are `HtmlOutcomeTargetButton` and `HtmlOutcomeTargetLink`. The corresponding `UIComponent` tags are `h:link` and `h:outcome`. Using preemptive navigation, the destination URL of `h:link` and `h:button` components are predetermined during the render response phase and navigated to when a user activates the components. Using preemptive navigation, the navigation case, including the target URL and target view ID, is evaluated/resolved during the render response phase before a user has activated the component, adding the provision for bookmarkable non-Faces requests. The preemptive/predetermined navigation is implemented and the target URL is retrieved when a user activates a hyperlink and the response is rendered. In contrast, a pre–JSF 2.0 `UICommand` component resolves and implements navigation at the same time after the invoke application phase.

`ConfigurableNavigationHandler` is a new class in JSF 2.0 with a provision to modify the navigation rules in an action method in the managed bean before rendering a view. `ConfigurableNavigationHandler` is a subclass of `NavigationHandler` with a provision to probe the navigation rules and navigation cases and to preemptively retrieve the target view ID and URL. With retrieval of navigation rules, possibly during the render response phase, a different navigation may be implemented than configured in faces-config.xml. Navigation rules can be modified dynamically using the `ConfigurableNavigationHandler` API. Two new methods are provided to retrieve the navigation rules dynamically, which are discussed in Table 5.1.

Table 5.1 `ConfigurableNavigationHandler` Methods

Method Name	Return Value	Parameters
`getNavigationCases()`	`java.util.Map<java.lang.String,java.util.Set<NavigationCase>>`	None
`getNavigationCase()`	`NavigationCase`	`FacesContext context, java.lang.String fromAction, java.lang.String outcome`

`javax.faces.application.NavigationCase` is a new class in JSF 2.0 that represents a navigation case. The `NavigationCase` object may be used to obtain all the information about a `navigation-case` using methods discussed in Table 5.2.

Table 5.2 `NavigationCase` Methods

Method Name	Description
`getActionURL`	Returns a URL to the navigation case
`getBookmarkableURL`	Returns a bookmarkable URL
`getCondition`	Evaluates the `<if/>` for the navigation case (if any) and returns a Boolean
`getFromAction`	Returns the `<from-action/>` as a string
`getFromOutcome`	Returns the `<from-outcome/>` as a string
`getFromViewId`	Returns the `<from-view-id>` as a string
`getToViewId`	Returns the `<to-view-id>` as a string
`hasCondition`	Returns a Boolean indicating whether an `<if/>` has been specified

Next, we will discuss using the `ConfigurableNavigationHandler` API to obtain or modify the navigation cases associated with a `from-view-id` in faces-config.xml, in a managed bean action method. Follow these steps:

1. Add a navigation rule without any navigation cases associated with it to faces-config .xml:

```
<navigation-rule>
    <from-view-id>/input.xhtml</from-view-id>
</navigation-rule>
```

2. We have kept the navigation rule empty to demonstrate adding navigation cases using the `ConfigurableNavigationHandler` API. You will add a navigation case using the `NavigationCase` API in the `Catalog.java` managed bean class. First, create a `ConfigurableNavigationHandler` object:

```
ConfigurableNavigationHandler navigationHandler =
(ConfigurableNavigationHandler)FacesContext.getCurrentInstance().getApplication
().getNavigationHandler();
```

3. Obtain the set of navigation cases associated with a `from-view-id` using the navigation handler:

```
String fromViewId = "/input.xhtml";
Set<NavigationCase> navigationCases =
                navigationHandler.getNavigationCases().get(fromViewId);
```

4. Create a new `NavigationCase` object.

```
NavigationCase nc =
                new NavigationCase(fromViewId, null, "output", null,
                                "/output2.xhtml", null, false, false);
```

5. If the set of navigation cases is `null`, create a new empty `LinkedHashSet` for `NavigationCase` objects and put the `LinkedHashSet` in the `NavigationCase` set associated with the `from-view-id`:

```
if (navigationCases == null) {
    navigationCases = new LinkedHashSet<NavigationCase>();
navigationHandler.getNavigationCases().put(fromViewId,
                                            navigationCases);
}
```

6. Add the new `NavigationCase` to the set of `NavigationCases` associated with the `from-view-id`.

```
navigationCases.add(nc);
```

7. Specify an outcome of `"output"`. The modified `Catalog.java` managed bean class appears in Listing 5.7.

Listing 5.7   Modified Catalog.java

```
package view;

import javax.faces.component.html.HtmlInputText;
import java.sql.*;
import java.util.LinkedHashSet;
import java.util.Set;
import javax.faces.application.ConfigurableNavigationHandler;
import javax.faces.application.NavigationCase;
import javax.faces.bean.ManagedBean;
import javax.faces.component.html.HtmlCommandButton;
import javax.faces.context.FacesContext;
```

```
@ManagedBean(name = "catalog")
public class Catalog {
    private HtmlInputText inputText1;
    private HtmlCommandButton commandButton1;
    private Statement stmt;
    private Connection connection;
    private ResultSet resultSet;
    private boolean navigate;
    public void setInputText1(HtmlInputText inputText1) {
        this.inputText1 = inputText1;
    }

    public HtmlInputText getInputText1() {
        return inputText1;
    }
    public void setNavigate(boolean navigate) {
        this.navigate = navigate;
    }
    public boolean getNavigate() {
        return navigate;
    }
    public void setCommandButton1(HtmlCommandButton commandButton1) {
        this.commandButton1 = commandButton1;
    }
    public HtmlCommandButton getCommandButton1() {
        return commandButton1;
    }
    public void setResultSet(ResultSet resultSet) {
        this.resultSet = resultSet;
    }
    public ResultSet getResultSet() {
        return resultSet;
    }
    public String commandButton_action() {
        try {
            Class.forName("oracle.jdbc.OracleDriver");
            String url = "jdbc:oracle:thin:@localhost:1521:XE";
            connection = DriverManager.getConnection(url, "OE", "OE");
            stmt =
connection.createStatement(ResultSet.TYPE_SCROLL_INSENSITIVE,
                        ResultSet.CONCUR_READ_ONLY);
            resultSet = stmt.executeQuery((String)inputText1.getValue());
```

```
        if (resultSet != null) {
            this.setResultSet(resultSet);
        }
        ConfigurableNavigationHandler navigationHandler =
(ConfigurableNavigationHandler)FacesContext.getCurrentInstance().getApplication()
.getNavigationHandler();
        String fromViewId = "/input.xhtml";
        Set<NavigationCase> navigationCases =
            navigationHandler.getNavigationCases().get(fromViewId);
        NavigationCase nc =
            new NavigationCase(fromViewId, null, "output", null,
                            "/output2.xhtml", null, false, false);
        if (navigationCases == null) {
            navigationCases = new LinkedHashSet<NavigationCase>();
            navigationHandler.getNavigationCases().put(fromViewId,
                                                navigationCases);

        }
        navigationCases.add(nc);
    }
    catch (SQLException e) {
        System.out.println(e.getMessage());
        return "error";
    } catch (ClassNotFoundException e) {
        System.out.println(e.getMessage());
        return "error";
    } catch (Exception e) {
        System.out.println(e.getMessage());
        return "error";
    } finally {
    }
    navigate = true;
    return "output";
    }
}
```

8. Redeploy the application and run the input.xhtml with the following URL: http://localhost:7101/webapp1/faces/input.xhtml.

9. Specify an SQL query and click Submit, as shown in Figure 5.23. Input.xhtml is not associated with any navigation cases in faces-config.xml. You added a navigation case to navigate to output2.xhtml if the outcome is "output". When the SQL query is submitted, the managed bean configures the new navigation case and output2.xhtml is rendered, as shown in Figure 5.24.

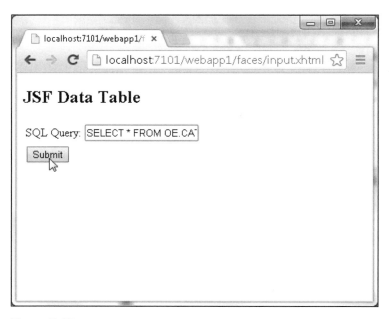

Figure 5.23
Submitting an SQL query.

Google and the Google logo are registered trademarks of Google Inc., used with permission.

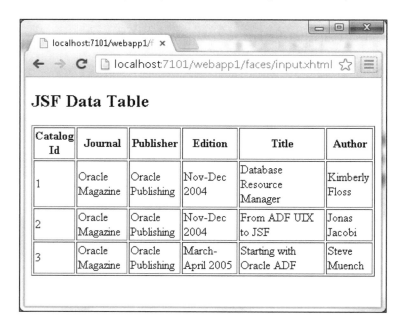

Figure 5.24
Output2.xhtml rendered by `ConfigurableNavigationHandler`.

Google and the Google logo are registered trademarks of Google Inc., used with permission.

10. In a variation of `ConfigurableNavigationHandler`, add a navigation case associated with the input.xhtml view ID in faces-config.xml:

```
<navigation-rule>
    <from-view-id>/input.xhtml</from-view-id>
    <navigation-case>
      <from-outcome>output</from-outcome>
      <to-view-id>/error.xhtml</to-view-id>
    </navigation-case>
</navigation-rule>
```

11. If you were to programmatically add another navigation case associated with outcome `"output"` for `from-view-id` input.xhtml, the new navigation case wouldn't get added. That's because a navigation case associated input.xhtml with outcome `"output"` is already defined. You would first need to remove the `to-view-id/error` .xhtml and add another `to-view-id`. As before, create a `ConfigurableNavigationHandler` object. Obtain the set of `NavigationCases` associated with the view ID. Then create a `NavigationCase` object for the error.xhtml view object as follows:

```
NavigationCase ncRemove =
            new NavigationCase(fromViewId, null, "output", null,"/error.xhtml",
null, false, false);
```

12. Remove the `NavigationCase` using the `remove` method:

```
navigationCases.remove(ncRemove);
```

13. Having removed the navigation case associated with input.xhtml, add a new navigation case, as discussed earlier. The `Catalog.java` managed bean class with a navigation case modified using the `ConfigurableNavigationHandler` appears in Listing 5.8.

Listing 5.8   Catalog.java, Including the `ConfigurableNavigationHandler`

```
package view;

import javax.faces.component.html.HtmlInputText;
import java.sql.*;
import java.util.LinkedHashSet;
import java.util.Set;
import javax.faces.application.ConfigurableNavigationHandler;
import javax.faces.application.NavigationCase;
import javax.faces.bean.ManagedBean;
```

```java
import javax.faces.bean.RequestScoped;
import javax.faces.component.html.HtmlCommandButton;
import javax.faces.context.FacesContext;

@ManagedBean(name = "catalog")
@RequestScoped
public class Catalog {

    private HtmlInputText inputText1;
    private HtmlCommandButton commandButton1;
    private Statement stmt;
    private Connection connection;
    private ResultSet resultSet;
    private boolean navigate;
    public void setInputText1(HtmlInputText inputText1) {
        this.inputText1 = inputText1;
    }
    public HtmlInputText getInputText1() {
        return inputText1;
    }
    public void setNavigate(boolean navigate) {
        this.navigate = navigate;
    }
    public boolean getNavigate() {
        return navigate;
    }
    public void setCommandButton1(HtmlCommandButton commandButton1) {
        this.commandButton1 = commandButton1;
    }
    public HtmlCommandButton getCommandButton1() {
        return commandButton1;
    }
    public void setResultSet(ResultSet resultSet) {
        this.resultSet = resultSet;
    }
    public ResultSet getResultSet() {
        return resultSet;
    }
    public String commandButton_action() {
        try {
            Class.forName("oracle.jdbc.OracleDriver");
            String url = "jdbc:oracle:thin:@localhost:1521:XE";
```

```
                connection = DriverManager.getConnection(url, "OE", "OE");
                stmt =
connection.createStatement(ResultSet.TYPE_SCROLL_INSENSITIVE,
ResultSet.CONCUR_READ_ONLY);
                resultSet = stmt.executeQuery((String) inputText1.getValue());
                if (resultSet != null) {
                    this.setResultSet(resultSet);
                }
                ConfigurableNavigationHandler navigationHandler =
                    (ConfigurableNavigationHandler)
FacesContext.getCurrentInstance().getApplication().getNavigationHandler();
                String fromViewId = "/input.xhtml";
                Set<NavigationCase> navigationCases =
navigationHandler.getNavigationCases().get(fromViewId);
                NavigationCase ncAdd =
                    new NavigationCase(fromViewId, null, "output", null, "/output2.xhtml",
null, false, false);
                NavigationCase ncRemove =
                    new NavigationCase(fromViewId, null, "output", null, "/error.xhtml",
null, false, false);

                if (navigationCases == null) {
                    navigationCases = new LinkedHashSet<NavigationCase>();
                    navigationHandler.getNavigationCases().put(fromViewId,
navigationCases);
                }
                navigationCases.remove(ncRemove);
                navigationCases.add(ncAdd);
            }
        catch (SQLException e) {
            System.out.println(e.getMessage());
            return "error";
        } catch (ClassNotFoundException e) {
            System.out.println(e.getMessage());
            return "error";
        } catch (Exception e) {
            System.out.println(e.getMessage());
            return "error";
        } finally {
        }
        navigate = true;
        return "output";
    }
}
```

14. Redeploy, run input.xhtml, and submit an SQL query. The navigation handler navigates the Facelets application to output2.xhtml as before, and a JSF data table is rendered. The difference is that you had to remove the navigation case already associated and add another.

SUMMARY

This chapter discussed the new navigation features in JSF 2.0. JSF 2.0 has added support for implicit navigation, which implies that in the absence of a navigation rule in faces-config.xml, the outcome value is used to ascertain the view ID to navigate to. Conditional navigation has been added to provide navigation based on evaluation of a Boolean expression. Preemptive navigation, which is discussed in more detail in Chapter 7, "View Parameters," is used to ascertain the navigation URL prior to selecting a hyperlink or button. The `ConfigurableNavigationHandler` API has been added to configure the navigation handler programmatically. The next chapter discusses the enhanced validation provided by JSF 2.0.

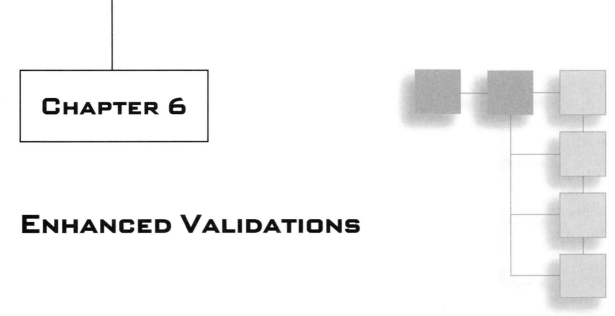

CHAPTER 6

ENHANCED VALIDATIONS

Validation is the process of validating the value of an input component (`EditableValueHolder`) with a validation constraint. JSF 2.0 has introduced several new validation features, including the following:

- Validation of empty fields
- Integration with bean validation
- A validator tag for regular expressions
- A validator tag for a required value
- Bean validation with custom validators

This chapter discusses each of these new features.

SETTING THE ENVIRONMENT

As a first step, download and install the following software:

- Oracle JDeveloper 12c (12.1.2.0.0) (www.oracle.com/technetwork/developer-tools/jdev/downloads/index.html)
- Oracle WebLogic Server 12c (included with JDeveloper 12c)
- Oracle Database Express Edition (XE) 11g (www.oracle.com/technetwork/database/database-technologies/express-edition/downloads/index.html)
- Bean validation API JAR (validation-api-1.0.0.GA.jar) (http://mvnrepository.com/artifact/javax.validation/validation-api/1.0.0.GA)

- Hibernate's bean validation reference implementation (hibernate-validator-4.0.0.GA.jar) (http://mvnrepository.com/artifact/org.hibernate/hibernate-validator/4.0.0.GA)

- Simple Logging Facade for Java (slf4j-1.7.6.zip) (www.slf4j.org/download.html)

To generate a JSF data table, you need a data source from which to create a database table in Oracle Database 11g XE. Use the SQL script in Listing 6.1 to specify one. (The database table is the same as the one used in previous chapters. If you've already created it, you don't have to create it again.)

Listing 6.1   SQL Script to Create an Oracle Database Table

```
CREATE USER OE IDENTIFIED BY OE;
GRANT CONNECT, RESOURCE to OE;
CREATE TABLE OE.Catalog(CatalogId INTEGER
PRIMARY KEY, Journal VARCHAR(25), Publisher VARCHAR(25),
 Edition VARCHAR(25), Title Varchar(45), Author Varchar(25));
INSERT INTO OE.Catalog VALUES('1', 'Oracle Magazine',
 'Oracle Publishing', 'Nov-Dec 2004', 'Database Resource
Manager', 'Kimberly Floss');
INSERT INTO OE.Catalog VALUES('2', 'Oracle Magazine',
 'Oracle Publishing', 'Nov-Dec 2004', 'From ADF UIX to JSF',
'Jonas Jacobi');
INSERT INTO OE.Catalog VALUES('3', 'Oracle Magazine',
 'Oracle Publishing', 'March-April 2005', 'Starting with
Oracle ADF ', 'Steve Muench');
```

Run the SQL script in SQL Command Line to create a database table OE.CATALOG. Add the Hibernate validator, the validation API, and Simple Logging Facade for Java JAR files to the CLASSPATH variable in the \\DefaultDomain\bin\startWebLogic script:

```
set CLASSPATH=%SAVE_CLASSPATH%;C:\JSF2.0\hibernate-validator-
4.0.0.GA.jar;C:\JSF2.0\validation-api-1.0.0.GA.jar;C:\JSF2.0\slf4j-1.7.6\slf4j-
api-1.7.6.jar;C:\JSF2.0\slf4j-1.7.6\slf4j-log4j12-
1.7.6.jar;C:\JSF2.0\slf4j-1.7.6\slf4j-simple-1.7.6.jar
```

As in Chapter 2, "Templating with Facelets," configure and start the IntegratedWebLogicServer.

Creating a Java EE Application

To grasp the new validation features in JSF 2.0, you will create a Java EE Web application consisting of an input.xhtml page and an output.xhtml page. The input.xhtml page has an input field for an SQL query and a Submit button to submit the SQL query.

The output.xhtml page consists of a JSF data table generated from the SQL query specified in input.xhtml. The input.xhtml will require modifications as you add different tags to explore different validation features. Follow these steps:

1. Add an input2.xhtml file, a copy of input.xhtml, to be used as a modifiable input JSF page.

2. Add an error.xhtml file, to be rendered if an error is generated.

3. Create the Java EE Web application in JDeveloper. To do so, start by choosing File > New > From Gallery.

4. In the New Gallery dialog box, choose General > Applications in the Categories pane and select Java EE Web Application in the Items pane. Then click OK.

5. In the Application Name field of the Name Your Application screen, type `Validations` as shown in Figure 6.1 and click Next.

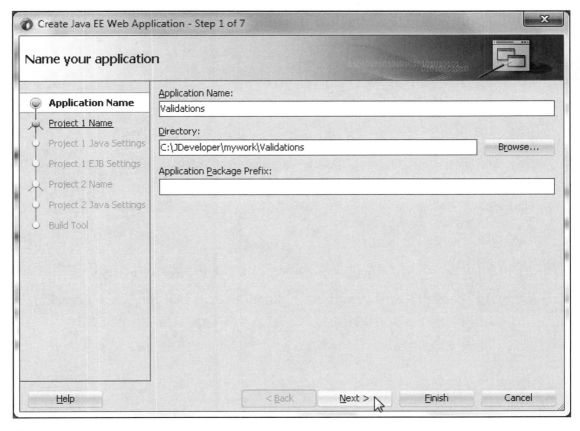

Figure 6.1
Creating a Java EE Web application called "Validations."
Source: Oracle Corporation.

6. Select the default settings for the Model project name and click Next.

7. Select the default Java settings for the Model project and click Next.

8. Select the default EJB settings for the Model project and click Next.

9. For the ViewController project, select the default name, select JSF under Project Features, and click Next.

10. Select the default Java settings for the ViewController project and click Next.

11. Select the default settings in the Select the Build Environment screen and click Finish. A Java EE Web application consisting of a Model and a ViewController project is created, as shown in Figure 6.2.

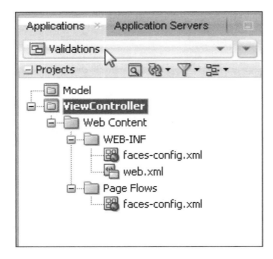

Figure 6.2
The Validations Java EE Web application.
Source: Oracle Corporation.

12. Right-click the ViewController project and select Project Properties.

13. Click Add Jar/Directory to add the Validations API JAR file (see Figure 6.3).

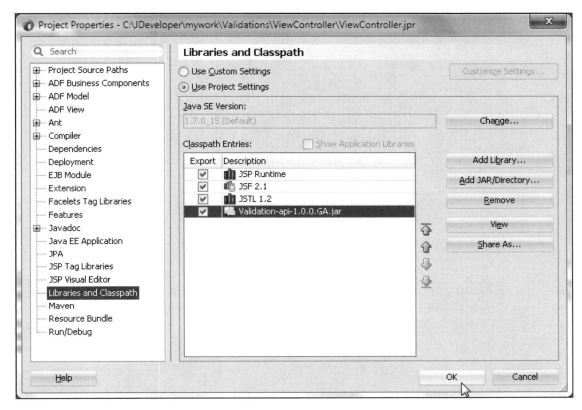

Figure 6.3
Adding the Validations API JAR file to the Java build path.
Source: Oracle Corporation.

14. For the JSF pages, create a managed bean. To begin, right-click faces-config.xml and select Open.

15. Click the Overview tab and the Managed Beans node.

16. Click the Add button to add a new managed bean.

17. In the Create Managed Bean dialog box, type catalog in the Bean Name field, type Catalog in the Class Name field, type view in the Package field, select the appropriate option from the Scope drop-down list (the default is request), and select the Annotations option button. Then click OK. (See Figure 6.4.) A new managed bean is created and a managed bean class, Catalog.java, is added.

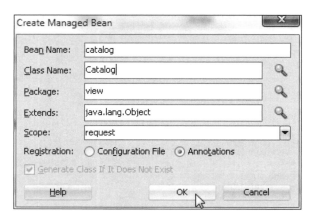

Figure 6.4
Creating a managed bean called "catalog."
Source: Oracle Corporation.

18. Because you are using the default view definition language in JSF 2.0, Facelets, you will create XHTML pages for the JSF pages. To begin, select the ViewController project in the Application navigator. Then, in the New Gallery dialog box, select Web Tier > HTML in the Categories pane and choose HTML Page in the Items pane. Then click OK.

19. In the Create HTML File dialog box, select the Create as XML File checkbox, type `input.xhtml` in the File Name field, and click OK, as shown in Figure 6.5.

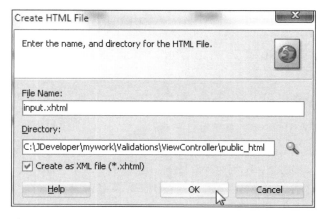

Figure 6.5
Creating a JSF page, input.xhtml.
Source: Oracle Corporation.

20. Similarly, add an input2.xhtml page as an alternative input JSF page, as well as output.xhtml and error.xhtml JSF pages. The directory structure of the Validations application is shown in Figure 6.6.

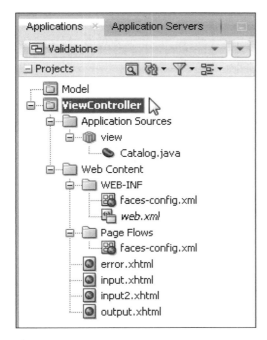

Figure 6.6
The directory structure of the Validations application.
Source: Oracle Corporation.

The web.xml file consists of the FacesServlet because you selected the JSF Project technology. The web.xml file appears in Listing 6.2.

Listing 6.2   The web.xml File

```xml
<?xml version = '1.0' encoding = 'windows-1252'?>
<web-app xmlns="http://java.sun.com/xml/ns/javaee"
xmlns:xsi="http://www.w3.org/2001/XMLSchema-instance"
        xsi:schemaLocation="http://java.sun.com/xml/ns/javaee
http://java.sun.com/xml/ns/javaee/web-app_3_0.xsd"
        version="3.0">
  <servlet>
    <servlet-name>Faces Servlet</servlet-name>
    <servlet-class>javax.faces.webapp.FacesServlet</servlet-class>
    <load-on-startup>1</load-on-startup>
  </servlet>
```

```
<servlet-mapping>
  <servlet-name>Faces Servlet</servlet-name>
  <url-pattern>/faces/*</url-pattern>
</servlet-mapping>
</web-app>
```

Because you are making use of JSF 2.0 support for implicit navigation and annotation-based configuration for managed bean (@ManagedBean) and managed bean scope (@RequestScoped), faces-config.xml is an empty file:

```
<?xml version="1.0" encoding="windows-1252"?>
<faces-config version="2.1" xmlns="http://java.sun.com/xml/ns/javaee">
</faces-config>
```

The input.xhtml JSF page consists of an h:outputLabel for a label for the input field, an h:inputText for an input text field to specify an SQL query, and an h:commandButton to submit the SQL query. The h:inputText tag has binding to a managed bean property inputText1. Add an h:message element to output a validation error message, like so:

```
<h:message for="inputText1" style="color:red" />
```

The h:commandButton tag has binding to a managed bean property commandButton1, and has action binding to a managed bean method commandButton_action. The input.xhtml page appears in Listing 6.3.

Listing 6.3   The input.xhtml Page

```
<!DOCTYPE html PUBLIC "-//W3C//DTD XHTML 1.0 Transitional//EN"
    "http://www.w3.org/TR/xhtml1/DTD/xhtml1-transitional.dtd">
<html xmlns="http://www.w3.org/1999/xhtml"
      xmlns:ui="http://java.sun.com/jsf/facelets"
      xmlns:h="http://java.sun.com/jsf/html"
      xmlns:f="http://java.sun.com/jsf/core">
<f:view>
 <h:head>
  <title></title>
</h:head>
  <h:body>
  <h:form id="form1">
   <h2>JSF Data Table</h2>
    <h:panelGrid columns="3">
        <h:outputLabel for="inputText1"
                       value="SQL Query : "/>
```

```
    <h:inputText id="inputText1" binding="#{catalog.inputText1}"
value="#{catalog.sqlQuery}" required="true">
    </h:inputText>
    <h:message for="inputText1" style="color:red" />
    <h:commandButton binding="#{catalog.commandButton1}"
action="#{catalog.commandButton_action}" value="Submit"/>
  </h:panelGrid>
  </h:form>
</h:body>
</f:view>
</html>
```

The output.xhtml page consists of an h:dataTable element with value binding to a managed bean property resultSet. This is the JDBC ResultSet for an SQL query specified in the input field and submitted using the Submit button. The var attribute of h:dataTable specifies the iteration variable to be used to iterate over the data model. It is set to "resultset". The h:column elements within h:dataTable have value binding to the ResultSet columns accessed using the iteration variable specified in the var attribute. The output.xhtml JSF page appears in Listing 6.4.

Listing 6.4   The output.xhtml Page

```
<!DOCTYPE html PUBLIC "-//W3C//DTD XHTML 1.0 Transitional//EN"
    "http://www.w3.org/TR/xhtml1/DTD/xhtml1-transitional.dtd">
<html xmlns="http://www.w3.org/1999/xhtml"
    xmlns:ui="http://java.sun.com/jsf/facelets"
    xmlns:h="http://java.sun.com/jsf/html"
    xmlns:f="http://java.sun.com/jsf/core">
<f:view>
 <h:head>
  <title></title>
</h:head>
  <h:body>
  <h:form id="form1">
   <h2>JSF Data Table</h2>
   <h:dataTable id="dataTable1" value="#{catalog.resultSet}" var="resultset"
                border="1" rows="4">
   <h:column id="column1">
    <f:facet name="header">
     <h:outputText value="Catalog Id"/>
    </f:facet>
    <h:outputText id="outputText1" value="#{resultset.catalogid}"/>
   </h:column>
```

```
    <h:column id="column2">
     <f:facet name="header">
      <h:outputText value="Journal"/>
     </f:facet>
     <h:outputText id="outputText2" value="#{resultset.journal}"/>
    </h:column>
    <h:column id="column3">
     <f:facet name="header">
      <h:outputText value="Publisher"/>
     </f:facet>
     <h:outputText id="outputText3" value="#{resultset.publisher}"/>
    </h:column>
    <h:column id="column4">
     <f:facet name="header">
      <h:outputText value="Edition"/>
     </f:facet>
     <h:outputText id="outputText4" value="#{resultset.edition}"/>
    </h:column>
    <h:column id="column5">
     <f:facet name="header">
      <h:outputText value="Title"/>
     </f:facet>
     <h:outputText id="outputText5" value="#{resultset.title}"/>
    </h:column>
    <h:column id="column6">
     <f:facet name="header">
      <h:outputText value="Author"/>
     </f:facet>
     <h:outputText id="outputText6" value="#{resultset.author}"/>
    </h:column>
   </h:dataTable>
  </h:form>
 </h:body>
</f:view>
</html>
```

The error.xhtml page consists of an error message. It appears in Listing 6.5.

Listing 6.5   The error.xhtml Page

```
<!DOCTYPE html PUBLIC "-//W3C//DTD XHTML 1.0 Transitional//EN"
    "http://www.w3.org/TR/xhtml1/DTD/xhtml1-transitional.dtd">
<html xmlns="http://www.w3.org/1999/xhtml"
      xmlns:ui="http://java.sun.com/jsf/facelets"
      xmlns:h="http://java.sun.com/jsf/html"
      xmlns:f="http://java.sun.com/jsf/core">
<f:view>
 <h:head>
  <title></title>
</h:head>
  <h:body>Error Page</h:body>
</f:view>
</html>
```

You want to make input2.xhtml the same as input.xhtml. You will be adding and removing tags to input2.xhtml to explore the different validation features. Follow these steps:

1. In the managed bean, specify the properties `inputText1`, `commandButton1`, and `resultSet`.

2. Add accessor (getter/setter) methods for the managed bean properties.

3. Add an action method, `commandButton_action`. This has action binding to the Submit button in input.xhtml. In the action method, the SQL query specified in the input text field is retrieved and run in the Oracle Database to generate a `ResultSet`, whose value is set on the `resultSet` managed bean property. The action method has a return value of `"output"` and a return value of `"error"` if an error is generated. You implement implicit navigation using the return value (outcome).

`Catalog.java` appears in Listing 6.6. some of the code sections have been commented; you will remove these comments in later sections.

Listing 6.6   Managed Bean Catalog.java

```
package view;
import javax.faces.bean.RequestScoped;
import javax.faces.component.html.HtmlInputText;
import javax.validation.constraints.*;
import java.sql.*;
import javax.faces.application.FacesMessage;
import javax.faces.bean.ManagedBean;
import javax.faces.component.UIComponent;
```

```java
import javax.faces.component.html.HtmlCommandButton;
import javax.faces.context.FacesContext;
import javax.faces.validator.ValidatorException;
@ManagedBean(name = "catalog")
@RequestScoped
public class Catalog {
    public Catalog() {
    }
    private HtmlCommandButton commandButton1;
    private Statement stmt;
    private Connection connection;
    private ResultSet resultSet;
    private HtmlInputText inputText1;
    private Long maxValue;
    // @Size(min=15, max=100)
    //@Pattern(regexp="SELECT+[a-z]+FROM+[a-z]+", message="The SQL Query should
start with SELECT and include a FROM clause")
    // @Size(min=15, max=10000, message= "SQL Query must be at least 15 and
at most 10000 characters long. ")
    //@Size(min=15, max=100, groups = {javax.validation.groups.Default.class})
    // @SQLQuery
    private String sqlQuery;
    public String getSqlQuery() {
        return sqlQuery;
    }
    public void setSqlQuery(String sqlQuery) {
        this.sqlQuery = sqlQuery;
    }
    // @Min(value=1)
    // @Max(value=10)
    private int catalogId;
    public int getCatalogId() {
        return catalogId;
    }
    public void setCatalogId(int catalogId) {
        this.catalogId = catalogId;
    }
    public void setMaxValue(Long maxValue) {
        this.maxValue = maxValue;
    }
    public Long getMaxValue() {
        return maxValue;
    }
```

```java
    public void setInputText1(HtmlInputText inputText1) {
        this.inputText1 = inputText1;
    }
    public HtmlInputText getInputText1() {
        return inputText1;
    }
    public void setCommandButton1(HtmlCommandButton commandButton1) {
        this.commandButton1 = commandButton1;
    }
    public HtmlCommandButton getCommandButton1() {
        return commandButton1;
    }
    public void setResultSet(ResultSet resultSet) {
        this.resultSet = resultSet;
    }
    public ResultSet getResultSet() {
        return resultSet;
    }
    public String commandButton_action() {

        try {
            Class.forName("oracle.jdbc.OracleDriver");
            String url = "jdbc:oracle:thin:@localhost:1521:XE";
            connection = DriverManager.getConnection(url, "OE", "OE");
            stmt =
connection.createStatement(ResultSet.TYPE_SCROLL_INSENSITIVE, ResultSet.
CONCUR_READ_ONLY);
            String sqlQuery = (String)(inputText1.getValue());
            //catalogId=((Integer)(inputText1.getValue())).intValue();
            // String sqlQuery = "SELECT * FROM OE.CATALOG WHERE CATALOGID=" +
catalogId;
            // String query = "SELECT * FROM OE.CATALOG WHERE CATALOGID=" +
(String)inputText1.getValue();
            resultSet = stmt.executeQuery((sqlQuery));
            if (resultSet != null) {
                this.setResultSet(resultSet);
            }
        }
        catch (SQLException e) {
            System.out.println(e.getMessage());
            return "error";
```

```
    } catch (ClassNotFoundException e) {
        System.out.println(e.getMessage());
        return "error";
    } catch (Exception e) {
        System.out.println(e.getMessage());
        return "error";
    } finally {
    }
    return "output";
    }
}
```

VALIDATION CONSTRAINT ANNOTATIONS

In JSF 1.2, validation constraints could be applied only using validator tags on the input component(s) in the JSF page. JSF 2.0 introduces validation constraints, which you can apply using annotations. Annotations were introduced in J2SE 5.0, on the managed bean properties that bind to the input components in the JSF page. The validation constraints are defined in the `javax.validation.constraints` package. Some of the validation constraints are discussed in Table 6.1.

Table 6.1 Validation Constraints

Validation Annotation	Description
@AssertFalse	This asserts that the annotated element must be false.
@AssertTrue	This asserts that the annotated element must be true.
@DecimalMax	This validates that the annotated element is a number whose value is less than or equal to the specified maximum.
@DecimalMin	This validates that the annotated element is a number whose value is greater than or equal to the specified minimum.
@Digits	This validates that the annotated element is a number within a specified range.
@Future	This validates that the annotated element is a date in the future.

@Max	This validates that the annotated element is a number with a value less than or equal to the specified maximum.
@Min	This validates that the annotated element is a number with a value greater than or equal to the specified minimum.
@NotNull	This validates that the annotated element must not be null.
@Null	This validates that the annotated element must be null.
@Past	This validates that the annotated element must be a date in the past.
@Pattern	This validates that the annotated string matches the specified regular expression.
@Size	This validates that the annotated element must be within the specified minimum and maximum constraints inclusive of the boundaries.

This section discusses some of these constraints. First, however, it covers a familiar validation example from JSF 1.2. The required attribute of the h:inputText component validates that a value has been specified for the input text field. In input.xhtml, you specify the following h:inputText element with the required attribute set to true:

```
<h:inputText id="inputText1" binding="#{catalog.inputText1}"
value="#{catalog.sqlQuery}" required="true"></h:inputText>
```

Then follow these steps:

1. Create a deployment profile, webapp1, for the ViewController project.

2. Start the IntegratedWebLogicServer if it's not already running.

3. Right-click the ViewController project and select Deploy > webapp1 to deploy the deployment profile to the IntegratedWebLogicServer.

4. Run the input.xhtml page with the following URL: http://localhost:7101/webapp1/faces/input.xhtml.

5. Do not specify a value in the input field, but click Submit. The application outputs a validation message indicating that a value is required, as shown in Figure 6.7.

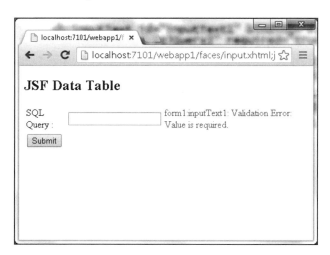

Figure 6.7
The required value validation message.
Google and the Google logo are registered trademarks of Google Inc., used with permission.

Next, we will discuss a validation constraint example using the @Size annotation. The @Size constraint validates whether the annotated element is within the specified size range, including the boundary values. The @Size constraint may be used on the types discussed in Table 6.2.

Table 6.2 Types Supported by @Size

Type	Evaluated parameter
String	String length
Collection	Collection size
Map	Map size
Array	Array length

You can annotate null elements with the @Size annotation. In the Catalog.java managed bean, annotate the sqlQuery property with the @Size annotation. Specify a min and a max value for the String length of an SQL query and specify a message to output if a validation error is generated.

```
@Size(min=15, max=10000, message= "SQL Query must be at least 15 and at most
10000 characters long. ")
    private String sqlQuery;
    public String getSqlQuery() {
        return sqlQuery;
    }
    public void setSqlQuery(String sqlQuery) {
        this.sqlQuery = sqlQuery;
    }
```

The h:inputText element has a value binding with the sqlQuery property:

```
<h:inputText id="inputText1" binding="#{catalog.inputText1}"
value="#{catalog.sqlQuery}"/>
```

For each example discussed, you would need to uncomment the corresponding code section in the managed bean and input.xhtml or use the input2.xhtml JSF page and then redeploy the application after each set of modifications.

Run the input.xhtml Facelets page with the following URL: http://localhost:7101/webapp1/faces/input.xhtml. Specify an incomplete SQL query with a string length of fewer than 15 characters and click Submit. The application outputs a validation error message indicating that the size of the SQL query must be between 15 and 10,000 characters, as shown in Figure 6.8.

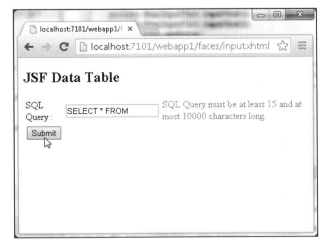

Figure 6.8
A validation error message for an @Size constraint.
Google and the Google logo are registered trademarks of Google Inc., used with permission.

In JSF 2.0 empty/null fields are validated by default. Try removing the "required" attribute from the h:inputText component tag and clicking Submit with an empty SQL Query field. The validation error message for the @Size constraint is displayed even though the input field is empty, as shown in Figure 6.9.

Figure 6.9
The @Size constraint is validated even though the input field is empty.
Google and the Google logo are registered trademarks of Google Inc., used with permission.

To prevent the validation of empty fields, JSF 2.0 provides a javax.faces.VALIDATE_EMPTY_FIELDS context parameter, which should be set to false in web.xml to disable validation of empty fields. To demonstrate the use of the context parameter, set the context parameter in web.xml as follows:

```
<context-param>
    <param-name>javax.faces.VALIDATE_EMPTY_FIELDS </param-name>
    <param-value>false</param-value>
</context-param>
```

Redeploy the application and rerun the input.xhtml JSF page. Then click the Submit button without specifying an SQL query, as shown in Figure 6.10.

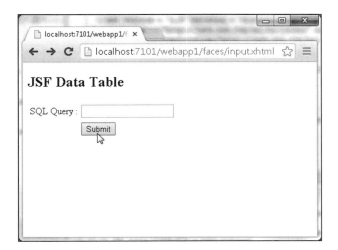

Figure 6.10
Submitting an empty SQL query.

Google and the Google logo are registered trademarks of Google Inc., used with permission.

A validation message is not displayed. Instead, an error page is rendered as an SQLException and is generated in the managed bean action method. The error outcome renders the error.xhtml JSF page, as shown in Figure 6.11.

Figure 6.11
An error message instead of a validation message.

Google and the Google logo are registered trademarks of Google Inc., used with permission.

Next, we will discuss an example with the @Min and @Max validation constraints. Follow these steps:

1. Annotate the variable declaration for catalogId in Catalog.java with the @Min and @Max annotations to specify the minimum and maximum values that a catalog ID may have:

```
@Min(value=1)
 @Max(value=10)
    private int catalogId;
    public int getCatalogId() {
        return catalogId;
    }
    public void setCatalogId(int catalogId) {
        this.catalogId = catalogId;
    }
```

2. Modify input2.xhtml with a value binding in the input field with the catalogId managed bean property.

```
<h:inputText id="inputText1" binding="#{catalog.inputText1}"
                    value="#{catalog.catalogId}"/>
```

3. Redeploy the ViewController project.

4. Run the input2.xhtml JSF page with the following URL: http://localhost:7101/ webapp1/faces/input2.xhtml.

5. Specify a catalog ID of 0 in the SQL Query field and click Submit. The application outputs a validation error message, "must be greater than or equal to 1," as shown in Figure 6.12.

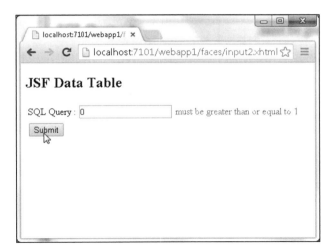

Figure 6.12
The validation message for an input value that is less than the @Min constraint value.

Google and the Google logo are registered trademarks of Google Inc., used with permission.

6. Specify a catalog ID value of 11 in the SQL Query field and click Submit. The validation error message "must be less than or equal to 10" is displayed, as shown in Figure 6.13.

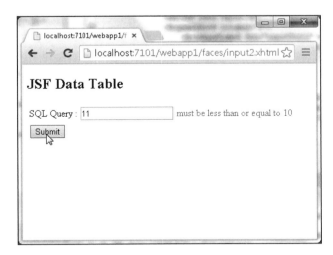

Figure 6.13
The validation message for an input value that is more than the @Max constraint value.

Google and the Google logo are registered trademarks of Google Inc., used with permission.

Next, we will discuss the @Pattern annotation, which validates a string with a regular expression. Follow these steps:

1. Annotate the sqlQuery String with the @Pattern annotation, including the regular expression to match and the validation error message to output:

```
@Pattern(regexp = "SELECT+[\\s]+[a-zA-Z]+[,]+[\\s]+[a-zA-Z]+[,]+[\\s]+[a-zA-Z]+[,]+
[\\s]+[a-zA-Z]+[,]+[\\s]+[a-zA-Z]+[,]+[\\s]+[a-zA-Z]+[\\s]+FROM+[\\s]+[a-zA-Z]+")
    private String sqlQuery;
    public String getSqlQuery() {
        return sqlQuery;
    }
    public void setSqlQuery(String sqlQuery) {
        this.sqlQuery = sqlQuery;
    }
```

2. In the input.xhtml JSF page, specify a value binding in the h:inputText field to the sqlQuery managed bean property:

```
<h:inputText id="inputText1" binding="#{catalog.inputText1}"
value="#{catalog.sqlQuery}"/>
```

3. Redeploy the ViewController project and run the input.xhtml JSF page with the following URL http://localhost:7101/webapp1/faces/input.xhtml.

4. Specify an SQL query that does not match the regular expression. For example, type SELECT * FROM CATALOG and click Submit. A validation error message indicates that the SQL query does not match the regular expression specified in the @Pattern annotation, as shown in Figure 6.14.

Figure 6.14
A validation error message for the @Pattern constraint.

Google and the Google logo are registered trademarks of Google Inc., used with permission.

5. Specify an SQL query that matches the regular expression. For example, type SELECT CATALOGID, JOURNAL, PUBLISHER, EDITION, TITLE, AUTHOR FROM CATALOG and click Submit, as shown in Figure 6.15. A data table is rendered, as shown in Figure 6.16.

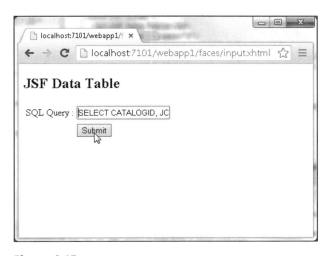

Figure 6.15
Specifying a valid SQL query.

Google and the Google logo are registered trademarks of Google Inc., used with permission.

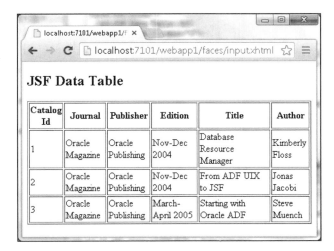

Figure 6.16
Rendering a JSF data table.

Google and the Google logo are registered trademarks of Google Inc., used with permission.

New Validators

JSF 2.0 introduces two new validators: `f:validateRequired` and `f:validateRegex`. `f:validateRequired` is similar to the `required` attribute in an input `UIInput` component. If it is specified for a `UIInput` component, and if the `disabled` attribute is not set to `false`, a value is required for the input component.

To explore the use of `f:validateRequired`, follow these steps:

1. In the input2.xhtml page, add a `f:validateRequired` tag within the `h:inputText` tag:

```
<h:inputText id="inputText1" binding="#{catalog.inputText1}"
value="#{catalog.sqlQuery}">
    <f:validateRequired />
    </h:inputText>
```

2. Before you can test the `f:validateRequired` tag, you must comment out the `javax.faces.VALIDATE_EMPTY_FIELDS` settings to `true` in web.xml:

```
<!--<context-param>
        <param-name>javax.faces.VALIDATE_EMPTY_FIELDS</param-name>
        <param-value>false</param-value>
    </context-param>-->
```

3. Redeploy the application and run the input2.xhtml JSF page.

4. Do not specify an SQL Query but click Submit. The application displays a validation error message, "Value is required," as shown in Figure 6.17.

Figure 6.17
A validation error message for `f:validateRequired`.

Google and the Google logo are registered trademarks of Google Inc., used with permission.

The f:validateRegex tag validates the String value of the wrapping component with a regular expression specified in the pattern attribute, which is a required attribute. To explore the use of the f:validateRegex tag, follow these steps:

1. Modify the input2.xhtml page to add a f:validateRegex tag within the h:inputText tag.

2. Remove any other tags, such as f:validateRequired, that may have been previously added.

```
<h:inputText id="inputText1" binding="#{catalog.inputText1}"
value="#{catalog.sqlQuery}">
                        <f:validateRegex
pattern="SELECT+[\s]+[*]+[\s]+FROM+[\s]+[a-zA-Z]+"/>
</h:inputText>
```

3. Redeploy the application and run the input2.xhtml JSF page with the following URL: http://localhost:7101/webapp1/faces/input2.xhtml.

4. Specify an SQL Query that does not match the regular expression specified in the f:validateRegex tag. For example, type SELECT * FROM OE.CATALOG, and click Submit. As shown in Figure 6.18, the application outputs a validation error message indicating that the Regex pattern is not matched. In this case, the OE. prefix in the table name does not match the regular expression.

Figure 6.18
A validation error message for f:validateRegex.

5. Remove the OE. prefix and click Submit, as shown in Figure 6.19. Because the SQL query SELECT * FROM CATALOG matches the regular expression, a data table is rendered, as shown in Figure 6.20.

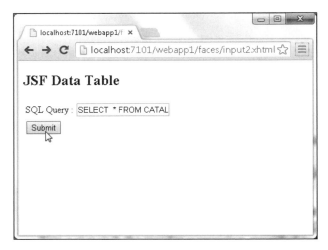

Figure 6.19
Submitting an SQL query that matches the regular expression.

Google and the Google logo are registered trademarks of Google Inc., used with permission.

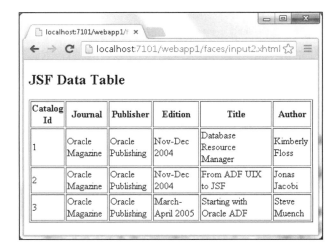

Figure 6.20
Rendering a JSF data table with a valid SQL query.

Google and the Google logo are registered trademarks of Google Inc., used with permission.

Bean Validation Integration

The JSR 303 specification defines a metadata model and an API—the default metadata source being annotations—that may be used to specify validation constraints in an application layer–independent manner. The application developer is not required to specify validators for each of the input (`EditableValueHolder`) components, but the bean validator is automatically applied to all the fields in a JSF page and the validation constraints are applied by the bean validation provider.

The bean validation constraints are defined in the `javax.validation.constraints` package, and custom constraints may also be defined. In the "Validation Constraint Annotations" section earlier in this chapter, you used some bean validation constraints. You did not have to add any configuration for the validation constraints. JSF 2.0 provides built-in integration with the bean validation constraints and automatically validates validation constraints that annotate input components in a managed bean.

You can customize bean validation using the `<f:validateBean/>` tag. For example, you can turn off bean validation by using the `disabled` attribute:

```
<f:validateBean disabled="true" />
```

You can also turn off bean validation by doing one of the following:

- Adding the following tag to faces-config.xml:

```
<application>
      <default-validators/>
   </application>
```

- Setting the `javax.faces.validator.DISABLE_DEFAULT_BEAN_VALIDATOR` context-param to `true` in web.xml:

```
<context-param>
      <param-name>javax.faces.validator.DISABLE_DEFAULT_BEAN_VALIDATOR</param-name>
      <param-value>true</param-value>
   </context-param>
```

If bean validation is turned off using one of these methods and `f:validateBean` is used in a JSF page, then `f:validateBean` overrides the settings in web.xml and faces-config.xml. For example, if bean validation is turned off in web.xml or faces-config.xml and the `<f:validateBean/>` tag is included in a component in a JSF page, bean validation is activated because of the `<f:validateBean/>` tag. You can specify `f:validateBean` within an input component tag; alternatively, you can specify one or more input components within the f:validateBean tag. In the following example, the f:validateBean tag is specified within the h:inputText component in input2.xhtml:

```
<h:inputText id="inputText1" binding="#{catalog.inputText1}"
                    value="#{catalog.sqlQuery}">
    <f:validateBean/>
</h:inputText>
```

In the managed bean, the sqlQuery managed bean property is annotated with the @Size validation constraint like so:

```
@Size(min=15, max=100)
    private String sqlQuery;
    public String getSqlQuery() {
        return sqlQuery;
    }
    public void setSqlQuery(String sqlQuery) {
        this.sqlQuery = sqlQuery;
    }
```

To see all this in action, follow these steps:

1. Redeploy the ViewController project and run the input2.xhtml page with the following URL: http://localhost:7101/webapp1/faces/input2.xhtml.

2. Specify an SQL query containing fewer than 15 characters and click Submit, as shown in Figure 6.21. The application displays a validation message, "size must be between 15 and 100," as shown in Figure 6.22.

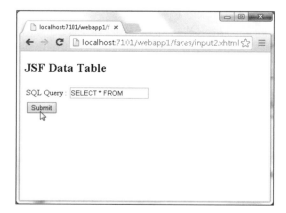

Figure 6.21
Submitting an SQL query to validate with the @Size constraint.
Google and the Google logo are registered trademarks of Google Inc., used with permission.

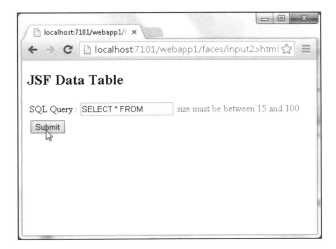

Figure 6.22
A validation error message for the @Size constraint.

Google and the Google logo are registered trademarks of Google Inc., used with permission.

You did not have to specify the f:validateBean tag for bean validation because bean validation is used by default. You can use the f:validateBean tag to specify validation groups, which are just fully qualified class names, for an input component or a set of input components using the validationGroups attribute. The validation groups are associated with validation constraints in the managed bean and group constrain the validation constraints that are to be applied to an input component or a set of input components. The default validation group is javax.validation.groups.Default.

To see this in action, follow these steps:

1. Create an empty interface view.CustomValidationGroup.

2. Modify the input2.xhtml JSF page to specify a validation group, the view.CustomValidationGroup, using the validationGroups attribute in the f:validateBean tag within the h:inputText component:

```
<h:inputText id="inputText1" binding="#{catalog.inputText1}"
                value="#{catalog.sqlQuery}">
    <f:validateBean validationGroups="view.CustomValidationGroup"/>
</h:inputText>
```

3. In the `Catalog.java` managed bean class, specify the `view.CustomValidationGroup.class` validation group in the `@Size` validation constraint annotating the `sqlQuery` property using the `groups` attribute:

```
@Size(min=15, max=100, groups = { view.CustomValidationGroup.class })
    private String sqlQuery;
    public String getSqlQuery() {
        return sqlQuery;
    }
    public void setSqlQuery(String sqlQuery) {
        this.sqlQuery = sqlQuery;
    }
```

4. Apply some other validation constraints, such as the `@Pattern` constraint discussed earlier to the `sqlQuery` property.

5. Redeploy and rerun the input2.xhtml JSF page. Only the `@Size` validation constraint is applied to the input text component. Any other validation constraint annotating the `sqlQuery` managed bean property does not get applied. The `Default` group represents all validation constraints and is validated by default. But, when specifying a specific group to be validated, the `Default` group is not validated by default for the annotated managed bean property. Only the `@Size` validation constraint is validated in the preceding example. To validate the validation constraints in the `Default` group, the `Default` class must be added to the list of validation groups:

```
<h:inputText id="inputText1" binding="#{catalog.inputText1}"
value="#{catalog.sqlQuery}">
    <f:validateBean validationGroups="view.CustomValidationGroup,
javax.validation.groups.Default"/>
</h:inputText>
```

If more than one validation constraint is specified in the managed bean, and the `h:message` tag is used to output the validation error message, the validation message is for only one of the validation constraints. For example, if the following validation constraints are applied to the `sqlQuery` property,

```
@Size(min=15, max=100)
@Pattern(regexp ="SELECT+[\\s]+[a-zA-Z]+[,]+[\\s]+[a-zA-Z]+[,]+[\\s]+[a-zA-Z]+[,]+
[\\s]+[a-zA-Z]+[,]+[\\s]+[a-zA-Z]+[,]+[\\s]+[a-zA-Z]+[\\s]+FROM+[\\s]+[a-zA-Z]+")
```

only the @Size validation constraint message or the @Pattern validation constraint message is output. To output the validation message for both the validation constraints, use the h:messages tag instead of the h:message tag:

```
<h:messages for="inputText1" style="color:red" />
```

The validation error messages for all the constraints are output, as shown in Figure 6.23.

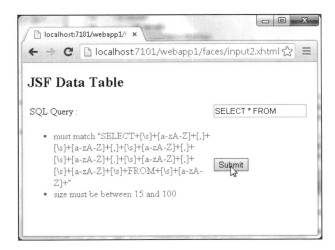

Figure 6.23
Validation error messages for multiple constraints.

Google and the Google logo are registered trademarks of Google Inc., used with permission.

CUSTOM VALIDATORS AND NULL AND EMPTY VALUES

You can create custom validators by implementing the javax.faces.validator.Validator interface. Custom validators are a not a new feature in JSF 2.0. However, support for null/empty fields in custom validators *is* a new feature in JSF 2.0. In this section, you will create a custom validator to validate an input component for an SQL query with a regular expression. Follow these steps:

1. Create a ValidatorBean Java class that implements the Validator interface, as shown in Figure 6.24.

Figure 6.24
Creating a custom validator class, `ValidatorBean`.
Source: Oracle Corporation.

2. Annotate the class with the `@FacesValidator` annotation, which is a new feature in JSF 2.0:

```
@FacesValidator("view.ValidatorBean")
public class ValidatorBean implements Validator {
}
```

3. Specify a regular expression in a `String` constant:

```
private static final String SQLQuery_REGEXP
="SELECT+[\\s]+[*]+[\\s]+FROM+[\\s]+[a-zA-Z]*";
```

4. In the `validate` method, compile the regular expression pattern and match the pattern with the SQL query:

```
String sqlquery = (String)val;
Pattern mask = Pattern.compile(SQLQuery_REGEXP);
 Matcher matcher = mask.matcher(sqlquery);
```

5. If the SQL query does not match the regular expression pattern, throw a
   ValidatorException consisting of a FacesMessage. The custom validator class
   appears in Listing 6.7.

```
if (!matcher.matches()) {
    throw new ValidatorException(message);
}
```

Listing 6.7 Custom Validator Class ValidatorBean.java

```java
package view;

import java.util.regex.*;
import javax.faces.application.FacesMessage;
import javax.faces.component.UIComponent;
import javax.faces.context.FacesContext;
import javax.faces.validator.*;
@FacesValidator("view.ValidatorBean")
public class ValidatorBean implements Validator {
    private static final String SQLQuery_REGEXP
="SELECT+[\\s]+[*]+[\\s]+FROM+[\\s]+[a-zA-Z]*";
    @Override
 public void validate(FacesContext context, UIComponent c,
                    Object val) throws ValidatorException
    {
        String sqlquery = (String)val;
        Pattern mask = Pattern.compile(SQLQuery_REGEXP);
        Matcher matcher = mask.matcher(sqlquery);
        if (!matcher.matches()) {
            FacesMessage message = new FacesMessage();
        message.setDetail("Please enter a valid SQL Query");
            message.setSummary("SQL Query not valid");
          message.setSeverity(FacesMessage.SEVERITY_ERROR);
            throw new ValidatorException(message);
        }
    }
}
```

6. Specify the custom validator on the input component for an SQL query using the
   f:validator tag:

```
<f:validator validatorId="view.ValidatorBean"/>
```

7. If you prefer, you can configure the validator in the faces-config.xml, as in JSF 1.2, instead of using the @FacesValidator annotation:

```
<?xml version="1.0" encoding="windows-1252"?>
<faces-config version="2.1" xmlns="http://java.sun.com/xml/ns/javaee">
  <validator>
    <validator-id>model.ValidatorBean</validator-id>
    <validator-class>view.ValidatorBean</validator-class>
  </validator>
</faces-config>
```

8. You can include the other validation constraints for validation of h:inputText. The h:inputText tag in the input2.xhtml JSF page with the custom validator and the bean validation follows:

```
<h:inputText id="inputText1" binding="#{catalog.inputText1}"
value="#{catalog.sqlQuery}">
                        <f:validator validatorId="view.ValidatorBean"/>
                            <f:validateBean
validationGroups="javax.validation.groups.Default"/>
                        </h:inputText>
```

9. Redeploy the application and run the input2.xhtml JSF page.

10. Specify an SQL query that does not match the regular expression in the custom validator and click Submit. The application outputs the custom validator exception message. Other validation error messages are also output if h:messages is used, as shown in Figure 6.25.

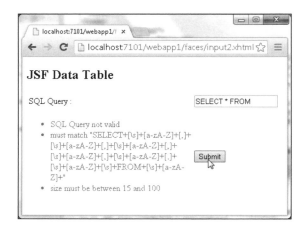

Figure 6.25
A validation error message for a custom validator and other validation constraints.

Google and the Google logo are registered trademarks of Google Inc., used with permission.

11. A new feature in JSF 2.0 for custom validators is support for null/empty values in the validation method. To see this in action, leave the SQL Query field empty and click Submit. The application still outputs the custom validator exception message, as shown in Figure 6.26.

Figure 6.26
Validating an empty field.

Google and the Google logo are registered trademarks of Google Inc., used with permission.

CUSTOM VALIDATORS WITH BEAN VALIDATION

As discussed earlier, JSF 2.0 provides integrated support for JSR 303 validation constraints. We discussed some of the validation constraints in the `javax.validation.constraints` package. In this section, you will create a custom validation constraint and use it with bean validation. Follow these steps:

1. First, you need to define an annotation for a validation constraint. In this case, create an annotation called `SQLQuery`. To begin, select File > New > From Gallery.

2. In the New Gallery dialog box, choose General > Java in the Categories pane, choose Annotation in the Items pane, and click OK, as shown in Figure 6.27.

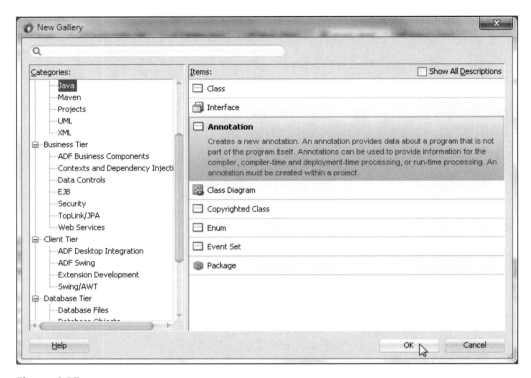

Figure 6.27
Selecting Annotation in the New Gallery dialog box.
Source: Oracle Corporation.

3. In the Create Annotation dialog box, type SQLQuery in the Name field, type view in the Package field, and click OK, as shown in Figure 6.28.

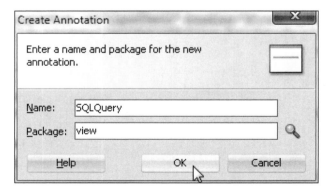

Figure 6.28
Creating an annotation.
Source: Oracle Corporation.

4. Add the SQLQuery annotation:

```
public @interface SQLQuery {
}
```

5. Add the @Constraint annotation, which specifies the validation class that implements the validator:

```
@Constraint(validatedBy = SQLQueryValidator.class)
```

6. Specify the default error message:

```
String message() default "SQL Query not valid";
```

The SQLQuery annotation type appears in Listing 6.8.

Listing 6.8   Annotation Type SQLQuery

```
package view;

import java.lang.annotation.Documented;
import java.lang.annotation.ElementType;
import java.lang.annotation.Retention;
import java.lang.annotation.RetentionPolicy;
import java.lang.annotation.Target;

import javax.validation.Constraint;
import javax.validation.Payload;

@Target( { ElementType.METHOD, ElementType.FIELD,
          ElementType.ANNOTATION_TYPE })
@Retention(RetentionPolicy.RUNTIME)
@Constraint(validatedBy = SQLQueryValidator.class)
@Documented
public @interface SQLQuery {
    String message() default "SQL Query is not a valid SQL Query";
    Class<?>[] groups() default { };
    Class<? extends Payload>[] payload() default { };
}
```

7. Create the validation class that implements the annotation. The validation class is required to implement the ConstraintValidator interface, which takes two parameters: the annotation and the type for the input value. To begin, create a Java class SQLQueryValidator that implements the javax.validation.ConstraintValidator interface, as shown in Figure 6.29.

Figure 6.29
Creating a validation class that implements the annotation type.
Source: Oracle Corporation.

8. `ConstraintValidator<A extends java.lang.annotation.Annotation,T>` is a generic type, and you will use the parameterized type `ConstraintValidator<SQLQuery, String>`:

```
public class SQLQueryValidator implements ConstraintValidator<SQLQuery, String> {
}
```

9. In the `isValid` method, compile a regular expression for the SQL query and match the SQL query input with the regular expression. If the SQL query matches the regular expression, return `true`. If it doesn't, return `false`.

```
Pattern mask =Pattern.compile("SELECT+[\\s]+[*]+[\\s]+FROM+[\\s]+[a-zA-Z]+");
  Matcher matcher = mask.matcher(value);
  if (!matcher.matches()) {
      return false;
  }
  return true;
```

The validation class SQLQueryValidator appears in Listing 6.9.

Listing 6.9   SQLQueryValidator.java

```
package view;

import javax.validation.ConstraintValidator;
import javax.validation.ConstraintValidatorContext;
import javax.faces.validator.*;

import java.util.regex.*;
import javax.faces.component.UIComponent;
import javax.faces.context.FacesContext;
import javax.faces.validator.FacesValidator;
@FacesValidator("view.SQLQueryValidator")
public class SQLQueryValidator implements ConstraintValidator<SQLQuery, String>
{
    @Override
    public void initialize(SQLQuery constraintAnnotation) {
    }
    public boolean isValid(String value, ConstraintValidatorContext context) {
        Pattern mask = Pattern.compile("SELECT+[\\s]+[*]+[\\s]+FROM+[\\s]+
[a-zA-Z]+");
        Matcher matcher = mask.matcher(value);
        if (!matcher.matches()) {
            return false;
        }
        return true;
    }
}
```

10. Having created an annotation, annotate the sqlQuery managed bean property with
    the @SQLQuery annotation in addition to other validation constraints:

```
    @Size(min = 15, max = 100)
    @Pattern(regexp =
            "SELECT+[\\s]+[a-zA-Z]+[,]+[\\s]+[a-zA-Z]+[,]+[\\s]+[a-zA-Z]+[,]+[\\s]+
    [a-zA-Z]+[,]+[\\s]+[a-zA-Z]+[,]+[\\s]+[a-zA-Z]+[\\s]+FROM+[\\s]+[a-zA-Z]+")
    @SQLQuery
    private String sqlQuery;
    public String getSqlQuery() {
        return sqlQuery;
    }
    public void setSqlQuery(String sqlQuery) {
        this.sqlQuery = sqlQuery;
    }
```

11. If the bean validation has been deactivated by any other method, add bean validation with the `f:validateBean` tag. The directory structure of the Validations application with the custom validator interfaces and classes is shown in Figure 6.30.

```
<h:inputText id="inputText1" binding="#{catalog.inputText1}"
                value="#{catalog.sqlQuery}">
<f:validateBean/>
</h:inputText>
```

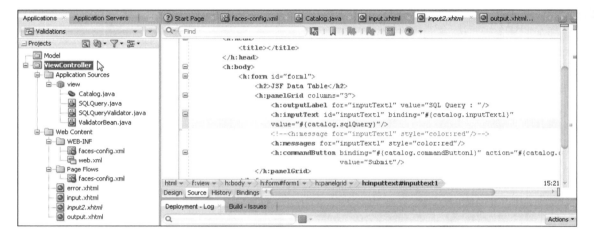

Figure 6.30
The directory structure of the Validations application.
Source: Oracle Corporation.

12. Redeploy the ViewController project and run the input2.xhtml JSF page.

13. Specify an SQL query that does not match the regular expression specified in the validation class for the `@SQLQuery` validation constraint annotation. Then click Submit. The application outputs a validation message from the custom validation class in addition to other validation messages, as shown in Figure 6.31.

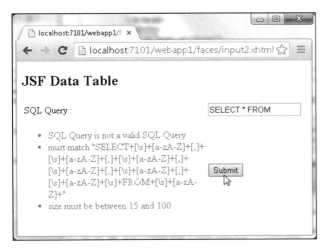

Figure 6.31
A validation message from the custom validation class.

Google and the Google logo are registered trademarks of Google Inc., used with permission.

SUMMARY

This chapter discussed the new validation features in JSF 2.0. These include bean validation, including bean validation with custom validators; new validators for regular expressions and required values; and validation of empty fields. The next chapter discusses view parameters, another new feature in JSF 2.0.

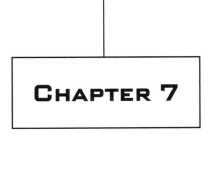

CHAPTER 7

VIEW PARAMETERS

JSF 1.2 does not provide support for sending parameters to the managed bean in a GET request. Instead, request parameters are specified in the request URL using the `?paramname1=paramvalue1&paramname2=paramvalue2` format. Seam framework, a Java EE based framework, supports sending page parameters with a page action. For example, the following page action binding also includes some page parameters:

```
<page view-id="/catalog.jsp" action="#{catalog.commandButton_action}">
        <param name="catalogId" value="#{catalog.catalogId}"/>
  <param name="sqlQuery"
value="#{catalog.sqlQuery}"/>
  </page>
```

When a GET request is made for the catalog.jsp view ID and request parameters catalogId and sqlQuery are included in the request, the request parameter values are set on the model object using the binding specified in the mapping for the page action. For example, if the GET request is `http://localhost:7001/webapp1/faces/catalog.jsp?catalogId=1&sql Query=SELECT * FROM CATALOG`, the request parameters' values are set on the catalogId and sqlQuery model object properties.

JSF 2.0 has added support for view parameters, which are similar to page parameters in Seam. You can specify the view parameters' binding in the JSF page metadata and the view parameter values in a GET request. You set the GET request parameter values on the managed bean properties, as specified in the view parameters mapping.

This chapter discusses view parameters in a JSF 2.0 page. It also discusses the application of view parameters in bookmarking links.

Setting the Environment

As a first step, download and install the following software:

- Oracle JDeveloper 12c (12.1.2.0.0) (www.oracle.com/technetwork/developer-tools/jdev/downloads/index.html)

- Oracle WebLogic Server 12c (included with JDeveloper 12c)

- Oracle Database Express Edition (XE) 11g (www.oracle.com/technetwork/database/database-technologies/express-edition/downloads/index.html)

- Bean validation API JAR (validation-api-1.0.0.GA.jar) (http://mvnrepository.com/artifact/javax.validation/validation-api/1.0.0.GA)

- Hibernate's bean validation reference implementation (hibernate-validator-4.0.0.GA.jar) (http://mvnrepository.com/artifact/org.hibernate/hibernate-validator/4.0.0.GA)

- Simple logging facade for Java (slf4j-1.7.6.zip) (www.slf4j.org/download.html)

To generate a JSF data table, you we need a data source from which to create a database table in Oracle Database 11g XE. Use the SQL script in Listing 7.1 to specify one. (The database table is the same as the one used in previous chapters. If you have already created it, you don't have to create it again.)

Listing 7.1   SQL Script to Create an Oracle Database Table

```
CREATE USER OE IDENTIFIED BY OE;
GRANT CONNECT, RESOURCE to OE;
CREATE TABLE OE.Catalog(CatalogId INTEGER
PRIMARY KEY, Journal VARCHAR(25), Publisher VARCHAR(25),
 Edition VARCHAR(25), Title Varchar(45), Author Varchar(25));
INSERT INTO OE.Catalog VALUES('1', 'Oracle Magazine',
 'Oracle Publishing', 'Nov-Dec 2004', 'Database Resource
```

```
Manager', 'Kimberly Floss');
INSERT INTO OE.Catalog VALUES('2', 'Oracle Magazine',
 'Oracle Publishing', 'Nov-Dec 2004', 'From ADF UIX to JSF',
'Jonas Jacobi');
INSERT INTO OE.Catalog VALUES('3', 'Oracle Magazine',
 'Oracle Publishing', 'March-April 2005', 'Starting with
Oracle ADF ', 'Steve Muench');
COMMIT;
```

Run the SQL script in SQL Command Line to create a database table OE.CATALOG. Add the Hibernate validator, the validation API, and Simple Logging Facade for Java JAR files to the CLASSPATH variable in the \\DefaultDomain\bin\startWebLogic script:

```
set CLASSPATH=%SAVE_CLASSPATH%;C:\JSF2.0\hibernate-validator-4.0.0.GA.jar;C:\JSF2.0\
validation-api-1.0.0.GA.jar;C:\JSF2.0\slf4j-1.7.6\slf4j-api-1.7.6.jar;C:\JSF2.0\
slf4j-1.7.6\slf4j-log4j12-1.7.6.jar;C:\JSF2.0\slf4j-1.7.6\slf4j-simple-1.7.6.jar
```

As in Chapter 2, "Templating with Facelets," configure and start the Integrated WebLogicServer.

CREATING A JAVA EE WEB APPLICATION

To grasp the view parameter feature in JSF 2.0 you will create a Java EE Web application consisting of an input.xhtml page and an output.xhtml page. The input.xhtml page has an input field for an SQL query and a Submit button to submit the SQL query. The output.xhtml page consists of a JSF data table generated from the SQL query specified in input.xhtml. An error.xhtml page is also included in case an error is generated. Follow these steps:

1. Select File > New > From Gallery.

2. In the New Gallery dialog box, select Applications in Categories in the General pane and select Java EE Web Application in the Items pane. Then click OK.

3. In the Name Your Application screen, type ViewParams in the Application Name field and click Next, as shown in Figure 7.1.

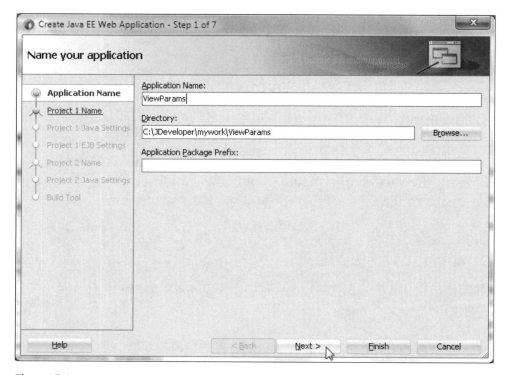

Figure 7.1
Creating a Java EE Web application called "ViewParams."
Source: Oracle Corporation.

4. Select the default settings for the Model project name and click Next.

5. Select the default Java settings for the Model project and click Next.

6. Select the default EJB settings and click Next.

7. In the ViewController project, select the JavaServer Faces project feature and click Next.

8. Select the default Java settings for the ViewController project and click Next.

9. Select the default Select Build Environment settings and click Finish. A Java EE Web application, ViewParams, consisting of a Model and a ViewController project, is created. (See Figure 7.2.)

Figure 7.2
Java EE Web application called "ViewParams."
Source: Oracle Corporation.

10. Right-click the ViewController project and select Project Properties.

11. Select Libraries and Classpath in the pane on the left.

12. Click the Validation-api-1.0.0.GA.jar entry in the pane on the right, as shown in Figure 7.3.

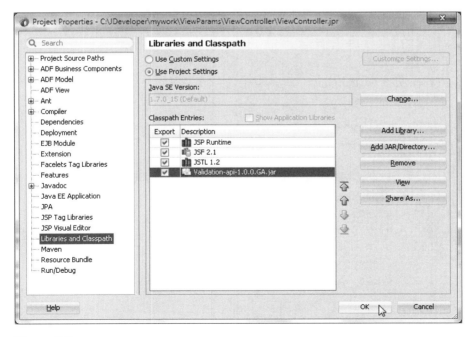

Figure 7.3
Adding Validation API to the Java Build Path.
Source: Oracle Corporation.

13. For the JSF pages, create a managed bean. To begin, right-click faces-config.xml and select Open.

14. Click the Overview tab and the Managed Beans node.

15. Click the Add button to add a new managed bean.

16. In the Create Managed Bean dialog box, type `catalog` in the Bean Name field, type `Catalog.java` in the Class Name field, and type `view` in the Package field. Then choose the desired option from the Scope drop-down list (the default is request) and select the Annotations option button. Finally, click OK. A new managed bean is created and a managed bean class, `Catalog.java`, is added.

17. In the managed bean, specify `catalogId` for the catalog ID, `inputText1` for a input text field, `commandButton1` for a command button, `sqlQuery` for an SQL query, and `resultSet` for a JDBC result set.

18. Add accessor methods for the managed bean properties.

19. Add an action method, `commandButton_action`, which has action binding to the Submit button in input.xhtml. In the action method, the SQL query specified in the input text field is retrieved and run in the Oracle Database to generate a `ResultSet`, whose value is set on the `resultSet` managed bean property. The action method has a return value of `"output"` and a return value of `"error"` if an error is generated. Implicit navigation is implemented using the return value (outcome). `Catalog.java` appears in Listing 7.2.

Listing 7.2 Managed Bean Class Catalog.java

```java
package view;

import javax.faces.component.html.HtmlInputText;
import javax.validation.constraints.*;
import java.sql.*;
import javax.faces.application.FacesMessage;
import javax.faces.bean.ManagedBean;
import javax.faces.bean.RequestScoped;
import javax.faces.component.UIComponent;
import javax.faces.component.html.HtmlCommandButton;
import javax.faces.context.FacesContext;
import javax.faces.validator.ValidatorException;

@ManagedBean(name = "catalog")
@RequestScoped
```

```java
public class Catalog {
    public Catalog() {
    }
    private HtmlCommandButton commandButton1;
    private Statement stmt;
    private Connection connection;
    private ResultSet resultSet;

    private HtmlInputText inputText1;

    private String sqlQuery;

    public String getSqlQuery() {
        return sqlQuery;
    }

    public void setSqlQuery(String sqlQuery) {
        this.sqlQuery = sqlQuery;
    }


    private int catalogId;

    public int getCatalogId() {
        return catalogId;
    }

    public void setCatalogId(int catalogId) {
        this.catalogId = catalogId;
    }

    public void setInputText1(HtmlInputText inputText1) {
        this.inputText1 = inputText1;
    }

    public HtmlInputText getInputText1() {
        return inputText1;
    }

    public void setCommandButton1(HtmlCommandButton commandButton1) {
        this.commandButton1 = commandButton1;
    }

    public HtmlCommandButton getCommandButton1() {
        return commandButton1;
    }

    public void setResultSet(ResultSet resultSet) {
        this.resultSet = resultSet;
    }
```

```java
    public ResultSet getResultSet() {
        return resultSet;
    }

    public String commandButton_action() {
        try {
            Class.forName("oracle.jdbc.OracleDriver");
            String url = "jdbc:oracle:thin:@localhost:1521:XE";
            connection = DriverManager.getConnection(url, "OE", "OE");
            stmt =
connection.createStatement(ResultSet.TYPE_SCROLL_INSENSITIVE,
                        ResultSet.CONCUR_READ_ONLY);
                catalogId = ((Integer) (inputText1.getValue()));
              sqlQuery =
                 "SELECT * FROM OE.CATALOG WHERE CATALOGID=" + catalogId;
            resultSet = stmt.executeQuery((sqlQuery));
            if (resultSet != null) {
                this.setResultSet(resultSet);
            }
        }
        catch (SQLException e) {
            System.out.println(e.getMessage());
            return "error";
        } catch (ClassNotFoundException e) {
            System.out.println(e.getMessage());
            return "error";
        } catch (Exception e) {
            System.out.println(e.getMessage());
            return "error";
        } finally {
        }
        return "output";
    }
}
```

20. Create six JSF pages (XHTML pages)—input.xhtml, input2.xhtml, input3.xhtml, input4.xhtml, output.xhtml, and error.xhtml—as explained in Chapter 2. The directory structure of the ViewParams application is shown in Figure 7.4.

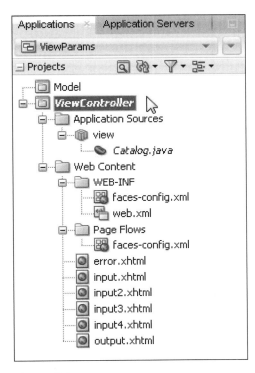

Figure 7.4
The directory structure of the ViewParams application.

Source: Oracle Corporation.

The web.xml page consists of the Faces servlet because you selected the JSF project technology. The web.xml page appears in Listing 7.3.

Listing 7.3   The web.xml Page

```
<?xml version = '1.0' encoding = 'windows-1252'?>
<web-app xmlns="http://java.sun.com/xml/ns/javaee"
xmlns:xsi="http://www.w3.org/2001/XMLSchema-instance"
        xsi:schemaLocation="http://java.sun.com/xml/ns/javaee
http://java.sun.com/xml/ns/javaee/web-app_3_0.xsd"
        version="3.0">
  <servlet>
    <servlet-name>Faces Servlet</servlet-name>
```

```
  <servlet-class>javax.faces.webapp.FacesServlet</servlet-class>
  <load-on-startup>1</load-on-startup>
 </servlet>
 <servlet-mapping>
  <servlet-name>Faces Servlet</servlet-name>
  <url-pattern>/faces/*</url-pattern>
 </servlet-mapping>
</web-app>
```

Because you are using implicit navigation and using annotations to configure the scope and managed bean, the faces-config.xml is an empty file:

```
<?xml version="1.0" encoding="windows-1252"?>
<faces-config version="2.1" xmlns="http://java.sun.com/xml/ns/javaee">
</faces-config>
```

The input.xhtml page consists of an h:outputLabel for a label for the input field, an h:inputText for an input text field to specify an SQL query, and an h:commandButton to submit the SQL query. The h:inputText field binds to a managed bean property inputText1. Add an h:message element to output the validation error message. The h:commandButton binds to a managed bean property commandButton1 and has an action binding to a managed bean method commandButton_action. The input.xhtml page appears in Listing 7.4.

Listing 7.4   The input.xhtml Page

```
<!DOCTYPE html PUBLIC "-//W3C//DTD XHTML 1.0 Transitional//EN"
    "http://www.w3.org/TR/xhtml1/DTD/xhtml1-transitional.dtd">
<html xmlns="http://www.w3.org/1999/xhtml"
     xmlns:ui="http://java.sun.com/jsf/facelets"
     xmlns:h="http://java.sun.com/jsf/html"
     xmlns:f="http://java.sun.com/jsf/core">
<f:view>
  <h:body>
<h:messages />
  <h:form id="form1">
   <h2>JSF Data Table</h2>
    <h:panelGrid columns="3">
        <h:outputLabel for="inputText1"
                        value="SQL Query Catalog ID: "/>
 <h:inputText id="inputText1" binding="#{catalog.inputText1}"
value="#{catalog.catalogId}">
    </h:inputText>
```

```
  <h:message for="inputText1" style="color:red" />
  <h:commandButton binding="#{catalog.commandButton1}"
action="#{catalog.commandButton_action}" value="Create DataTable"/>
  </h:panelGrid>
  </h:form>
</h:body>
</f:view>
</html>
```

The output.xhtml page consists of an `h:dataTable` element with value binding to a managed bean property `resultSet`, which is the JDBC `ResultSet` for an SQL query specified in the input field and submitted using the Submit button. The `var` attribute of `h:dataTable` specifies the iteration variable to be used to iterate over the data model and is set to `"resultset"`. The `h:column` elements within the `h:dataTable` have value binding to the `ResultSet` columns accessed using the iteration variable specified in the `var` attribute. Add an `h:outputText` element for the SQL query. The output.xhtml page appears in Listing 7.5.

Listing 7.5 The output.xhtml Page

```
<!DOCTYPE html PUBLIC "-//W3C//DTD XHTML 1.0 Transitional//EN"
    "http://www.w3.org/TR/xhtml1/DTD/xhtml1-transitional.dtd">
<html xmlns="http://www.w3.org/1999/xhtml"
    xmlns:ui="http://java.sun.com/jsf/facelets"
    xmlns:h="http://java.sun.com/jsf/html"
    xmlns:f="http://java.sun.com/jsf/core">
<f:view>
 <h:head>
  <title></title>
</h:head>

  <h:body>
  <h:form id="form1">
   <h2>JSF Data Table</h2>
<!-- <h:outputText value="SQL Query: #{catalog.sqlQuery}" />-->
   <h:dataTable id="dataTable1" value="#{catalog.resultSet}" var="resultset"
              border="1" rows="4">
    <h:column id="column1">
     <f:facet name="header">
      <h:outputText value="Catalog Id"/>
     </f:facet>
     <h:outputText id="outputText1" value="#{resultset.catalogid}"/>
    </h:column>
```

```
    <h:column id="column2">
     <f:facet name="header">
      <h:outputText value="Journal"/>
     </f:facet>
     <h:outputText id="outputText2" value="#{resultset.journal}"/>
    </h:column>
    <h:column id="column3">
     <f:facet name="header">
      <h:outputText value="Publisher"/>
     </f:facet>
     <h:outputText id="outputText3" value="#{resultset.publisher}"/>
    </h:column>
    <h:column id="column4">
     <f:facet name="header">
      <h:outputText value="Edition"/>
     </f:facet>
     <h:outputText id="outputText4" value="#{resultset.edition}"/>
    </h:column>
    <h:column id="column5">
     <f:facet name="header">
      <h:outputText value="Title"/>
     </f:facet>
     <h:outputText id="outputText5" value="#{resultset.title}"/>
    </h:column>
    <h:column id="column6">
     <f:facet name="header">
      <h:outputText value="Author"/>
     </f:facet>
     <h:outputText id="outputText6" value="#{resultset.author}"/>
    </h:column>
   </h:dataTable>
  </h:form>
 </h:body>
</f:view>
</html>
```

The error.xhtml page consists of an error message. It appears in Listing 7.6.

Listing 7.6   The error.xhtml Page

```
<!DOCTYPE html PUBLIC "-//W3C//DTD XHTML 1.0 Transitional//EN"
    "http://www.w3.org/TR/xhtml1/DTD/xhtml1-transitional.dtd">
<html xmlns="http://www.w3.org/1999/xhtml"
    xmlns:ui="http://java.sun.com/jsf/facelets"
    xmlns:h="http://java.sun.com/jsf/html"
    xmlns:f="http://java.sun.com/jsf/core">
<f:view>
 <h:head>
  <title></title>
</h:head>
  <h:body>Error Page</h:body>
</f:view>
</html>
```

POST REQUEST PARAMETERS IN JSF 1.2

In JSF 1.2, you can send request parameters to the managed bean only in a POST request. You can specify the mapping for the request parameter catalogId to a managed bean property in the faces-config.xml as follows:

```
<managed-bean>
    <managed-bean-name>catalog</managed-bean-name>
    <managed-bean-class>model.Catalog</managed-bean-class>
    <managed-bean-scope>request</managed-bean-scope>
    <managed-property>
      <property-name>catalogId</property-name>
      <value>#{param['catalogId']}</value>
    </managed-property>
  </managed-bean>
```

In the managed bean, the catalogId property and the accessor methods are specified as follows:

```
public class Catalog {
    private int catalogId;
    public int getCatalogId() {
        return catalogId;
    }
    public void setCatalogId(int catalogId) {
        this.catalogId = catalogId;
    }
}
```

In the JSF page, the `catalogId` managed bean property is specified in a value binding for an `h:inputText` component:

```
<h:inputText id="inputText1" binding="#{catalog.inputText1}"
value="#{catalog.catalogId}"/>
```

When the JSF page is submitted in a POST request with a value in the `h:inputText` field, the value is set on the `catalogId` property. But no provision to include request parameters in a GET request is provided in JSF 1.2.

VIEW PARAMETERS IN JSF 2.0

View parameters add the provision to send request parameters in a GET request. A view parameter is a UI component represented with the `UIViewParameter` class. Just like other UI components, it is saved in the UI component tree for a JSF page and may be associated with validators and converters. A view parameter is an `EditableValueHolder` because it implements the interface.

You specify the mappings for the view parameters to managed bean properties in `f:viewParam` tags, which are specified within the `f:metadata` tag. The `f:metadata` tag must be specified at the top level within a JSF view. For example, add the following `f:viewParam` tag to the `f:metadata` tag:

```
<f:metadata>
  <f:viewParam id="catalogId" name="catalogId" value="#{catalog.catalogId}"/>
</f:metadata>
```

The `f:viewParam` tag specifies a value binding from a view parameter named `catalogId` to a managed bean property named `catalogId`. An `h:outputText` tag with the `catalogId` value is also specified. The input.xhtml JSF page with the `f:viewParam` tag appears in Listing 7.7.

Listing 7.7   The input.xhtml Page with `f:viewParam`

```
<!DOCTYPE html PUBLIC "-//W3C//DTD XHTML 1.0 Transitional//EN"
    "http://www.w3.org/TR/xhtml1/DTD/xhtml1-transitional.dtd">
<html xmlns="http://www.w3.org/1999/xhtml"
xmlns:ui="http://java.sun.com/jsf/facelets"
    xmlns:h="http://java.sun.com/jsf/html"
xmlns:f="http://java.sun.com/jsf/core">
    <f:metadata>
        <f:viewParam id="catalogId" name="catalogId"
value="#{catalog.catalogId}"/>
    </f:metadata>
```

```
<f:view>
    <h:outputText value="CatalogId: #{catalog.catalogId}"/>
    <h:body>
        <h:form id="form1">
            <h2>JSF Data Table</h2>
            <h:panelGrid columns="3">
                <h:outputLabel for="inputText1" value="SQL Query Catalog ID: "/>
                <h:inputText id="inputText1"
binding="#{catalog.inputText1}" value="#{catalog.catalogId}"></h:inputText>
                <h:message for="inputText1" style="color:red"/>
                <h:commandButton binding="#{catalog.commandButton1}"
action="#{catalog.commandButton_action}"
                                    value="Create DataTable"/>
            </h:panelGrid>
        </h:form>
    </h:body>
</f:view>
</html>
```

Because the value binding for the `catalogId` property is specified using view parameters, you don't need to retrieve the `catalogId` property value in the managed bean. The following line may be commented out in the action method `commandButton_action`:

```
//catalogId=((Integer)(inputText1.getValue()));
```

To see all this in action, follow these steps:

1. Create a deployment profile, webapp1, for the ViewController project with Java EE Web Context root as webapp1.

2. To run the Web application on the WebLogic Server, start the IntegratedWebLogicServer if it's not already started.

3. Right-click the ViewController project and select Deploy > webapp1 to deploy the deployment profile to the IntegratedWebLogicServer.

4. Run the input.xhtml JSF page with the following URL: http://localhost:7101/webapp1/faces/input.xhtml?catalogId=2. This includes a request parameter. The Catalog ID value is filled in the `CatalogId type` field.

5. Click Create DataTable, as shown in Figure 7.5. The `commandButton_action` method of the managed bean is invoked with an outcome of `"output"`, which causes the application to navigate to output.xhtml. In the postback (submit the page to itself), output.xhtml is rendered in the browser, but the URL in the browser is still for

input.xhtml because the JSF controller servlet performs server forwarding by default during navigation. The browser renders the output.xhtml JSF page and generates the data table for Catalog ID 2, as shown in Figure 7.6.

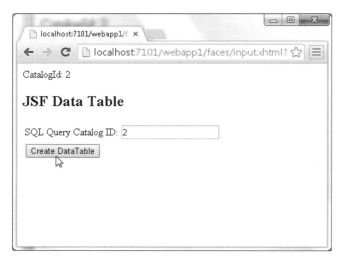

Figure 7.5
Including a view parameter in a GET request.

Google and the Google logo are registered trademarks of Google Inc., used with permission.

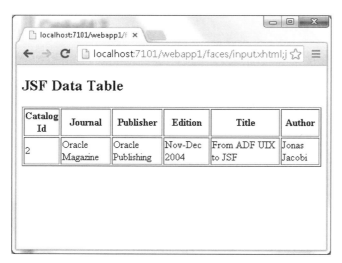

Figure 7.6
Rendering a JSF data table using Catalog ID from ViewParam.

Google and the Google logo are registered trademarks of Google Inc., used with permission.

As discussed, view parameters are saved in the UI component tree. Their value does not have to re-specified in a component tree postback when a JSF page is submitted. In the previous example, the h:inputText field is included, but it is not required. The input.xhtml JSF page with just a command button appears in Listing 7.8.

Listing 7.8   The input.xhtml Page Without h:inputText

```
<!DOCTYPE html PUBLIC "-//W3C//DTD XHTML 1.0 Transitional//EN"
    "http://www.w3.org/TR/xhtml1/DTD/xhtml1-transitional.dtd">
<html xmlns="http://www.w3.org/1999/xhtml"
    xmlns:ui="http://java.sun.com/jsf/facelets"
    xmlns:h="http://java.sun.com/jsf/html"
    xmlns:f="http://java.sun.com/jsf/core">
<f:metadata>
  <f:viewParam id="catalogId" name="catalogId" value="#{catalog.catalogId}"/>
 </f:metadata>
<f:view>
 <h:outputText value="CatalogId: #{catalog.catalogId}" />
  <h:body>
  <h:form id="form1">
   <h2>JSF Data Table</h2>
    <h:panelGrid columns="3">
    <h:commandButton binding="#{catalog.commandButton1}"
action="#{catalog.commandButton_action}" value="Create DataTable"/>
  </h:panelGrid>
  </h:form>
</h:body>
</f:view>
</html>
```

6. Redeploy and run the modified input.xhtml JSF page with the following URL: http://localhost:7101/webapp1/faces/input.xhtml?catalogId=2. The view parameter catalogId updates the model during the update model phase. The component tree is created during the render response phase, as is the response. The catalogId view parameter value is output using the h:outputText tag, which has a value binding to the catalogId property, as shown in Figure 7.7. The view parameter value is saved in the component tree when rendering of a JSF page (a view) is complete. When the form is submitted, the view parameter values are applied to the managed bean model object. In the postback, the output.xhtml JSF page is rendered and the JSF data table is generated, as shown in Figure 7.8.

Figure 7.7
Submitting a form using a view parameter, without an input text field.

Google and the Google logo are registered trademarks of Google Inc., used with permission.

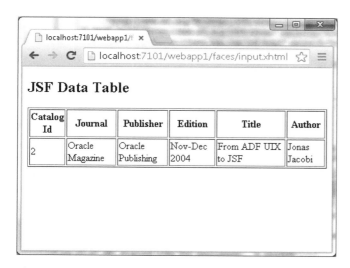

Figure 7.8
Rendering a JSF data table using a view parameter.

Google and the Google logo are registered trademarks of Google Inc., used with permission.

ADDING VALIDATION WITH VIEW PARAMETERS

As mentioned, a view parameter, specified with the `f:viewParam` tag, is just an `EditablevalueHolder` UI component. You can configure validators and converters with a view parameter just as with any other `EditableValueHolder`. In the following example, an `f:validateLength` validator is configured with the `f:viewParam` tag and the validation message is output using the `validatorMessage` attribute of the `f:viewParam` tag. To output a validator message, add the `h:messages` tag:

```
<f:metadata>
<f:viewParam id="catalogId" name="catalogId" value="#{catalog.catalogId}"
validatorMessage="Text must
be  1 chars long">
                    <f:validateLength maximum="1"/>
  </f:viewParam>
 </f:metadata>
<h:messages />
```

The input2.xhtml JSF page with the validator appears in Listing 7.9. The validator validates the `h:inputText` field length to be a maximum of 1.

Listing 7.9   Including a Validator

```
<!DOCTYPE html PUBLIC "-//W3C//DTD XHTML 1.0 Transitional//EN"
    "http://www.w3.org/TR/xhtml1/DTD/xhtml1-transitional.dtd">
<html xmlns="http://www.w3.org/1999/xhtml"
      xmlns:ui="http://java.sun.com/jsf/facelets"
      xmlns:h="http://java.sun.com/jsf/html"
      xmlns:f="http://java.sun.com/jsf/core">
<f:metadata>
  <f:viewParam id="catalogId" name="catalogId" value="#{catalog.catalogId}"
    validatorMessage="Text must be 1 chars long">
                    <f:validateLength maximum="1"/>
  </f:viewParam>
 </f:metadata>
<f:view>
 <h:messages />
 <h:outputText value="CatalogId: #{catalog.catalogId}" /><br/>
<!-- <h:outputText value="SQL Query: #{catalog.sqlQuery}" />

->
  <h:body>
  <h:form id="form1">
   <h2>JSF Data Table</h2>
    <h:panelGrid columns="3">
    <h:commandButton binding="#{catalog.commandButton1}"
action="#{catalog.commandButton_action}" value="Create DataTable"/>
```

```
   </h:panelGrid>
   </h:form>
</h:body>
</f:view>
</html>
```

Redeploy the ViewController project and run the JSF page with the following URL: http://localhost:7101/webapp1/faces/input2.xhtml?catalogId=12. It includes a request parameter `catalogId` with a value of 12. Because the `catalogId` value length is more than 1, the application outputs a validator error message, as shown in Figure 7.9. The default value for `int` (0) is set on `catalogId`.

Figure 7.9
Using validation in conjunction with view parameters.

Google and the Google logo are registered trademarks of Google Inc., used with permission.

You can add an `h:outputText` tag to output.xhtml to output the SQL query:

```
<h:outputText value="SQL Query: #{catalog.sqlQuery}" />
```

Redeploy and rerun the JSF page, but set the `catalogId` request parameter value to 2, which is a valid value, with the following URL: http://localhost:7101/webapp1/faces/input2.xhtml?catalogId=2. Then click the Create DataTable button, as shown in Figure 7.10.

Figure 7.10
Submitting a form with a validated view parameter value.

In the postback, the data table in output.xhtml is rendered and displayed, as shown in Figure 7.11.

Figure 7.11
Rendering a JSF table using a validated view parameter value.

PreRenderView Event Handling

JSF 2.0 provides a new system event, PreRenderView, which is dispatched after the view parameters have been processed but before the view has been rendered. A listener for the event is registered using the f:event tag and its listener attribute. For example, try adding an f:event tag. Specify its type as preRenderView and the listener as a method createSQLQuery in the managed bean:

```
<f:metadata>
  <f:viewParam id="catalogId" name="catalogId" value="#{catalog.catalogId}"
   validatorMessage="Text must be 1 chars long">
  <f:validateLength maximum="1"/>
  </f:viewParam>
 <f:event type="preRenderView" listener="#{catalog.createSQLQuery}" />
 </f:metadata>
```

The input2.xhtml JSF page with a preRenderView event appears in Listing 7.10.

Listing 7.10   The input2.xhtml Page with the preRenderView Event

```
<!DOCTYPE html PUBLIC "-//W3C//DTD XHTML 1.0 Transitional//EN"
    "http://www.w3.org/TR/xhtml1/DTD/xhtml1-transitional.dtd">
<html xmlns="http://www.w3.org/1999/xhtml"
xmlns:ui="http://java.sun.com/jsf/facelets"
     xmlns:h="http://java.sun.com/jsf/html"
xmlns:f="http://java.sun.com/jsf/core">
    <f:metadata>
        <f:viewParam id="catalogId" name="catalogId"
value="#{catalog.catalogId}"
                     validatorMessage="Text must be 1 chars long">
            <f:validateLength maximum="1"/>
        </f:viewParam>
    </f:metadata>
    <f:view>
        <h:messages/>
        <h:outputText value="SQL Query: #{catalog.sqlQuery}"/>
<h:body>
            <f:event type="preRenderView" listener="#{catalog.createSQLQuery}"/>
        </h:body>
    </f:view>
</html>
```

Some of the applications of a preRenderView event are as follows:

- Loading application data prior to rendering a view

- Setting application context prior to rendering a view

- Navigating to a different view, not the view to be rendered prior to which the event is dispatched

In the previous example on using validators with view parameters, you rendered a view with a command button from which you invoked a managed bean action method to generate a JSF data table. You don't need to invoke the managed bean action method using a command button, however. You can add a listener method createSQLQuery to the f:event tag to create and run an SQL query to generate a result set that is used to create a data table. The createSQLQuery method is the same as the commandButton_action action method except that you have added navigation using the NavigationHandler to navigate to a different view, output.xhtml. You have also added a validation test so that the JSF application navigates to output.xhtml using implicit navigation only if the validation does not fail. The createSQLQuery listener method for the preRenderView event appears in Listing 7.11.

Listing 7.11   Listener Method for preRenderView Event

```
public String createSQLQuery() {
        try {
            Class.forName("oracle.jdbc.OracleDriver");
            String url = "jdbc:oracle:thin:@localhost:1521:XE";
            connection = DriverManager.getConnection(url, "OE", "OE");
            stmt =
connection.createStatement(ResultSet.TYPE_SCROLL_INSENSITIVE,ResultSet.
CONCUR_READ_ONLY);
            sqlQuery = "SELECT * FROM OE.CATALOG WHERE CATALOGID=" + catalogId;
            resultSet = stmt.executeQuery((sqlQuery));

            if (resultSet != null) {
                this.setResultSet(resultSet);
            }
        }
        catch (SQLException e) {
            System.out.println(e.getMessage());
            return "error";
        } catch (ClassNotFoundException e) {
            System.out.println(e.getMessage());
            return "error";
```

```
        } catch (Exception e) {
            System.out.println(e.getMessage());
            return "error";
        } finally {
        }
        FacesContext ctx = FacesContext.getCurrentInstance();

        if (!ctx.isValidationFailed()) {
            ctx.getApplication().getNavigationHandler().handleNavigation(ctx,
null, "output");
        }
        return "error";

    }
```

Redeploy and rerun the JSF page with the following URL: http://localhost:7101/webapp1/ faces/input2.xhtml?catalogId=2. Because you have specified a `preRenderView` event and navigation to output.xhtml in the event listener, output.xhtml is rendered (see Figure 7.12). You did not need to fill an input form or click a command button.

Figure 7.12
Using a listener method instead of an action method to render a data table.

Google and the Google logo are registered trademarks of Google Inc., used with permission.

PREEMPTIVE NAVIGATION AND BOOKMARKING

JSF 2.0 has introduced two new components: `h:link` and `h:button`. They render a hyperlink and a button, respectively, and generate a `GET` request when clicked. Preemptive navigation is a JSF 2.0 feature in which the outcome specified in the `h:link` or `h:`

`button` component is used to determine the target view ID by the navigation handler during the pre-rendering phase to construct the destination URL. The resulting destination URLs are bookmarkable. You can include view parameters in the resulting destination URLs using the `includeViewParams` attribute. For example, the following `h:link` constructs the destination URL from the outcome (input2.xhtml) and the view parameters, if any:

```
<h:link outcome="/input2.xhtml" includeViewParams="true"
value="Create DataTable">
```

You add the view parameters to the destination URL using the `paramname=paramvalue` format. The `includeViewParams` may also be specified in the outcome itself:

```
<h:link outcome="/input2.xhtml?includeViewParams=true"
        value="Create DataTable">
```

To add an `h:link` to the input3.xhtml JSF page, follow these steps:

1. Select Outcome Target Hyperlink in the JSF > HTML Components palette, as shown in Figure 7.13.

Figure 7.13
Selecting Outcome Target Hyperlink in the Components palette.
Source: Oracle Corporation.

2. In the Insert Outcome Target Hyperlink dialog box, type the label you want for the link in the Value field and click OK, as shown in Figure 7.14.

Figure 7.14
Adding an Outcome Target Hyperlink.
Source: Oracle Corporation.

3. Click the `h:link` tag and select the `outcome` attribute from the attribute list, as shown in Figure 7.15.

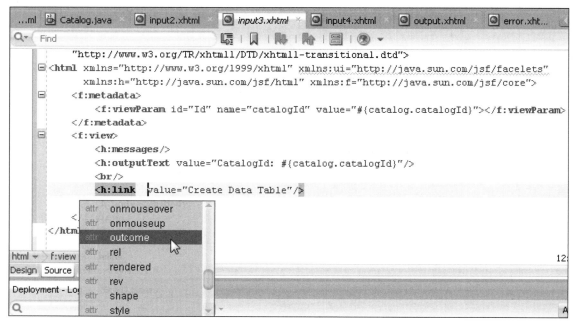

Figure 7.15
Adding the `outcome` attribute to `h:link`.
Source: Oracle Corporation.

4. Similarly, add the `includeViewParams` attribute to the `h:link` tag, as shown in Figure 7.16.

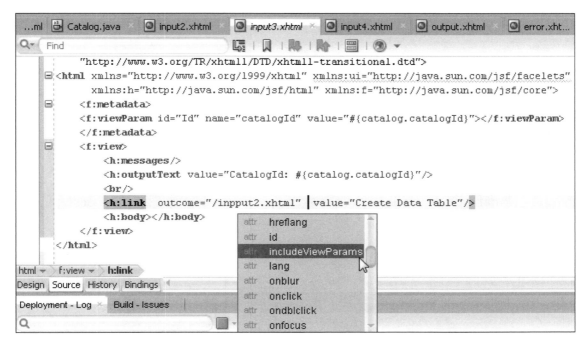

Figure 7.16
Adding the includeViewParams attribute to h:link.
Source: Oracle Corporation.

The input3.xhtml JSF page with a bookmarkable h:link appears in Listing 7.12.
The includeViewParams attribute is set to true, which implies that the catalogId view
parameter is included in the destination URL for the h:link.

Listing 7.12   The input3.xhtml Page with a Bookmarkable h:link

```
<!DOCTYPE html PUBLIC "-//W3C//DTD XHTML 1.0 Transitional//EN"
    "http://www.w3.org/TR/xhtml1/DTD/xhtml1-transitional.dtd">
<html xmlns="http://www.w3.org/1999/xhtml"
xmlns:ui="http://java.sun.com/jsf/facelets"
    xmlns:h="http://java.sun.com/jsf/html"
xmlns:f="http://java.sun.com/jsf/core">
    <f:metadata>
    <f:viewParam id="Id" name="catalogId"
value="#{catalog.catalogId}"></f:viewParam>
    </f:metadata>
    <f:view>
<h:body>
```

```
<h:messages/>
        <h:outputText value="CatalogId: #{catalog.catalogId}"/>
        <br/>
        <h:link outcome="/input2.xhtml" value="Create Data Table"
includeViewParams="true"/>
</h:body>
    </f:view>
</html>
```

5. Redeploy and run the JSF page with the following URL: http://localhost:7101/
   webapp1/faces/input3.xhtml?catalogId=2. It includes a request parameter. A
   bookmarkable hyperlink is rendered, as shown in Figure 7.17. The destination URL
   for the link is constructed during the rendering phase.

Figure 7.17
Demonstrating preemptive navigation with a bookmarkable link.
Google and the Google logo are registered trademarks of Google Inc., used with permission.

6. Position the cursor on the link to display the destination URL. The destination
   URL includes the view parameter catalogId as a GET request parameter (refer to
   Figure 7.17). An outcome of "input2.xhtml" includes the input2.xhtml view in the
   destination URL and the includeViewParams attribute being set to true if the
   destination URL includes the view parameters.

7. Click the Create DataTable link. This invokes the following URL in the browser:
   http://localhost:7101/webapp1/faces/input2.xhtml?catalogId=2. The input2.xhtml JSF
   page has a preRenderView event configured that navigates to output.xhtml. A JSF data
   table is rendered, as shown in Figure 7.18. Note that you did not have to hard-code
   the destination URL in h:link. The destination URL is variable based on the request
   parameters' values.

Figure 7.18
Rendering a JSF data table from a bookmarkable link.

Google and the Google logo are registered trademarks of Google Inc., used with permission.

COMPONENT PARAMETERS WITH VIEW PARAMETERS

View parameters are not the only source of parameters for a destination URL for an
h:link or an h:button. Parameters from different sources are included in the following order:

1. Component parameters

2. Navigation case parameters

3. View parameters

If a component parameter has the same name as a view parameter, the component
parameter overrides the view parameter. For example, follow these steps:

1. Add a component parameter using the f:param tag to the bookmarkable link example
   in the previous section. The component parameter (catalogId) has the same name as
   the view parameter in input3.xhtml. We have set the component parameter value to
   be one less than the view parameter value to demonstrate which parameter value is
   added to the destination URL for the h:link.

   ```
   <h:link outcome="/input2.xhtml" includeViewParams="true"
           value="Create DataTable">
     <f:param name="catalogId" value="#{catalog.catalogId - 1}"/>
   </h:link>
   ```

2. Redeploy the application and rerun the input3.xhtml JSF page with the same URL
   (http://localhost:7101/webapp1/faces/input3.xhtml?catalogId=2). The hyperlink is
   displayed as before, with the view parameter value included.

3. Position the cursor on the hyperlink as before. The destination URL has the request parameter `catalogId` value as 1, which is the value set in the component parameter for `h:link`.

4. Click the Create DataTable link to invoke the input2.xhtml page, which has a `preRenderView` event configured to a listener that navigates to output.xhtml, as shown in Figure 7.19. Note that the `catalogId` value in the data table shown in Figure 7.20 is 1, not 2, which was specified in the URL for input3.xhtml.

Figure 7.19
Component parameter value used in bookmarkable link.
Google and the Google logo are registered trademarks of Google Inc., used with permission.

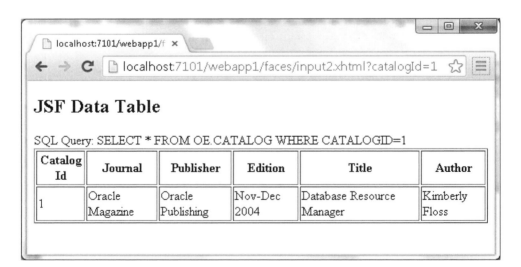

Figure 7.20
Data table rendered from a bookmarkable link generated with a component parameter.
Google and the Google logo are registered trademarks of Google Inc., used with permission.

VIEW PARAMETERS IN REDIRECTS

In a JSF redirect, the JSF controller servlet redirects to another URL and displays the redirected URL in the browser. This is in contrast to a forward, in which the JSF servlet internally forwards the request to another resource and the URL in the browser is the same as the URL from which the forward request is initiated.

To see how this works, you will use the input4.xhtml, input3.xhtml, input2.xhtml JSF pages. In input4.xhtml, view parameters for catalogId and sqlQuery are defined, and a panel grid consisting of an h:outputLabel, an h:inputText, and an h:commandButton is specified. The input4.xhtml page appears in Listing 7.13.

Listing 7.13   The input4.xhtml Page

```
<!DOCTYPE html PUBLIC "-//W3C//DTD XHTML 1.0 Transitional//EN"
    "http://www.w3.org/TR/xhtml1/DTD/xhtml1-transitional.dtd">
<html xmlns="http://www.w3.org/1999/xhtml"
xmlns:ui="http://java.sun.com/jsf/facelets"
    xmlns:h="http://java.sun.com/jsf/html"
xmlns:f="http://java.sun.com/jsf/core">
      <f:metadata>
          <f:viewParam id="catalogId" name="catalogId"
value="#{catalog.catalogId}"/>
          <f:viewParam id="Id" name="sqlQuery" value="#{catalog.sqlQuery}"/>
      </f:metadata>
    <f:view>
<h:body>
      <h:messages/>
      <h:outputText value="CatalogId: #{catalog.catalogId}"/>
          <h:form id="form1">
              <h2>JSF Data Table</h2>
              <h:panelGrid columns="3">
                  <h:outputLabel for="inputText1" value="SQL Query Catalog ID: "/>
                  <h:inputText id="inputText1"
binding="#{catalog.inputText1}" value="#{catalog.catalogId}"></h:inputText>
                  <h:message for="inputText1" style="color:red"/>
                  <h:commandButton binding="#{catalog.commandButton1}"
action="#{catalog.commandButton_action}"
                                     value="Create DataTable"></h:commandButton>
              </h:panelGrid>
          </h:form>
      </h:body>
    </f:view>
</html>
```

In input3.xhtml, view parameters for `catalogId` and `sqlQuery` are specified. In addition, an `h:link`, which has an `includeViewParams` attribute set to `true`, and an `f:param` component parameter are specified.

```
<f:metadata>
   <f:viewParam id="Id" name="catalogId"
value="#{catalog.catalogId}"></f:viewParam>
   <f:viewParam id="Id" name="sqlQuery"
value="#{catalog.sqlQuery}"></f:viewParam>

   </f:metadata>
```

In input2.xhtml, an `f:viewParam` with a validator is specified. Another view parameter for `sqlQuery` is also specified. In addition, an `f:event` tag of type `preRenderView` is specified. The listener method creates a JDBC result set and navigates to output.xhtml, as shown in Listing 7.14.

Listing 7.14   The input2.xhtml Page with `f:event`

```
<!DOCTYPE html PUBLIC "-//W3C//DTD XHTML 1.0 Transitional//EN"
    "http://www.w3.org/TR/xhtml1/DTD/xhtml1-transitional.dtd">
<html xmlns="http://www.w3.org/1999/xhtml"
xmlns:ui="http://java.sun.com/jsf/facelets"
     xmlns:h="http://java.sun.com/jsf/html"
xmlns:f="http://java.sun.com/jsf/core">
   <f:metadata>
       <f:viewParam id="catalogId" name="catalogId"
value="#{catalog.catalogId}"
                      validatorMessage="Text must be 1 chars long">
           <f:validateLength maximum="1"/>
       </f:viewParam>

       <f:viewParam id="Id" name="sqlQuery"
value="#{catalog.sqlQuery}"></f:viewParam>

   </f:metadata>
   <f:view>
       <h:body> <f:event type="preRenderView"
listener="#{catalog.createSQLQuery}"/>
       <h:messages/>
       <h:outputText value="CatalogId: #{catalog.catalogId}"/>
       <br/>
```

```
      <h:outputText value="SQL Query: #{catalog.sqlQuery}"/>
            <!-- <h:form id="form1">
  <h2>JSF Data Table</h2>
    <h:panelGrid columns="3">
    <h:commandButton binding="#{catalog.commandButton1}"
action="#{catalog.commandButton_action}" value="Create DataTable"/>
  </h:panelGrid>
  </h:form>-->
        </h:body>
    </f:view>
</html>
```

Redirecting Without View Parameters

First, let's cover redirecting without including view parameters. Follow these steps:

1. In faces-config.xml, specify a navigation rule for redirecting to input3.xhtml from input4.xhtml:

```
<navigation-rule>
    <from-view-id>/input4.xhtml</from-view-id>
    <navigation-case>
      <from-outcome>input3</from-outcome>
      <to-view-id>/input3.xhtml</to-view-id>
      <redirect/>
    </navigation-case>
  </navigation-rule>
```

2. In the managed bean, specify the return value of commandButton_action as "input3":

```
return "input3";
```

3. Redeploy and run input4.xhtml with the following URL: http://localhost:7101/webapp1/faces/input4.xhtml?catalogId=3.

4. Click the Create DataTable button, as shown in Figure 7.21. The application navigates and redirects to input3.xhtml and does not include the view parameters from input4.xhtml. As a result, the catalogId value is output as 0, which is the default value for int, as shown in Figure 7.22. In the bookmarkable link, the destination URL has catalogId=-1 because a component parameter catalogId value overrides the view parameter catalogId value.

Figure 7.21
Submitting a form to demonstrate redirection without view parameters.
Google and the Google logo are registered trademarks of Google Inc., used with permission.

Figure 7.22
A component parameter overriding a view parameter.
Google and the Google logo are registered trademarks of Google Inc., used with permission.

Redirecting with View Parameters

In this section, you will include the view parameters in a redirect. Follow these steps:

1. Add the `redirect` tag attribute `include-view-params`, set to `"true"`:

```
<navigation-rule>
    <from-view-id>/input4.xhtml</from-view-id>
    <navigation-case>
      <from-outcome>input3</from-outcome>
```

```
        <to-view-id>/input3.xhtml</to-view-id>
        <redirect include-view-params="true"/>
    </navigation-case>
  </navigation-rule>
```

The return type of the `commandButton_action` method is still the same:

`return "input3";`

2. Redeploy and run input4.xhtml with the following URL: http://localhost:7101/ webapp1/faces/input4.xhtml?catalogId=2.

3. Click the Create DataTable button, as shown in Figure 7.23. The application navigates to input3.xhtml and the redirect URL includes the view parameter `catalogId`. In a redirect, the view ID (input3.xhtml) in the browser is the same as the view ID served on the server.

Figure 7.23
Submitting a form to demonstrate redirection with view parameters.
Google and the Google logo are registered trademarks of Google Inc., used with permission.

4. Click the Create DataTable link, as shown in Figure 7.24. The application navigates to input2.xhtml, with the `catalogId` in the destination URL. In addition, the `preRenderView` event is dispatched and the output.xhtml page is rendered, as shown in Figure 7.25.

Figure 7.24
Including view parameters with the redirect.

Google and the Google logo are registered trademarks of Google Inc., used with permission.

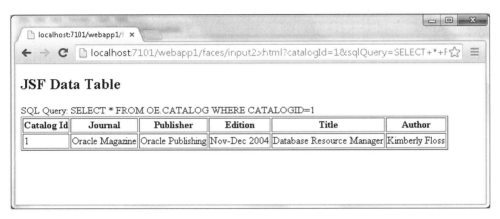

Figure 7.25
Rendering a JSF data table by including view parameters in the redirect.

Source: Google and the Google logo are registered trademarks of Google Inc., used with permission.

You can also configure the redirect with view parameters in the managed bean action method outcome. Follow these steps:

1. Modify the return value of the commandButton_action method as follows:

   ```
   return "input3?faces-redirect=true&amp;includeViewParams=true";
   ```

2. In the faces-config.xml navigation rule, remove the <redirect/> tag. The redirect or the include view parameters are not configured in the faces-config.xml.

   ```
   <navigation-rule>
       <from-view-id>/input4.xhtml</from-view-id>
       <navigation-case>
   ```

```
        <from-outcome>input3</from-outcome>
        <to-view-id>/input3.xhtml</to-view-id>
    </navigation-case>
</navigation-rule>
```

3. Redeploy and rerun the input4.xhtml page with the same result as in the preceding example.

Redirecting with View Parameters in `<redirect>` and from `f:viewParam`

With a JSF redirect, you can specify view parameters in the `<redirect/>` tag in faces-config.xml using `view-param` tags. To add a `view-param` tag, add a less-than symbol (`<`) within the `redirect` tag and select `view-param` (see Figure 7.26).

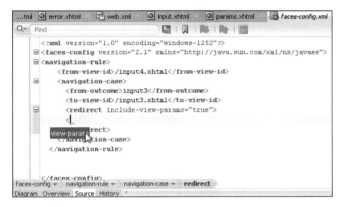

Figure 7.26
Adding a `view-param` tag to the `<redirect/>` tag.
Source: Oracle Corporation.

To explore this further, follow these steps:

1. Add two `view-param` tags to the `redirect` tag as follows:
```
<navigation-rule>
    <from-view-id>/input4.xhtml</from-view-id>
    <navigation-case>
        <from-outcome>input3</from-outcome>
```

```
        <to-view-id>/input3.xhtml</to-view-id>
        <redirect include-view-params="true">
                <view-param>
                        <name>viewparam1</name>
                        <value>1</value>
                </view-param>
                <view-param>
                        <name>viewparam2</name>
                        <value>2</value>
                </view-param>
        </redirect>
    </navigation-case>
  </navigation-rule>
```

As discussed, you can also add view parameters using the `f:viewParam` tag in the JSF page. The input4.xhtml page has two `f:viewParam` tags:

```
<f:viewParam id="catalogId" name="catalogId" value="#{catalog.catalogId}"/>
    <f:viewParam id="Id" name="sqlQuery"
value="#{catalog.sqlQuery}"></f:viewParam>
```

2. Set the outcome of the `commandButton_action` method to "input3":

```
return "input3";
```

3. Redeploy and run input4.xhtml with the following URL: http://localhost:7101/ webapp1/faces/input4.xhtml?catalogId=3&sqlQuery=null. The URL includes two request parameters, `catalogId` and `sqlQuery`, mapping for which is defined in the `f:metadata` tag.

4. Click the Create DataTable button, as shown in Figure 7.27. The navigation redirects to input3.xhtml using the following URL, which includes request parameters `viewparam1`, `viewparam2`, `catalogId` and `sqlQuery`: http://localhost:7001/webapp1/faces/ input3.xhtml?viewparam1=1&viewparam2=2&catalogId=3&sqlQuery=SELECT+* +FROM+OE.CATALOG+WHERE+CATALOGID%3D3. First, the view parameters in the `redirect` tag are specified; the view parameters in the `f:viewParam` tags are specified after that.

Figure 7.27
Submitting a form to demonstrate the inclusion of view parameters in `<redirect/>` and `<f:viewParam/>`.

5. Click the hyperlink, which is a bookmarkable link with the following target URL: http://localhost:7001/webapp1/faces/input2.xhtml?catalogId=2&sqlQuery=SELECT +*+FROM+OE.CATALOG+WHERE+CATALOGID%3D3. (See Figure 7.28.) As a `preRenderView` event is configured in input2.xhtml, the application navigates to output.xhtml and a data table is generated. (See Figure 7.29.)

Figure 7.28
The destination URL, including view parameters.

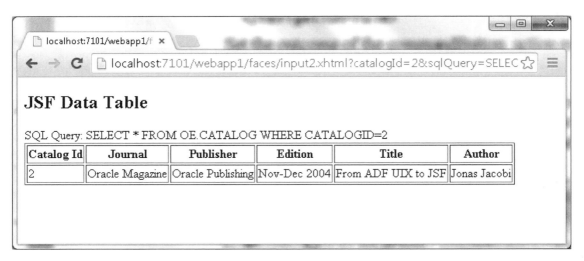

Figure 7.29
Rendering a JSF data table using view parameters for the catalog ID and SQL query.

Google and the Google logo are registered trademarks of Google Inc., used with permission.

Overriding View Parameters in `f:viewParam`

You can override the view parameters in the `f:viewParam` tags using view parameters with the same name in the `redirect` tag. To see this in action, follow these steps:

1. Specify a value for the `catalogId` view parameter in the `redirect` tag in faces-config.xml:

```
<navigation-rule>
    <from-view-id>/input4.xhtml</from-view-id>
    <navigation-case>
      <from-outcome>input3</from-outcome>
      <to-view-id>/input3.xhtml</to-view-id>
        <redirect>
                <view-param>
                    <name>catalogId</name>
                    <value>2</value>
                </view-param>
        </redirect>
    </navigation-case>
</navigation-rule>
```

2. Set the outcome of the `commandButton_action` method to `"input3"`:

```
return "input3";
```

3. Invoke the input4.xhtml page with a different value for the `catalogId` request parameter than specified in the faces-config.xml redirect tag—for example, http://localhost:7101/webapp1/faces/input4.xhtml?catalogId=3.

4. Click the Create DataTable button, as shown in Figure 7.30. The input3.xhtml page is invoked with a `catalogId` value of 2, which is specified in the `view-param` tag in the `redirect` tag. The `view-param` value in the `redirect` tag overrides the `catalogId` value in the GET request URL. The bookmarkable link has a `catalogId` value of 1 because the `f:param` in the `h:link` overrides the `catalogId` view parameter value of 2.

Figure 7.30
Submitting a form to demonstrate overriding view parameters.
Google and the Google logo are registered trademarks of Google Inc., used with permission.

5. Click the Create DataTable hyperlink, as shown in Figure 7.31. The `preRenderView` event is dispatched and the data table in output.xhtml is rendered, as shown in Figure 7.32.

Figure 7.31
Demonstrating the overriding of view parameters.
Google and the Google logo are registered trademarks of Google Inc., used with permission.

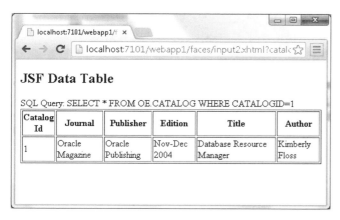

Figure 7.32
Rendering a JSF data table with an overridden view parameter.

Google and the Google logo are registered trademarks of Google Inc., used with permission.

SUMMARY

This chapter discussed using view parameters to send request parameters in a GET request. You specify the value of a view parameter using f:viewParam tags in the f:metadata tag. This chapter also discussed using validation with view parameters. You can dispatch the preRenderView event after the view parameters have been processed but before the view has been rendered.

One of the main benefits of view parameters is preemptive navigation, in which the destination URL for an h:link or h:button component is constructed during the PreRenderView phase. You can create bookmarkable links using preemptive navigation. You can also include view parameters in the destination URL for h:link or h:button to send request parameters.

This chapter also discussed using view parameters with component parameters and navigation case parameters, as well as with redirects. The next chapter discusses client behaviors.

CHAPTER 8

CLIENT BEHAVIORS

Behaviors are objects that are attached to user interface components to enhance a component's functionality. They are not explicitly defined by the component implementation. JSF 2.0 defines a component behavior model with Behavior as the root interface. Different types of behavior contracts and interactions between behaviors and components are supported by the behavior API.

Client behaviors are one implementation of behaviors. They define a mechanism for script-producing behaviors to attach scripts to components to be run on the client from client-side events. Client behaviors are a new feature in JSF 2.0, with which additional client-side functionality can be added to components using scripts. A component obtains the script associated with a client behavior using the getScript() method and wires up the script to a client-side event handler. Components that support/include client behaviors must implement the ClientBehaviorHolder interface. ClientBehaviorHolder is similar to EditableValueHolder for components that are required to support validators/converters.

Note

Chapter 3, "Ajax," discussed the f:ajax tag, which generated an AjaxBehaviorEvent that was broadcast to the listener registered with the f:ajax tag. AjaxBehaviorEvent is an implementation of ClientBehavior.

A basic requirement for the client behavior API is that the client behaviors and components should be loosely coupled. Components and client behaviors should be independent of each other, not dependent on a specific implementation from the other.

In this chapter, you will add a client behavior to a command button (h:commandButton) to display a confirmation dialog box when an SQL query is submitted to generate a data table.

OVERVIEW OF THE BEHAVIOR API

Table 8.1 outlines some of the classes and interfaces and an annotation in the Behavior API in the javax.faces.component.behavior package.

Table 8.1 Behavior API Classes and Interfaces in `javax.faces.component.behavior` Package

Class/Interface	Description	Some of the Methods
Behavior	Root interface of the component behavior model	Broadcast(BehaviorEvent): Broadcasts to all registered event listeners
ClientBehavior	Base interface for behaviors that attach scripts to client events that are exposed by ClientBehaviorHolder components	getScript: Returns the JavaScript script associated with the client behavior
AjaxBehavior	A ClientBehavior implementation that generates an Ajax request	addAjaxBehaviorListener (AjaxBehaviorListener): Adds a listener to receive event notifications from AjaxBehavior
BehaviorBase	A base class that provides default implementation of Behavior	addBehaviorListener, broadcast
ClientBehaviorBase	Base class for ClientBehavior	decode, getScript, getRenderer
ClientBehaviorHolder	Interface to be implemented by all UIComponents that are required to support client behaviors as defined by ClientBehavior	addClientBehavior: Adds the client behavior to the component for the specified event

		getClientBehaviors: **Returns all client behaviors attached to the component**
		getDefaultEventName: **Returns the default event name for the component implementing the** ClientBehaviorHolder **interface (If an event is not specified, the default event name, if provided by** ClientBehaviorHolder, **is used. The default component is** "action" **and the default event for the editable value holder components is** "valueChange".**)**
		getEventNames: **Returns a collection of event names supported by the component**
ClientBehaviorContext	Provides context information that may be used by the getScript method of a Behavior implementation	getComponent: **Returns the component that is requesting the** Behavior **script**
		getEventName: **Returns the behavior event name for which the** Behavior **script is requested**
@FacesBehavior	A class annotated with this annotation registers the class as a behavior with the runtime	N/A

Some of the `Behavior`-related API *not* included in the `javax.faces.component.behavior` package is discussed in Table 8.2.

Table 8.2 Behavior API Not in `javax.faces.component.behavior` Package

Class or Interface	Description	Some of the Methods
`javax.faces.view.` `facelets.BehaviorConfig`	Returns the ID of a behavior declared in a Facelets page.	`getBehaviorId`
`javax.faces.view.` `facelets.BehaviorHandler`	Specifies the `FaceletHandler` that corresponds to attached objects of type `ClientBehavior`. The current specification defines only one Facelet tag for this sort of attached object: `f:ajax`.	`getBehaviorId, getEventName`
`javax.faces.view.` `BehaviorHolderAttached` `ObjectHandler`	Represents an attached object that is a `Behavior Holder` in View Definition Language (VDL) page.	`getEventName()` returns the client event name to which the behavior applies
`javax.faces.view.` `BehaviorHolderAttached` `ObjectTarget`	Represents a `BehaviorHolder` attached object target in View Definition Language (VDL) page.	`isDefaultEvent()` returns a Boolean to indicate if it's a default event
`javax.faces.event.` `BehaviorEvent`	An event that can be generated by the `Behavior` component.	`getBehavior`: Returns the behavior that sent the event
`javax.faces.event.` `BehaviorListener`	Base interface for event listeners for `BehaviorEvents`	N/A

SETTING THE ENVIRONMENT

As a first step, download and install the following software:

- Oracle JDeveloper 12c (12.1.2.0.0) (www.oracle.com/technetwork/developer-tools/jdev/downloads/index.html)

- Oracle WebLogic Server 12c (included with JDeveloper 12c)

- Oracle Database Express Edition (XE) 11g (www.oracle.com/technetwork/database/database-technologies/express-edition/downloads/index.html)

To generate a JSF data table, you need a data source from which to create a database table in Oracle Database 11g XE. Use the SQL script in Listing 8.1. (The database table is the same as the one used in previous chapters. If you have already created it, you don't have to create it again.)

Listing 8.1   SQL Script to Create an Oracle Database Table

```
CREATE USER OE IDENTIFIED BY OE;
GRANT CONNECT, RESOURCE to OE;
CREATE TABLE OE.Catalog(CatalogId INTEGER
PRIMARY KEY, Journal VARCHAR(25), Publisher VARCHAR(25),
 Edition VARCHAR(25), Title Varchar(45), Author Varchar(25));
INSERT INTO OE.Catalog VALUES('1', 'Oracle Magazine',
 'Oracle Publishing', 'Nov-Dec 2004', 'Database Resource
Manager', 'Kimberly Floss');
INSERT INTO OE.Catalog VALUES('2', 'Oracle Magazine',
 'Oracle Publishing', 'Nov-Dec 2004', 'From ADF UIX to JSF',
'Jonas Jacobi');
INSERT INTO OE.Catalog VALUES('3', 'Oracle Magazine',
 'Oracle Publishing', 'March-April 2005', 'Starting with
Oracle ADF ', 'Steve Muench');
COMMIT;
```

Run the SQL script in SQL Command Line to create a database table OE.CATALOG. As in Chapter 2, "Templating with Facelets," configure and start the Integrated WebLogicServer.

CREATING A JAVA EE WEB APPLICATION

To grasp the new client behavior features in JSF 2.0, you will create a Java EE Web application consisting of an input.xhtml page and an output.xhtml page. The input.xhtml page has an input field for an SQL query and a Submit button to submit the SQL query. The output.xhtml page consists of a JSF data table generated from the SQL query specified in input.xhtml. An error.xhtml page is also included in case an error is generated. Follow these steps:

1. Select File > New > From Gallery.

2. Select General > Applications in the Categories pane and Java EE Web Application in the Items pane. Then click OK.

3. In the Application Name field, type `ClientBehaviors`. Then click Next, as shown in Figure 8.1. The Java EE Web Application template creates two projects: a Model project and a ViewController project. The ViewController project is the project you will use to develop a client behavior application.

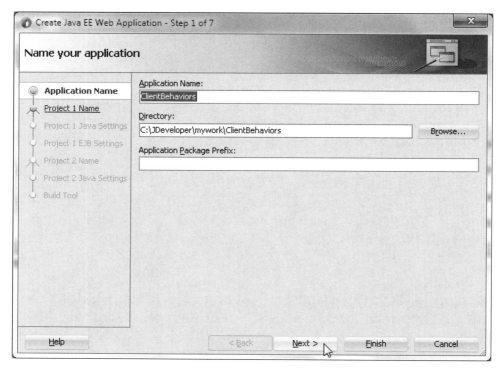

Figure 8.1
Creating a Java EE Web application called "ClientBehaviors."
Source: Oracle Corporation.

4. For project 1, select the default Project Name setting, Model, and click Next.

5. Select the default Java settings for the Model project and click Next.

6. Select the default EJB settings and click Next.

7. For project 2, select the default Project Name setting, ViewController.

8. Select the default directory.

9. Select JavaServer Faces (JSF) in the Project Features pane and click Next, as shown in Figure 8.2.

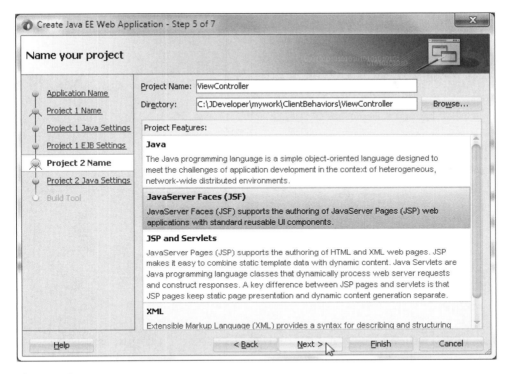

Figure 8.2
Selecting the JavaServer Faces project feature.
Source: Oracle Corporation.

10. Select the default Java settings for the ViewController project and click Next.

11. In the Build Tool screen, select the default settings, and click Finish. A Java EE Web application (ClientBehaviors) consisting of a Model and a ViewController project is created, as shown in Figure 8.3.

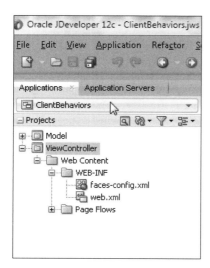

Figure 8.3
The ClientBehaviors application.
Source: Oracle Corporation.

12. Next, you will create XHTML pages for the JSF pages. To begin, select the ViewController project in the Applications navigator.

13. Select File > New > From Gallery.

14. In the New Gallery dialog box, select Web Tier > HTML in the Categories pane and HTML Page in the Items page. Then click OK.

15. In the Create HTML File dialog box, select the Create as XML File checkbox, type `input.xhtml` in the File Name field, and click OK.

16. Similarly, add output.xhtml and error.xhtml JSF pages. (See Figure 8.4.)

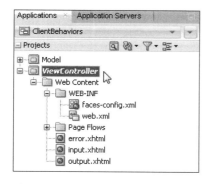

Figure 8.4
JSF pages in the ClientBehaviors application.
Source: Oracle Corporation.

17. You need to create a managed bean for the JSF pages. To begin, right-click faces-config.xml and select Open.

18. Select the Overview tab and select the Managed Beans node.

19. Click Add to add a new managed bean, as shown in Figure 8.5.

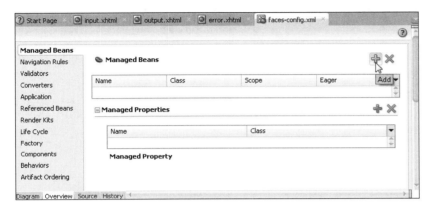

Figure 8.5
Adding a new managed bean.
Source: Oracle Corporation.

20. In the Create Managed Bean dialog box, type catalog in the Bean Name field, type Catalog in the Class Name field, type view in the Package field, and select request from the Scope drop-down list. Then select the Annotations option button and click OK. A managed bean class, Catalog.java, is added to the ClientBehaviors application, as shown in Figure 8.6.

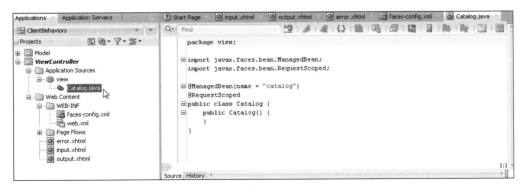

Figure 8.6
The Catalog.java managed bean class.
Source: Oracle Corporation.

The managed bean and scope are configured in faces-config.xml in JSF 1.2, but in JSF 2.0, the @ManagedBean annotation configures the POJO as a managed bean and the @RequestScoped annotation configures the managed bean class scope as request. The faces-config.xml is an empty file:

```
<?xml version="1.0" encoding="windows-1252"?>
<faces-config version="2.1" xmlns="http://java.sun.com/xml/ns/javaee">
</faces-config>
```

The input.xhtml page consists of an h:outputLabel for a label for the input field, an h:inputText for an input text field to specify an SQL query, and an h:commandButton to submit the SQL query. The h:inputText field binds to a managed bean property inputText1. The h:commandButton binds to a managed bean property commandButton1, and has action binding to a managed bean method commandButton_action. The input.xhtml page appears in Listing 8.2.

Listing 8.2   The input.xhtml Page

```
<!DOCTYPE html PUBLIC "-//W3C//DTD XHTML 1.0 Transitional//EN"
    "http://www.w3.org/TR/xhtml1/DTD/xhtml1-transitional.dtd">
<html xmlns="http://www.w3.org/1999/xhtml"
    xmlns:ui="http://java.sun.com/jsf/facelets"
    xmlns:h="http://java.sun.com/jsf/html"
    xmlns:f="http://java.sun.com/jsf/core">
<f:view>
 <h:head>
  <title></title>
</h:head>
  <h:body>
  <h:form id="form1">
   <h2>JSF Data Table</h2>
    <h:panelGrid columns="2">
        <h:outputLabel for="inputText1"
                       value="SQL Query: "/>
   <h:inputText id="inputText1" binding="#{catalog.inputText1}"
required="true"/>
   <h:commandButton binding="#{catalog.commandButton1}"
action="#{catalog.commandButton_action}" value="Submit"/>
   </h:panelGrid>
   </h:form>
</h:body>
</f:view>
</html>
```

The output.xhtml page consists of an h:dataTable element with value binding to a managed bean property resultSet, which is the JDBC ResultSet for an SQL query specified in the input field and submitted using the Submit button. The var attribute of h:dataTable specifies the iteration variable to be used to iterate over the data model and is set to "resultset". The h:column elements within h:dataTable have value binding to the ResultSet columns accessed using the iteration variable specified in the var attribute. The output.xhtml page appears in Listing 8.3.

Listing 8.3   The output.xhtml Page

```
<!DOCTYPE html PUBLIC "-//W3C//DTD XHTML 1.0 Transitional//EN"
    "http://www.w3.org/TR/xhtml1/DTD/xhtml1-transitional.dtd">
<html xmlns="http://www.w3.org/1999/xhtml"
    xmlns:ui="http://java.sun.com/jsf/facelets"
    xmlns:h="http://java.sun.com/jsf/html"
    xmlns:f="http://java.sun.com/jsf/core">
<f:view>
 <h:head>
  <title></title>
</h:head>
  <h:body>
  <h:form id="form1">
   <h2>JSF Data Table</h2>
   <h:dataTable id="dataTable1" value="#{catalog.resultSet}" var="resultset"
                border="1" rows="4">
    <h:column id="column1">
     <f:facet name="header">
      <h:outputText value="Catalog Id"/>
     </f:facet>
     <h:outputText id="outputText1" value="#{resultset.catalogid}"/>
    </h:column>
    <h:column id="column2">
     <f:facet name="header">
      <h:outputText value="Journal"/>
     </f:facet>
     <h:outputText id="outputText2" value="#{resultset.journal}"/>
    </h:column>
    <h:column id="column3">
     <f:facet name="header">
      <h:outputText value="Publisher"/>
     </f:facet>
```

```
        <h:outputText id="outputText3" value="#{resultset.publisher}"/>
       </h:column>
       <h:column id="column4">
        <f:facet name="header">
         <h:outputText value="Edition"/>
        </f:facet>
        <h:outputText id="outputText4" value="#{resultset.edition}"/>
       </h:column>
       <h:column id="column5">
        <f:facet name="header">
         <h:outputText value="Title"/>
        </f:facet>
        <h:outputText id="outputText5" value="#{resultset.title}"/>
       </h:column>
       <h:column id="column6">
        <f:facet name="header">
         <h:outputText value="Author"/>
        </f:facet>
        <h:outputText id="outputText6" value="#{resultset.author}"/>
       </h:column>
      </h:dataTable>
     </h:form>
</h:body></f:view>
</html>
```

The error.xhtml page consists of an error message and appears in Listing 8.4.

Listing 8.4   The error.xhtml Page

```
<!DOCTYPE html PUBLIC "-//W3C//DTD XHTML 1.0 Transitional//EN"
     "http://www.w3.org/TR/xhtml1/DTD/xhtml1-transitional.dtd">
<html xmlns="http://www.w3.org/1999/xhtml"
      xmlns:ui="http://java.sun.com/jsf/facelets"
      xmlns:h="http://java.sun.com/jsf/html"
      xmlns:f="http://java.sun.com/jsf/core">
<f:view>
 <h:head>
  <title></title>
 </h:head>
  <h:body>Error Page</h:body>
</f:view>
</html>
```

In the managed bean, which is a POJO, do the following:

1. Specify the properties inputText1, commandButton1, and resultSet.

2. Add accessor methods for the managed bean properties.

3. Add a commandButton_action action method, which has action binding to the Submit button in input.xhtml.

In the action method, the SQL query specified in the input text field is retrieved and run in the Oracle Database to generate a ResultSet, whose value is set on the ResultSet managed bean property. The action method has a return value of "output" or a return value of "error" if an error is generated. We will discuss the implicit navigation implemented using the return value (outcome). Catalog.java appears in Listing 8.5.

Listing 8.5   Managed Bean Catalog.java

```java
package view;
import javax.faces.component.html.HtmlInputText;
import java.sql.*;
import javax.faces.bean.ManagedBean;
import javax.faces.bean.RequestScoped;
import javax.faces.component.html.HtmlCommandButton;
@ManagedBean(name = "catalog")
@RequestScoped
public class Catalog {
    public Catalog() {
    }
    private HtmlCommandButton commandButton1;
    private Statement stmt;
    private Connection connection;
    private ResultSet resultSet;
    private HtmlInputText inputText1;
    private HtmlInputText inputText2;
    private String sqlQuery;
    public String getSqlQuery() {
        return sqlQuery;
    }
    public void setSqlQuery(String sqlQuery) {
        this.sqlQuery = sqlQuery;
    }
    private int catalogId;
    public int getCatalogId() {
```

```
            return catalogId;
    }
    public void setCatalogId(int catalogId) {
        this.catalogId = catalogId;
    }
    public void setInputText2(HtmlInputText inputText2) {
        this.inputText2 = inputText2;
    }
    public HtmlInputText getInputText2() {
        return inputText2;
    }
    public void setInputText1(HtmlInputText inputText1) {
        this.inputText1 = inputText1;
    }
    public HtmlInputText getInputText1() {
        return inputText1;
    }
    public void setCommandButton1(HtmlCommandButton commandButton1) {
        this.commandButton1 = commandButton1;
    }

    public HtmlCommandButton getCommandButton1() {
        return commandButton1;
    }
    public void setResultSet(ResultSet resultSet) {
        this.resultSet = resultSet;
    }
    public ResultSet getResultSet() {
        return resultSet;
    }
    public String commandButton_action() {
        try {
            Class.forName("oracle.jdbc.OracleDriver");
            String url = "jdbc:oracle:thin:@localhost:1521:XE";
            connection = DriverManager.getConnection(url, "OE", "OE");
            stmt =
connection.createStatement(ResultSet.TYPE_SCROLL_INSENSITIVE,
ResultSet.CONCUR_READ_ONLY);
            String sqlQuery = (String)(inputText1.getValue());
            resultSet = stmt.executeQuery((sqlQuery));
            if (resultSet != null) {
                this.setResultSet(resultSet);
            }
```

```
        }
    catch (SQLException e) {
        System.out.println(e.getMessage());
        return "error";
    } catch (ClassNotFoundException e) {
        System.out.println(e.getMessage());
        return "error";
    } catch (Exception e) {
        System.out.println(e.getMessage());
        return "error";
    } finally {
    }
    return "output";
    }
}
```

CREATING A FACELETS TAGLIB

Client behaviors are just tags enclosed within component tags in a Facelets page. Behaviors are exposed using Facelets taglibs. First, you need to create a Facelets tag library for the client behavior example to display a confirmation dialog box when an SQL query is submitted to create a data table. Follow these steps:

1. Select the WEB-INF folder in the Applications navigator.

2. Select File > New > From Gallery.

3. In the New Gallery dialog box, select General > XML in the Categories pane and select XML Document in the Items pane, as shown in Figure 8.7. Then click OK.

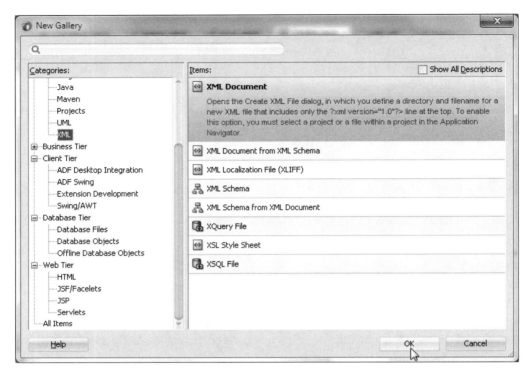

Figure 8.7
Creating an XML document.
Source: Oracle Corporation.

4. In the Create XML File dialog box, type `facelet.taglib.xml` in the File Name dialog box and click OK, as shown in Figure 8.8. The facelet.taglib.xml Facelets tag library is added to the WEB-INF directory.

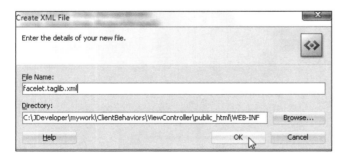

Figure 8.8
Creating facelet.taglib.xml.
Source: Oracle Corporation.

Note

A Facelets taglib file name must end with .taglib.xml.

5. The root element in a Facelets taglib is `facelet-taglib`. The namespace tag specifies the taglib's namespace that will be used in the Facelets page to add tags from the taglib. Add one or more tags using the `<tag>` element.

6. The `tag-name` tag specifies the name of the tag. Add a `tag-name` tag with `confirm` as the tag value.

7. The `behavior` tag is used to add a JSF 2.0 behavior. Specify the behavior ID with the `behavior-id` tag, which is a required tag for a `behavior` tag.

8. Optionally, you can add a handler class for the behavior with the `handler-class` tag and add one or more behavior extensions with the `behavior-extension` tags. A behavior extension contains implementation-specific content.

The Facelets taglib tags are defined in the web-facelettaglibrary_2_0.xsd XML schema. The facelet.taglib.xml file appears in Listing 8.6.

Listing 8.6   The facelet.taglib.xml File

```
<?xml version='1.0' encoding='UTF-8'?>
<facelet-taglib xmlns="http://java.sun.com/xml/ns/javaee" version="2.0">
  <namespace>http://example.org/datatable</namespace>
  <tag>
    <tag-name>confirm</tag-name>
    <behavior>
      <behavior-id>view.behavior.Confirm</behavior-id>
    </behavior>
    <attribute>
      <name>event</name>
      <required>true</required>
      <type>String</type>
    </attribute>
  </tag>
</facelet-taglib>
```

9. Copy the Facelets taglib listing to the facelet.taglib.xml file in the ClientBehaviors application, as shown in Figure 8.9.

Figure 8.9
The Facelets taglib listing.
Source: Oracle Corporation.

10. For a Facelets page to find a Facelets taglib, you need to specify the taglib in the web.xml file. Add the `javax.faces.FACELETS_LIBRARIES` context parameter and specify its value as the relative path (relative to the doc root of the Web application) to the facelet.taglib.xml file. To specify multiple taglib files, separate them with a semicolon (;).

```
<context-param>
        <param-name>javax.faces.FACELETS_LIBRARIES</param-name>
        <param-value>/WEB-INF/facelet.taglib.xml</param-value>
</context-param>
```

The web.xml page consists of the Faces servlet because you had selected the JSF project technology. The web.xml page appears in Listing 8.7.

Listing 8.7   The web.xml Page

```
<?xml version = '1.0' encoding = 'windows-1252'?>
<web-app xmlns="http://java.sun.com/xml/ns/javaee" xmlns:xsi="http://www.w3.org/2001/
XMLSchema-instance"
        xsi:schemaLocation="http://java.sun.com/xml/ns/javaee http://java.sun.com/
xml/ns/javaee/web-app_3_0.xsd"
        version="3.0">
    <context-param>
        <param-name>javax.faces.FACELETS_LIBRARIES</param-name>
        <param-value>/WEB-INF/facelet.taglib.xml</param-value>
    </context-param>
    <servlet>
```

```
        <servlet-name>Faces Servlet</servlet-name>
        <servlet-class>javax.faces.webapp.FacesServlet</servlet-class>
        <load-on-startup>1</load-on-startup>
    </servlet>
    <servlet-mapping>
        <servlet-name>Faces Servlet</servlet-name>
        <url-pattern>/faces/*</url-pattern>
    </servlet-mapping>
</web-app>
```

CONFIGURING THE CLIENT BEHAVIOR

Before you can use a client behavior in a Facelets page, you need to configure the behavior in the faces-config.xml file. Follow these steps:

1. Position the cursor in faces-config.xml and select Behavior from the JSF Configuration Elements Components palette, as shown in Figure 8.10.

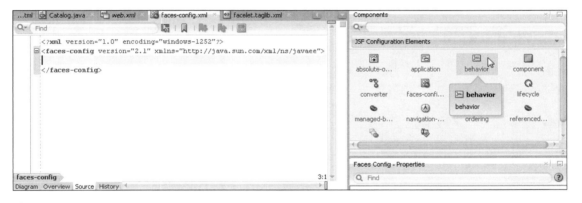

Figure 8.10
Adding behavior.
Source: Oracle Corporation.

2. In the Insert Behavior dialog box, type `view.behavior.Confirm` in the ID field, type `view.behavior.ConfirmBehavior` in the Class field, and click OK, as shown in Figure 8.11. As shown in Figure 8.12, a `behavior` tag is added to the faces-config.xml file. A `behavior` tag represents a unique behavior implementation class.

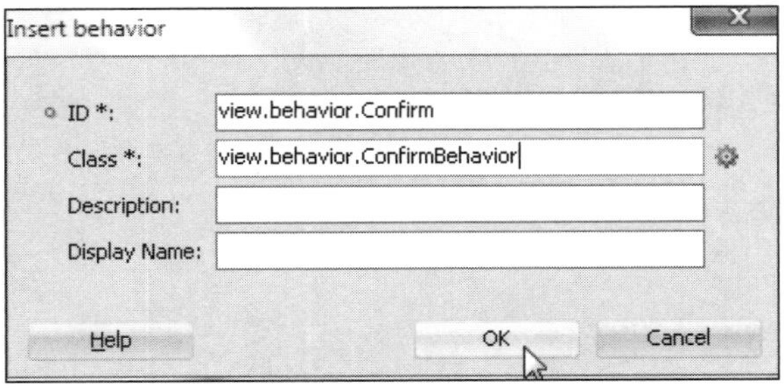

Figure 8.11
Specifying the behavior ID and class.
Source: Oracle Corporation.

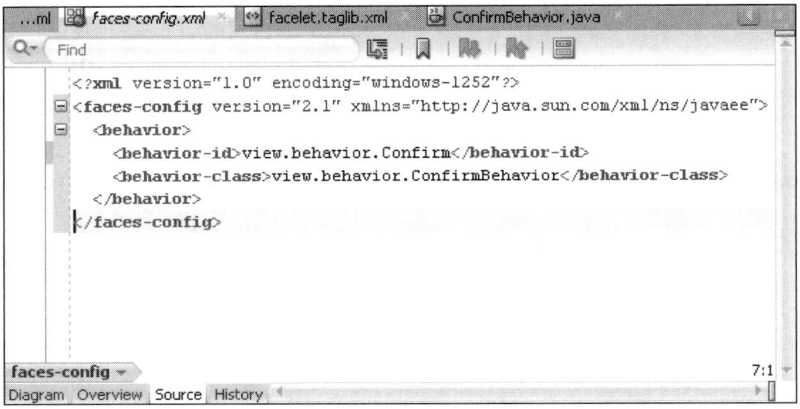

Figure 8.12
A behavior tag in faces-config.xml.
Source: Oracle Corporation.

Note

The ID and class are the only two required elements to define a behavior. A behavior ID must be unique within a Web application. The behavior class represents the fully qualified class name of the Behavior implementation class.

The faces-config.xml page appears in Listing 8.8.

Listing 8.8   The faces-config.xml Page

```
<?xml version="1.0" encoding="windows-1252"?>
<faces-config version="2.1" xmlns="http://java.sun.com/xml/ns/javaee">
  <behavior>
    <behavior-id>view.behavior.Confirm</behavior-id>
    <behavior-class>view.behavior.ConfirmBehavior</behavior-class>
  </behavior>
</faces-config>
```

The `behavior` tag provides two optional design-time features with the `attribute` and `property` tags. You can specify one or more `attribute` tags in the `behavior` tag to configure attributes on the UI component to affect the operation of the behavior. Note that the `attribute` tags don't have any effect at runtime; they are only for design tools. Similarly, you can add one or more `property` tags to identify JavaBean properties of the behavior implementation class that may be configured to affect the operation of the behavior. Properties are for design-time tools only and have no effect at runtime.

You can specify one or more client behavior renderers using the `client-behavior-renderer` tags in a `render-kit` tag. The `client-behavior-renderer` tag represents a concrete `ClientBehaviorRenderer` implementation class, which is specified with the `client-behavior-renderer-class` tag and must be unique within a `render-kit` tag. The standard components render the client behavior scripts as DOM event handlers, but other renderers/components may add the script into the markup differently. The tags in faces-config.xml are based on the http://java.sun.com/xml/ns/javaee/web-facesconfig_2_1.xsd XML schema.

In the faces-config.xml page, you specified a behavior implementation class, `view.behavior` `.ConfirmBehavior`, which you will create next. Follow these steps:

1. Add a Java class. To begin, choose File > New > From Gallery.

2. In the New Gallery dialog box, select General > Java in the Categories pane and select Class in the Items pane. Then click OK. (See Figure 8.13.)

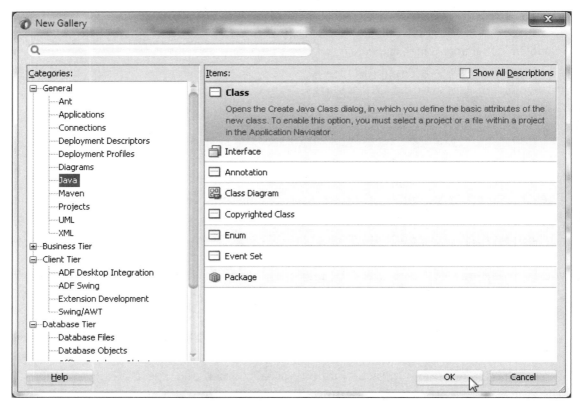

Figure 8.13
Adding a Java class.
Source: Oracle Corporation.

3. In the Create Java Class dialog box, type `ConfirmBehavior` in the Name field and type `view.behavior` in the Package field. Then click the Browse Classes button to the right of the Extends field to add the class to extend, as shown in Figure 8.14.

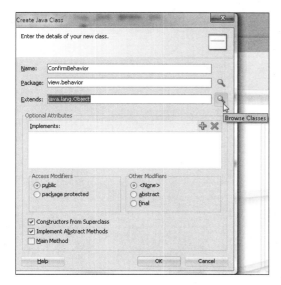

Figure 8.14
Click the Browse Classes button next to the Extends field.
Source: Oracle Corporation.

4. In the Class Browser dialog box, click the Search tab.

5. Type `ClientBehaviorBase` in the Match Class Name field.

6. Select javax.faces.component.behavior.ClientBehaviorBase in the Matching Classes pane and click OK, as shown in Figure 8.15.

Figure 8.15
Selecting `ClientBehaviorBase` as the class to extend.
Source: Oracle Corporation.

7. The `ClientBehaviorBase` class is added to the Extends field in the Create Java Class dialog box. (See Figure 8.16.) Click OK.

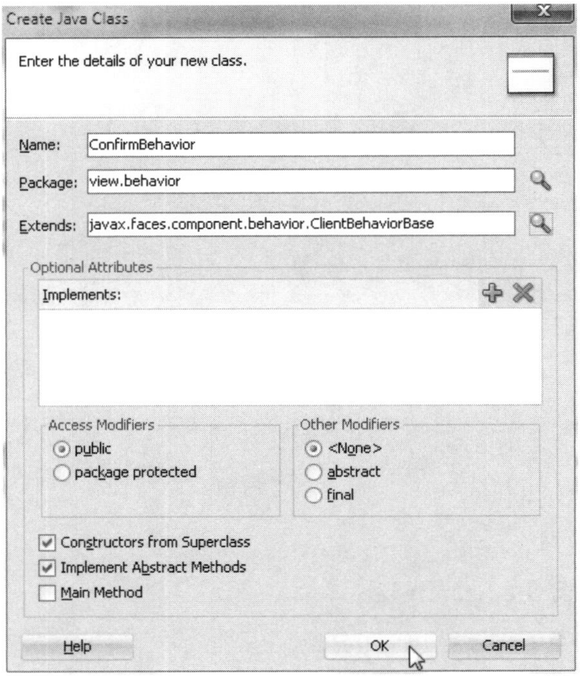

Figure 8.16
Creating the `ConfirmBehavior` class.
Source: Oracle Corporation.

8. The `ClientBehavior` class is added to the ClientBehaviors application. In the class, override the `getScript` method, which is used by a component to get the script associated with the component. The `getScript` method returns a String that further invokes the JavaScript function `confirm()`.

You have configured the `ClientBehavior` class in faces-config.xml. This class appears in Listing 8.9.

Listing 8.9   ConfirmBehavior.java

```
package view.behavior;

import javax.faces.component.behavior.ClientBehaviorBase;
import javax.faces.component.behavior.ClientBehaviorContext;
```

```
public class ConfirmBehavior extends ClientBehaviorBase {
    @Override
    public String getScript(
        ClientBehaviorContext behaviorContext) {
        return "return confirm('Create Data Table?')";
    }
}
```

The ConfirmBehavior class is shown in the ClientBehaviors application in Figure 8.17.

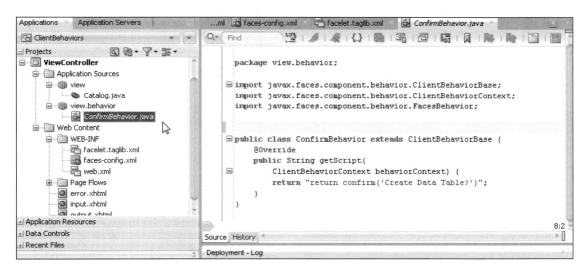

Figure 8.17
ConfirmBehavior class.
Source: Oracle Corporation.

USING A CLIENT BEHAVIOR

In this section, you will use the client behavior taglib tag(s) in a JSF page. Follow these steps:

1. Modify input.xhtml to configure a confirm tag with the h:commandButton tag. First, add the datatable namespace, which is the namespace for the Facelets taglib you created.

   ```
   <html xmlns="http://www.w3.org/1999/xhtml"
         xmlns:ui="http://java.sun.com/jsf/facelets"
         xmlns:h="http://java.sun.com/jsf/html"
         xmlns:f="http://java.sun.com/jsf/core"
         xmlns:datatable= "http://example.org/datatable">
   ```

2. Add a `datatable:confirm` tag to the `h:commandButton` tag to replace the `<h:commandButton/>` tag with `<h:commandButton> </h:commandButton>`, as shown in Figure 8.18.

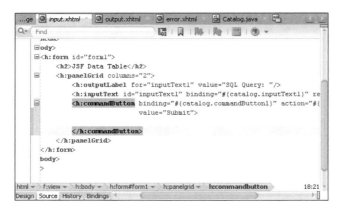

Figure 8.18
The `h:commandButton` tag.
Source: Oracle Corporation.

3. Position the cursor within the `<h:commandButton> </h:commandButton>` tags and add a less-than symbol (<). Then select `datatable:` from the drop-down list that appears, as shown in Figure 8.19.

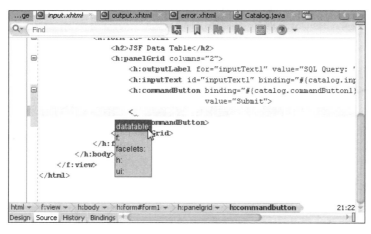

Figure 8.19
Selecting `datatable:`.
Source: Oracle Corporation.

4. A behavior is attached with a component using the `event` attribute, which specifies the event that shall invoke the associated behavior script. Add an `event` attribute to the `datatable:confirm` tag with the value as `click`, as shown in Figure 8.20.

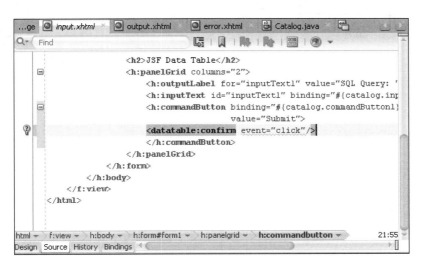

Figure 8.20
The `datatable:confirm` tag with an `event` attribute.
Source: Oracle Corporation.

If multiple scripts are registered for a behavior, the scripts are chained together and invoked in the order in which they appear on the page. If any of the sequenced scripts returns `false`, the subsequent scripts are not invoked. The `confirm` tag script runs on the client side, but client behaviors may send requests to the server, or postback to the server. The `AjaxBehaviorEvent` broadcast from the listener attribute of an `f:ajax` tag and processed on the server managed bean (refer to Chapter 3) is an example of client behavior event handling that extends across multiple tiers of an application. The input.xhtml page appears in Listing 8.10.

Listing 8.10   The input.xhtml Page

```
<!DOCTYPE html PUBLIC "-//W3C//DTD XHTML 1.0 Transitional//EN"
    "http://www.w3.org/TR/xhtml1/DTD/xhtml1-transitional.dtd">
<html xmlns="http://www.w3.org/1999/xhtml"
xmlns:ui="http://java.sun.com/jsf/facelets"
    xmlns:h="http://java.sun.com/jsf/html"
xmlns:f="http://java.sun.com/jsf/core"
    xmlns:datatable="http://example.org/datatable">
    <f:view>
```

```
<h:head>
    <title></title>
</h:head>
<h:body>
    <h:form id="form1">
        <h2>JSF Data Table</h2>
        <h:panelGrid columns="2">
            <h:outputLabel for="inputText1" value="SQL Query: "/>
            <h:inputText id="inputText1"
binding="#{catalog.inputText1}" required="true"/>
            <h:commandButton binding="#{catalog.commandButton1}"
action="#{catalog.commandButton_action}"
                                value="Submit">
                <datatable:confirm event="click"/>
            </h:commandButton>
        </h:panelGrid>
    </h:form>
</h:body>
</f:view>
</html>
```

TESTING CLIENT BEHAVIORS

In this section, you will run the ClientBehaviors application on the IntegratedWebLogic-Server. Follow these steps:

1. Create a deployment profile, webapp1, for the ViewController project, as explained in Chapter 2.

2. Right-click the ViewController project and select Deploy > webapp1 to deploy the webapp1 deployment profile to the IntegratedWebLogicServer server, discussed in detail in earlier chapters.

3. Run input.xhtml with the following URL: http://localhost:7101/webapp1/faces/input. xhtml.

4. Specify an SQL query, SELECT * FROM OE.CATALOG, and click Submit, as shown in Figure 8.21.

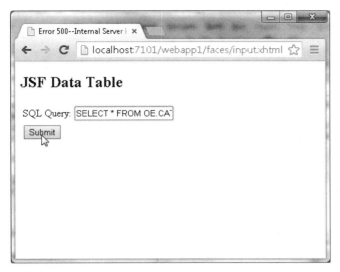

Figure 8.21
Testing client behaviors by submitting an SQL query.

Google and the Google logo are registered trademarks of Google Inc., used with permission.

5. Because the command button is configured with a client behavior to display a confirmation dialog box, the confirmation dialog box is displayed, as shown in Figure 8.22. Click OK. A data table is generated, as shown in Figure 8.23.

Figure 8.22
The confirmation dialog box.

Google and the Google logo are registered trademarks of Google Inc., used with permission.

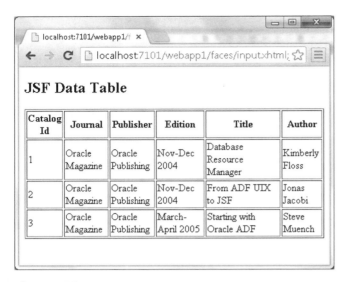

Figure 8.23
A JSF data table.

Google and the Google logo are registered trademarks of Google Inc., used with permission.

Summary

This chapter discussed the behavior API. You added a client behavior to a command button so that when the button is clicked, a confirmation dialog box is displayed. You created a behavior in a Facelets taglib and included the behavior using tags enclosed within component tags in a Facelets page. The next chapter discusses the new scopes introduced in JSF 2.0, configuration using annotations, as well as the state-saving features.

CHAPTER 9

SCOPES

JSF 1.2 provided only three scopes: request, session, and application. The session scope was used in applications that required a scope greater than request, but less than session. The request scope was too limited for some applications, such as a command button or a link to update or delete in a request-scoped page. The request scope was also limited in Faces redirects, which started a new request. JSF 2.0 has introduced three new scopes: view, flash, and custom. The view and flash scopes in JSF 2.0 fill in the requirement for an intermediate scope managed bean.

Another limitation in JSF 1.2 is the requirement for too much configuration in faces-config.xml for managed beans, managed properties, converters, validators, renderers, and even managed bean scopes. JSF 2.0 has introduced annotations based configuration to replace most of the faces-config.xml configurations.

OVERVIEW OF SCOPES

This section introduces the three new scopes: view, flash, and custom.

THE VIEW SCOPE

The view scope is scoped to a view only. It is greater in scope than the request scope, but lesser than the session scope. One problem with managed beans that had a request scope was that if the rendered attribute of a command component such as a command button was bound to the request-scoped bean, the command button wouldn't invoke the action method. If the Facelets application navigated away from a view page, the application became outside the view scope.

The view scope is started when you enter a view with a GET request. If a page is reloaded, the old view scope is lost and a new view scope is started. The managed bean in view scope is stored as an attribute in the view state. In a POST request, the old view is restored and the old view scope is reused. The view scope is generally used for CRUD (create, read, update, and delete) operations. To make a managed bean view scoped, specify that the scope should be view in the managed-bean-scope element in faces-config.xml:

```
<managed-bean>
    <managed-bean-name>catalog</managed-bean-name>
    <managed-bean-class>model.Catalog</managed-bean-class>
    <managed-bean-scope>view</managed-bean-scope>
</managed-bean>
```

Alternatively, you can configure a managed bean to be in view scope using the @ViewScoped annotation:

```
@ManagedBean(name = "catalogBean")
@ViewScoped
public class Catalog {
}
```

The #{viewScope} implicit object provides access to the view scope. The javax.faces.component.UIViewRoot.getViewMap(boolean create) method returns a map that is the interface to the data store represented by the view scope.

The Flash Scope

Flash is actually not a scope, but a method to transfer temporary objects between user views across two consecutive requests generated by the Faces lifecycle. The two consecutive requests may be to the same view IDs or to different view IDs.

The flash concept is taken from the Ruby on Rails ActionController::Flash module. The temporary objects placed in the flash scope are made available to the next view in the user session and subsequently removed. The flash scope is also available for redirects and adjacent GET requests, making the POST/REDIRECT/GET pattern available to Faces applications. A user may access flash using the EL implicit object flash, and with ExternalContext. getFlash(), which returns a flash object. The Flash class implements Map<String, Object> interface. Flash may be used in a JSP page or a Facelets page.

The Custom Scope

Custom scopes are configured using an EL expression in the `managed-bean-scope` element in faces-config.xml:

```
<managed-bean>
        <managed-bean-name>catalog</managed-bean-name>
  <managed-bean-class>view.Catalog</managed-bean-class>
        <managed-bean-scope>#{customScope}</managed-bean-scope>
</managed-bean>
```

`#{customScope}` specifies a map that contains the properties of the scope. An EL resolver is required for the custom scope to resolve the custom scope and the beans in the custom scope. A new custom-scoped bean instance is added to the map on instantiation. You can also custom-scope a managed bean using the `@CustomScoped` annotation:

```
@CustomScoped(value=#{customScope})
```

OVERVIEW OF SIMPLIFIED CONFIGURATION

The previous section discussed the `@ViewScoped` and `@CustomScoped` annotations. JSF 2.0 introduces some new annotations for simplified configuration that replace the faces-config.xml configuration. The new annotations are discussed in Table 9.1.

Table 9.1   New Annotations

Annotation	Description
@ViewScoped	Places the annotated managed bean class in the new view scope
@CustomScoped	Places the annotated managed bean class in the new custom scope
@SessionScoped	The session scope is not new, but the annotation for the session scope is
@RequestScoped	Annotation for the request scope
@ApplicationScoped	Annotation for the application scope
@ManagedBean	Annotation for a managed bean
@ManagedProperty	Annotation for a managed bean property
@FacesComponent	Specifies a UI component

(Continued)

Table 9.1 New Annotations (*Continued*)

Annotation	Description
@FacesRenderer	Specifies a renderer
@FacesConverter	Specifies a converter
@FacesValidator	Specifies a validator
@FacesBehavior	Specifies a behavior

JSF 2.0 introduces a new configuration option called "project stage" that provides a hint to the JSF implementation regarding the state of the application and the role of the deployment. The project stage is represented with the `javax.faces.application.ProjectStage` enum and can be obtained using the `Application.geProjectStage()` method. You can set the project stage using the `javax.faces.PROJECT_STAGE` context parameter or the `java:comp/env/jsf/ProjectStage` JNDI name. The `ProjectStage` enum constants are discussed in Table 9.2.

Table 9.2 ProjectStage Enum Constants

ProjectStage Value	Description
Development	Used during application development. Features include a verbose output.
Production	Used during production. The default value.
SystemTest	Indicates system testing.
UnitTest	Indicates unit testing.
Extension	Used to specify custom stage.

The `javax.faces.PROJECT_STAGE` context parameter value is used if specified. You specify the project stage value using a `context-param` in web.xml as follows:

```
<context-param>
<param-name>javax.faces.PROJECT_STAGE</param-name>
<param-value>Development</param-value>
</context-param>
```

The `java:comp/env/jsf/ProjectStage` in JNDI is used if specified. You can specify the project stage in web.xml using an `env-entry` as follows:

```
<env-entry>
<env-entry-name>jsf/ProjectStage</env-entry-name>
<env-entry-value>Development</env-entry-value>
<env-entry-type>java.lang.String</env-entry-type>
</env-entry>
```

The default value of `Production` is used.

SETTING THE ENVIRONMENT

As a first step, download and install the following software:

- Oracle JDeveloper 12c (12.1.2.0.0) (www.oracle.com/technetwork/developer-tools/jdev/downloads/index.html)

- Oracle WebLogic Server 12c (included with JDeveloper 12c)

- Oracle Database Express Edition (XE) 11g (www.oracle.com/technetwork/database/database-technologies/express-edition/downloads/index.html)

To generate a JSF data table, you need a data source from which to create a database table in Oracle Database 11g XE. Use the SQL script in Listing 9.1. (The database table is the same as the one used in previous chapters. If you have already created it, you don't have to create it again.)

Listing 9.1   SQL Script for Creating an Oracle Database Table

```
CREATE USER OE IDENTIFIED BY OE;
GRANT CONNECT, RESOURCE to OE;
CREATE TABLE OE.Catalog(CatalogId INTEGER
PRIMARY KEY, Journal VARCHAR(25), Publisher VARCHAR(25),
 Edition VARCHAR(25), Title Varchar(45), Author Varchar(25));
INSERT INTO OE.Catalog VALUES('1', 'Oracle Magazine',
 'Oracle Publishing', 'Nov-Dec 2004', 'Database Resource
Manager', 'Kimberly Floss');
INSERT INTO OE.Catalog VALUES('2', 'Oracle Magazine',
 'Oracle Publishing', 'Nov-Dec 2004', 'From ADF UIX to JSF',
'Jonas Jacobi');
INSERT INTO OE.Catalog VALUES('3', 'Oracle Magazine',
 'Oracle Publishing', 'March-April 2005', 'Starting with
Oracle ADF ', 'Steve Muench');
COMMIT;
```

Run the SQL script in SQL Command Line to create a database table OE.CATALOG. As in Chapter 2, "Templating with Facelets," configure and start the IntegratedWebLogicServer.

CREATING A JAVA EE WEB APPLICATION

To grasp the new scope features in JSF 2.0, you will create a Java EE Web application consisting of an input.xhtml page and an output.xhtml page. The input.xhtml page has an input field for an SQL query and a Submit button to submit the SQL query. The output.xhtml page consists of a JSF data table generated from the SQL query specified in input.xhtml. To demonstrate the view scope, you will use output2.xhtml. An error.xhtml page is also included in case an error is generated. Follow these steps:

1. Select File > New > From Gallery.

2. In the New Gallery dialog box, select General > Applications in the Categories pane and choose Java EE Web Application in the Items pane. Then click OK.

3. In the Name Your Application screen, type Scopes in the Application Name field and click Next, as shown in Figure 9.1.

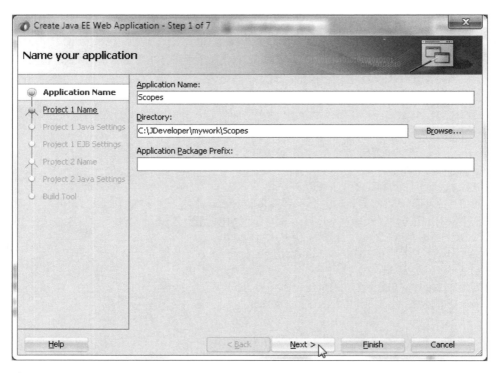

Figure 9.1
Creating a Java EE Web application called "Scopes."
Source: Oracle Corporation.

4. Select the default settings for the Model project name and click Next.

5. Select the default Java settings for the Model project and click Next.

6. Select the default EJB settings for the Model project and click Next.

7. For the ViewController project, select JavaServer Faces in Project Features pane and click Next, as shown in Figure 9.2.

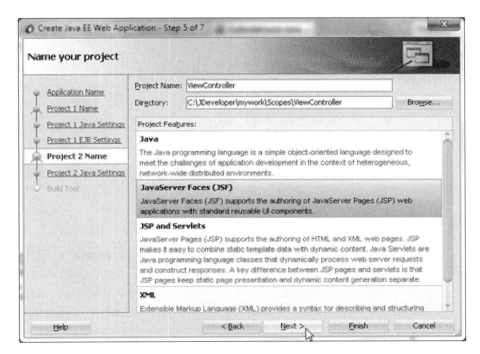

Figure 9.2
Selecting the JavaServer Faces project feature.
Source: Oracle Corporation.

8. Select the default Java settings for the ViewController project and click Next.

9. Select the default settings in the Select Build Environment screen and click Finish. A Java EE Web application called "Scopes" consisting of a Model project and a ViewController project is created, as shown in Figure 9.3.

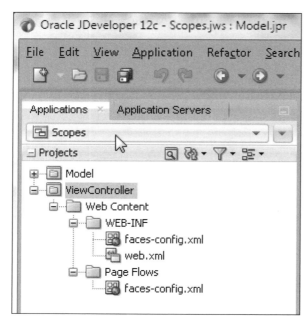

Figure 9.3
A Java EE Web application called "Scopes."
Source: Oracle Corporation.

10. Next, create XHTML pages for the JSF pages. Add input.xhtml, output.xhtml (for the view scope example), output2.xhtml (for the flash scope example and the custom scope example), and error.xhtml pages using the procedure described in earlier chapters.

11. For the JSF pages create a managed bean. To begin, right-click faces-config.xml and select Open.

12. Select the Overview tab and the Managed Beans node.

13. Click Add to add a new managed bean.

14. In the Create Managed Bean dialog box, type `catalogBean` in the Bean Name field, type `Catalog` in the Class Name field, type `view` in the Package field, and select view from the Scope drop-down list. Then select the Annotations option button and click OK. (See Figure 9.4.) A `catalogBean` managed bean is added to the Scopes application.

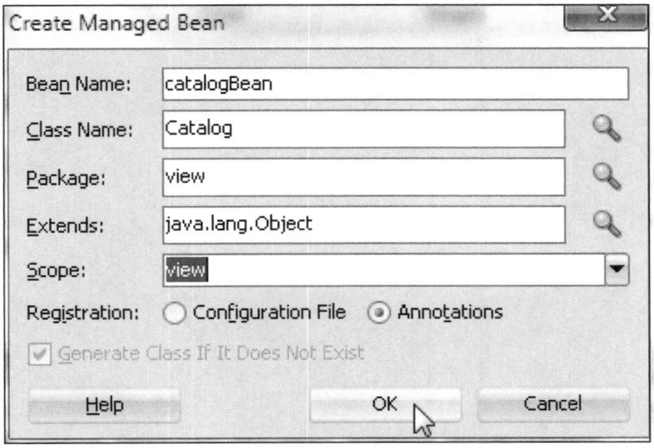

Figure 9.4
Selecting the view scope for the managed bean.
Source: Oracle Corporation.

15. Add another managed bean, catalog2, with the corresponding Java class Catalog2.java. Change the Scope setting to none for the catalog2 managed bean, as shown in Figure 9.5. We will use the catalog2 managed bean to demonstrate custom scope and flash scope. The directory structure of the Scopes application is shown in Figure 9.6.

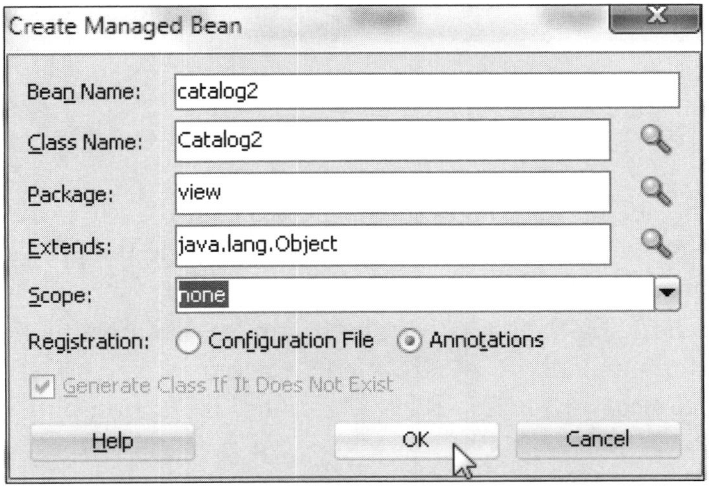

Figure 9.5
Selecting the none scope for the managed bean.
Source: Oracle Corporation.

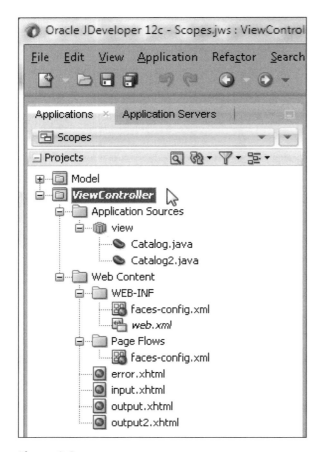

Figure 9.6
The directory structure of the Scopes application.
Source: Oracle Corporation.

16. The web.xml file consists of the FacesServlet because you selected the JSF project technology. Add a context-param javax.faces.PROJECT_STAGE to define the project state. The web.xml page appears in Listing 9.2.

Listing 9.2   The web.xml Page

```
<?xml version = '1.0' encoding = 'windows-1252'?>
<web-app xmlns="http://java.sun.com/xml/ns/javaee"
xmlns:xsi="http://www.w3.org/2001/XMLSchema-instance"
        xsi:schemaLocation="http://java.sun.com/xml/ns/javaee
http://java.sun.com/xml/ns/javaee/web-app_3_0.xsd"
        version="3.0">
```

```
<context-param>
    <param-name>javax.faces.PROJECT_STAGE</param-name>
    <param-value>Development</param-value>
</context-param>
<servlet>
    <servlet-name>Faces Servlet</servlet-name>
    <servlet-class>javax.faces.webapp.FacesServlet</servlet-class>
    <load-on-startup>1</load-on-startup>
</servlet>
<servlet-mapping>
    <servlet-name>Faces Servlet</servlet-name>
    <url-pattern>/faces/*</url-pattern>
</servlet-mapping>
</web-app>
```

The input.xhtml page binds to the catalog2 managed bean properties. The input.xhtml page consists of an h:outputLabel for a label for the input field, an h:inputText for an input text field to specify an SQL query, and an h:commandButton to submit the SQL query. The h:inputText field binds to a managed bean property inputText1. h:inputText is associated with a validator, f:validateRegex. Do not specify an h:messages tag for validation errors. You will see the use of the development project stage, which automatically adds the h:messages tag if it is not present to output validation error messages. h:commandButton binds to a managed bean property commandButton1, and has action binding to a managed bean method commandButton_action. The input.xhtml page appears in Listing 9.3.

Listing 9.3   The input.xhtml Page

```
<!DOCTYPE html PUBLIC "-//W3C//DTD XHTML 1.0 Transitional//EN"
    "http://www.w3.org/TR/xhtml1/DTD/xhtml1-transitional.dtd">
<html xmlns="http://www.w3.org/1999/xhtml"
    xmlns:ui="http://java.sun.com/jsf/facelets"
    xmlns:h="http://java.sun.com/jsf/html"
    xmlns:f="http://java.sun.com/jsf/core"
    >
<f:view>
 <h:head>
  <title></title>
 </h:head>
 <h:body>
  <h:form id="form1">
   <h2>JSF Data Table</h2>
```

```
    <h:panelGrid columns="2">
     <h:outputLabel for="inputText1"
                        value="SQL Query : "/>
     <h:inputText id="inputText1" binding="#{catalog2.inputText1}" value="#{
catalog2.sqlQuery}">
      <f:validateRegex pattern="SELECT+[\s]+[a-zA-Z]+[,]+[\s]+[a-zA-Z]+[,]+[\s]+
[a-zA-Z]+[,]+[\s]+[a-zA-Z]+[,]+[\s]+[a-zA-Z]+[,]+[\s]+[a-zA-Z]+[\s]+FROM+[\s]+
[a-zA-Z]+"/>
     </h:inputText>
      <h:commandButton binding="#{catalog2.commandButton1}"
                        action="#{catalog2.commandButton_action}" value="Submit">
     </h:commandButton>
    </h:panelGrid>
   </h:form>
  </h:body>
 </f:view>
</html>
```

The output.xhtml page consists of an h:dataTable element with value binding to a managed bean property resultSet, which is the JDBC ResultSet for an SQL query specified in the input field and submitted using the Submit button. The var attribute of h:dataTable specifies the iteration variable to be used to iterate over the data model and is set to "resultset". The h:column elements within the h:dataTable have value binding to the ResultSet columns accessed using the iteration variable specified in the var attribute. The output.xhtml JSF page appears in Listing 9.4.

Listing 9.4   The output.xhtml Page

```
<!DOCTYPE html PUBLIC "-//W3C//DTD XHTML 1.0 Transitional//EN"
    "http://www.w3.org/TR/xhtml1/DTD/xhtml1-transitional.dtd">
<html xmlns="http://www.w3.org/1999/xhtml"
     xmlns:ui="http://java.sun.com/jsf/facelets"
     xmlns:h="http://java.sun.com/jsf/html"
     xmlns:f="http://java.sun.com/jsf/core">
<f:view>
 <h:head>
  <title></title>
 </h:head>
  <h:body>
  <h:form id="form1">
   <h2>JSF Data Table</h2>
```

```
<h:dataTable id="dataTable1" value="#{catalogBean.resultSet}" var="row"
            border="1" rows="4">
  <h:column id="column1">
   <f:facet name="header">
    <h:outputText value="Catalog Id"/>
   </f:facet>
   <h:outputText id="outputText1" value="#{row.catalogid}"/>
  </h:column>
  <h:column id="column2">
   <f:facet name="header">
    <h:outputText value="Journal"/>
   </f:facet>
   <h:outputText id="outputText2" value="#{row.journal}"/>
  </h:column>
  <h:column id="column3">
   <f:facet name="header">
    <h:outputText value="Publisher"/>
   </f:facet>
   <h:outputText id="outputText3" value="#{row.publisher}"/>
  </h:column>
  <h:column id="column4">
   <f:facet name="header">
    <h:outputText value="Edition"/>
   </f:facet>
   <h:outputText id="outputText4" value="#{row.edition}"/>
  </h:column>
  <h:column id="column5">
   <f:facet name="header">
    <h:outputText value="Title"/>
   </f:facet>
   <h:outputText id="outputText5" value="#{row.title}"/>
  </h:column>
  <h:column id="column6">
   <f:facet name="header">
    <h:outputText value="Author"/>
   </f:facet>
   <h:outputText id="outputText6" value="#{row.author}"/>
  </h:column>
  <h:column>
        <h:commandLink action="#{catalogBean.deleteRow}" value="Delete"
reRender="dataTable1">
         </h:commandLink>
```

```
      </h:column>
    </h:dataTable>
   </h:form>
 </h:body>
</f:view>
</html>
```

The output2.xhtml page (for the flash scope example and the custom scope example) consists of an h:dataTable element with value binding to a managed bean property resultSet, which is the JDBC ResultSet for an SQL query specified in the input field and submitted using the Submit button. The var attribute of h:dataTable specifies the iteration variable to be used to iterate over the data model and is set to "resultset". The h:column elements within the h:dataTable have value binding to the ResultSet columns accessed using the iteration variable specified in the var attribute. The output2.xhtml JSF page appears in Listing 9.5.

Listing 9.5   The output2.xhtml Page

```
<!DOCTYPE html PUBLIC "-//W3C//DTD XHTML 1.0 Transitional//EN"
    "http://www.w3.org/TR/xhtml1/DTD/xhtml1-transitional.dtd">
<html xmlns="http://www.w3.org/1999/xhtml"
      xmlns:ui="http://java.sun.com/jsf/facelets"
      xmlns:h="http://java.sun.com/jsf/html"
      xmlns:f="http://java.sun.com/jsf/core">
<f:view>
 <h:head>
  <title></title>
</h:head>
  <h:body>
  <h:form id="form1">
   <h2>JSF Data Table</h2>
 <!-- <h:dataTable id="dataTable1" value="#{flash.catalog2.resultSet}"
var="resultset"
                 border="1" rows="4">-->
                <h:dataTable id="dataTable1" value="#{catalog2.resultSet}"
var="resultset"
                 border="1" rows="4">
    <h:column id="column1">
     <f:facet name="header">
      <h:outputText value="Catalog Id"/>
     </f:facet>
```

```
        <h:outputText id="outputText1" value="#{resultset.catalogid}"/>
      </h:column>
      <h:column id="column2">
       <f:facet name="header">
        <h:outputText value="Journal"/>
       </f:facet>
       <h:outputText id="outputText2" value="#{resultset.journal}"/>
      </h:column>
      <h:column id="column3">
       <f:facet name="header">
        <h:outputText value="Publisher"/>
       </f:facet>
       <h:outputText id="outputText3" value="#{resultset.publisher}"/>
      </h:column>
      <h:column id="column4">
       <f:facet name="header">
        <h:outputText value="Edition"/>
       </f:facet>
       <h:outputText id="outputText4" value="#{resultset.edition}"/>
      </h:column>
      <h:column id="column5">
       <f:facet name="header">
        <h:outputText value="Title"/>
       </f:facet>
       <h:outputText id="outputText5" value="#{resultset.title}"/>
      </h:column>
      <h:column id="column6">
       <f:facet name="header">
        <h:outputText value="Author"/>
       </f:facet>
       <h:outputText id="outputText6" value="#{resultset.author}"/>
      </h:column>
     </h:dataTable>
    </h:form>
  </h:body>
 </f:view>
</html>
```

The error.xhtml page consists of an error message, and appears in Listing 9.6.

Listing 9.6   The error.xhtml Page

```
<!DOCTYPE html PUBLIC "-//W3C//DTD XHTML 1.0 Transitional//EN"
    "http://www.w3.org/TR/xhtml1/DTD/xhtml1-transitional.dtd">
<html xmlns="http://www.w3.org/1999/xhtml"
      xmlns:ui="http://java.sun.com/jsf/facelets"
      xmlns:h="http://java.sun.com/jsf/html"
      xmlns:f="http://java.sun.com/jsf/core">
<f:view>
 <h:head>
  <title></title>
</h:head>
  <h:body>Error Page</h:body>
</f:view>
</html>
```

The managed bean `catalogBean` is view scoped with the `@ViewScoped` annotation, which is discussed in the next section. In the managed bean, do the following:

1. Specify the properties `inputText1`, `commandButton1`, and `resultSet`.

2. Add accessor methods for the managed bean properties.

3. Add an action method `commandButton_action`, which has action binding to the Submit button in input.xhtml.

In the action method, the SQL query specified in the input text field is retrieved and run in the Oracle Database to generate a `ResultSet`, whose value is set on the `ResultSet` managed bean property. The action method has a return value of `"output"` or of `"error"` if an error is generated. The `@PostConstruct` method initializes the `resultSet` property. The `deleteRow` method is used in the view scope section. `Catalog.java` appears in Listing 9.7.

Listing 9.7   Managed Bean Catalog.java

```
package view;
import java.sql.Connection;
import java.sql.DriverManager;
import java.sql.ResultSet;
import java.sql.SQLException;
import java.sql.Statement;
import javax.annotation.PostConstruct;
import javax.faces.bean.ManagedBean;
import javax.faces.bean.ManagedProperty;
import javax.faces.bean.ViewScoped;
```

```java
@ManagedBean(name = "catalogBean")
@ViewScoped
public class Catalog {
    public Catalog() {
    }
    private Statement stmt;
    private Connection connection;
    private ResultSet resultSet;
    public void setResultSet(ResultSet resultSet) {
        this.resultSet = resultSet;
    }
    public ResultSet getResultSet() {
        return resultSet;
    }
    @PostConstruct
    public void createResultSet() {
        try {
            Class.forName("oracle.jdbc.OracleDriver");
            String url = "jdbc:oracle:thin:@localhost:1521:XE";
            connection = DriverManager.getConnection(url, "OE", "OE");
            stmt =
connection.createStatement(ResultSet.TYPE_SCROLL_SENSITIVE,ResultSet.
CONCUR_UPDATABLE);
            String sqlQuery = "SELECT CATALOGID, JOURNAL, PUBLISHER, EDITION,
TITLE, AUTHOR FROM OE.CATALOG";
            resultSet = stmt.executeQuery((sqlQuery));
            if (resultSet != null) {
                this.setResultSet(resultSet);
            }
        }
        catch (SQLException e) {
            System.out.println(e.getMessage());

        } catch (ClassNotFoundException e) {
            System.out.println(e.getMessage());

        } catch (Exception e) {
            System.out.println(e.getMessage());
        } finally {
        }
    }
    public String deleteRow() {
```

```
        try {
            resultSet.moveToCurrentRow();
            resultSet.deleteRow();
        } catch (SQLException e) {
          System.out.println(e.getMessage());
        }
        return null;
    }
}
```

In the `catalog2` managed bean, which is also a POJO, do the following:

1. Specify the property for `catalogId`, `inputText1`, `sqlQuery`, `commandButton1`, and `resultSet`.

2. Add accessor methods for the managed bean properties.

3. Add an action method `commandButton_action`, which has action binding to the Submit button in input.xhtml.

In the action method, the SQL query specified in the input text field is retrieved and run in the Oracle Database to generate a `ResultSet`, whose value is set on the `ResultSet` type managed bean property. The action method has a return value of `"output2"` or of `"error"` if an error is generated. Implicit navigation is implemented using the return value (outcome). We will use `Catalog2.java` to discuss the flash scope and the custom scope.

We have added another managed bean class `Catalog.java` to discuss the view scope. Some of the code to be used in the flash scope section and the custom scope section is commented out and may be uncommented when required for testing a relevant scope. `Catalog2.java` appears in Listing 9.8.

Listing 9.8   Managed Bean Catalog2.java

```
package view;
import javax.faces.component.html.HtmlInputText;
import java.sql.*;
import javax.faces.bean.CustomScoped;
import javax.faces.bean.ManagedBean;
import javax.faces.bean.ManagedProperty;
import javax.faces.component.html.HtmlCommandButton;
import javax.faces.context.FacesContext;
import javax.faces.context.Flash;
@ManagedBean(name = "catalog2")
```

```java
//@CustomScoped(value="#{customScope}")
public class Catalog2 {
    public Catalog2() {
    }
    private HtmlCommandButton commandButton1;
    private Statement stmt;
    private Connection connection;
    private ResultSet resultSet;
    private HtmlInputText inputText1;
    @ManagedProperty(value =
                        "SELECT CATALOGID, JOURNAL, PUBLISHER, EDITION, TITLE,
AUTHOR FROM CATALOG")
    private String sqlQuery;
    public String getSqlQuery() {
        return sqlQuery;
    }
    public void setSqlQuery(String sqlQuery) {
        this.sqlQuery = sqlQuery;
    }
    private int catalogId;
    public int getCatalogId() {
        return catalogId;
    }
    public void setCatalogId(int catalogId) {
        this.catalogId = catalogId;
    }
    public void setInputText1(HtmlInputText inputText1) {
        this.inputText1 = inputText1;
    }
    public HtmlInputText getInputText1() {
        return inputText1;
    }
    public void setCommandButton1(HtmlCommandButton commandButton1) {
        this.commandButton1 = commandButton1;
    }
    public HtmlCommandButton getCommandButton1() {
        return commandButton1;
    }
    public void setResultSet(ResultSet resultSet) {
        this.resultSet = resultSet;
    }
    public ResultSet getResultSet() {
        return resultSet;
    }
```

```
    public String commandButton_action() {
        try {
            Class.forName("oracle.jdbc.OracleDriver");
            String url = "jdbc:oracle:thin:@localhost:1521:XE";
            connection = DriverManager.getConnection(url, "OE", "OE");
            stmt =
connection.createStatement(ResultSet.TYPE_SCROLL_INSENSITIVE,
                        ResultSet.CONCUR_READ_ONLY);
            String sqlQuery = (String)(inputText1.getValue());
            resultSet = stmt.executeQuery((sqlQuery));
            if (resultSet != null) {
                this.setResultSet(resultSet);
            }
        }
        catch (SQLException e) {
            System.out.println("SQLException: "+e.getMessage());
            return "error";
        } catch (ClassNotFoundException e) {
            System.out.println("ClassNotFoundException: "+e.getMessage());
            return "error";
        } catch (Exception e) {
            System.out.println("Exception: "+e.getMessage());
            return "error";
        } finally {
        }
//      Flash flash =
        // FacesContext.getCurrentInstance().getExternalContext().getFlash();
    // flash.put("catalog2", this);
    // return "output2?faces-redirect=true";
        return "output2";
    }
}
```

SIMPLIFIED CONFIGURATION

This section discusses some of the new features to simplify configuration. In JSF 1.2, you had to configure the managed bean in faces-config.xml. In JSF 2.0, you could still config-ure in faces-config.xml, but the @ManagedBean annotation has been provided to configure a managed bean in the POJO class. The `Catalog` and `Catalog2` POJOs are annotated with the `@ManagedBean` annotation to configure them as managed beans.

```
@ManagedBean(name = "catalogBean")
public class Catalog {
}
@ManagedBean(name = "catalog2")
public class Catalog2 {
}
```

You can use the `@ManagedProperty` annotation to specify a managed property. Annotate the `sqlQuery` property with `@ManagedProperty` and specify the initial value of the SQL query in the `value` element:

```
@ManagedProperty(value =
                        "SELECT CATALOGID, JOURNAL, PUBLISHER, EDITION, TITLE, AUTHOR FROM
CATALOG")
    private String sqlQuery;
    public String getSqlQuery() {
        return sqlQuery;
    }
    public void setSqlQuery(String sqlQuery) {
        this.sqlQuery = sqlQuery;
    }
```

To demonstrate the use of project stage, set the `javax.faces.PROJECT_STAGE` parameter to `Development`:

```
<context-param>
    <param-name>javax.faces.PROJECT_STAGE</param-name>
    <param-value>Development</param-value>
</context-param>
```

The `javax.faces.application.ProjectStage` enum has been introduced in JSF 2.0. The enum constants represent the different states of an application in a product development lifecycle. The enum constants are discussed in Table 9.2.

To demonstrate the use of `ProjectStage`, follow these steps:

1. Create a deployment profile webapp1 for the ViewController project as explained in Chapter 2.

2. Start the IntegratedWebLogicServer if it's not already started.

3. Right-click the ViewController project and select Deploy > webapp1 to deploy the deployment profile to the IntegratedWebLogicServer, as explained in Chapter 2.

4. Run the input.xhtml page with the following URL: http://localhost:7101/webapp1/faces/input.xhtml. A default SQL query specified with the @ManagedBeanProperty is entered, as shown in Figure 9.7.

Figure 9.7
The default SQL query in input.xhtml.

Google and the Google logo are registered trademarks of Google Inc., used with permission.

5. Enter an SQL query that does not match the regular expression specified in the f:validateRegex tag. As an example, omit the comma, as shown in Figure 9.8. Then click Submit. As shown in Figure 9.9, a validation error message is displayed. Because you set the project stage to Development, a validation error message is displayed even though you did not specify an h:messages tag in input.xhtml.

Figure 9.8
Submitting an SQL query that does not match the regular expression.
Google and the Google logo are registered trademarks of Google Inc., used with permission.

Figure 9.9
Validation error message.
Google and the Google logo are registered trademarks of Google Inc., used with permission.

SAME VIEW WITH VIEW SCOPE

The view scope starts with a GET request to a view page and ends when the application navigates away from the view or reloads it. We will use output.xhtml and the catalog managed bean to demonstrate the view scope, adding a Delete link in a data table to delete a row. The h:commandLink tag invokes the deleteRow method in the view-scoped managed bean catalogBean. The bean is stored in the view state. When the view is restored after a delete action, the view scope is reused. The request parameter state is kept while in the current page:

```
    <h:column>
<h:commandLink action="#{catalogBean.deleteRow()}" value="Delete"
reRender="dataTable1">
  </h:commandLink>
    </h:column>
```

Next, you use output.xhtml with a delete link to delete a row in the data table. The Catalog.java POJO is used for the view scoped managed bean. The Catalog.java managed bean class is annotated with the @ViewScoped annotation to specify a view scoped managed bean:

```
@ManagedBean(name = "catalogBean")
@ViewScoped
public class Catalog {
}
```

Because you are not submitting an SQL query to invoke a command action method in the managed bean, use the @PostConstruct annotation to annotate a method for initialization of the resultSet property:

```
@PostConstruct
    public void createResultSet() {
}
```

The Catalog.java managed bean class has a deleteRow method to delete a row when the Delete link is selected in the data table:

```
public String deleteRow() {
        try {
            resultSet.moveToCurrentRow();
            resultSet.deleteRow();
        } catch (SQLException e) {
```

```
            System.out.println(e.getMessage());
        }
        return null;
    }
```

The managed bean POJO `Catalog.java` is listed in an earlier section. Redeploy and run the output.xhtml page with the following URL: http://localhost:7101/webapp1/faces/output.xhtml. A data table is displayed. The last column has a Delete link. Click the Delete link, as shown in Figure 9.10.

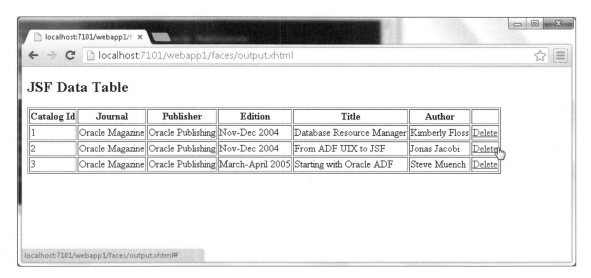

Figure 9.10
Clicking on the Delete link.
Google and the Google logo are registered trademarks of Google Inc., used with permission.

The `deleteRow` method is invoked and the current row is deleted. The view is restored in the postback and the view scope is reused. The data table with one row deleted is rendered, as shown in Figure 9.11.

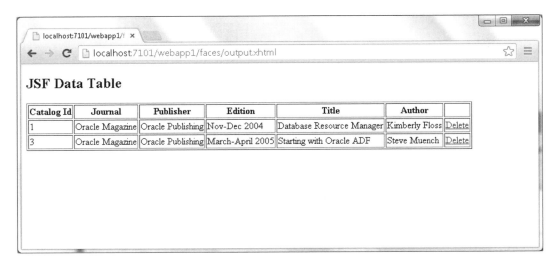

Figure 9.11
A data table with one row deleted.

Google and the Google logo are registered trademarks of Google Inc., used with permission.

REDIRECTING WITH FLASH SCOPE

The POST/REDIRECT/GET (PRG) pattern is recommended for form submissions to prevent a POST request from being resubmitted. But if the PRG pattern is used in a JSF application, in a JSF redirect, a new request to the redirect URL is generated, and the request-scoped objects from the previous request are not available in the new request. To demonstrate a JSF redirect with implicit navigation, follow these steps:

1. Modify the return value of the action method commandButton_action() in managed bean catalog2 class Catalog2.java in the request-scoped managed bean. Specifically, replace:

   ```
   return "output2";
   ```

   with the following:

   ```
   return "output2?faces-redirect=true";
   ```

2. Redeploy the application and run the input.xhtml page with the following URL: http://localhost:7101/webapp1/faces/input.xhtml. Specify an SQL query and click Submit, as shown in Figure 9.12.

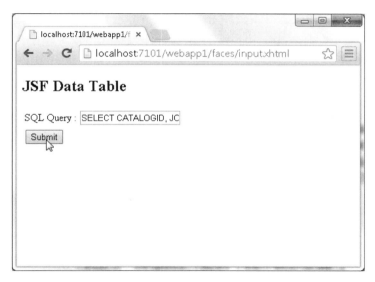

Figure 9.12
Submitting an SQL query.
Google and the Google logo are registered trademarks of Google Inc., used with permission.

3. Because you are using `faces-redirect`, a new request is sent to the redirect URL, http://localhost:7001/webapp1/faces/output2.xhtml. The request-scoped `resultSet` object generated in the request submitted from input.xhtml is not available in the new request. The data table generated is empty, as shown in Figure 9.13.

Figure 9.13
Empty data table.
Google and the Google logo are registered trademarks of Google Inc., used with permission.

4. The flash scope makes the PRG pattern feasible in a JSF application by making the objects placed in the flash scope available in the redirect URL (the new request). In the command action method, create a `flash` object using the `getFlash()` method of `ExternalContext`.

5. Add the `catalog2` bean to the `flash` object using the `put` method.

6. Add a `faces-redirect` to the implicit navigation.

```
Flash flash =FacesContext.getCurrentInstance().getExternalContext().getFlash();
flash.put("catalog2", this);
return "output2?faces-redirect=true";
// return "output2";
```

7. In output2.xhtml, use the implicit object `flash` to retrieve the `catalog2` bean and access the `resultSet` property. Replace:

```
<h:dataTable id="dataTable1" value="#{catalog2.resultSet}" var="resultset"
border="1" rows="4">
```

with:

```
<h:dataTable id="dataTable1" value="#{flash.catalog2.resultSet}" var="resultset"
border="1" rows="4">
```

8. Redeploy the application and rerun input.xhtml with the following URL: http://localhost:7101/webapp1/faces/input.xhtml.

9. Submit an SQL query, as shown in Figure 9.14. A JSF data table is rendered, as shown in Figure 9.15. Because you are using the flash scope with `faces-redirect`, the `catalog2` bean, which is in the flash scope, is available in the redirected URL using the EL implicit object `flash`.

Figure 9.14
Submitting an SQL query to demonstrate the flash scope.
Google and the Google logo are registered trademarks of Google Inc., used with permission.

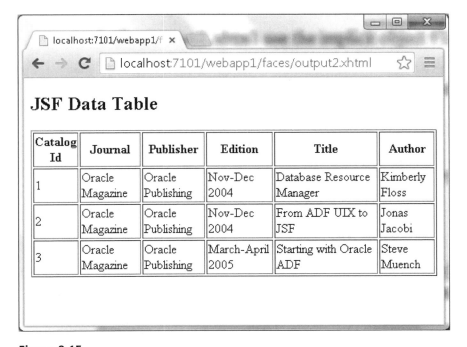

Figure 9.15
Demonstrating flash scope.
Google and the Google logo are registered trademarks of Google Inc., used with permission.

CREATING A CUSTOM SCOPED MANAGED BEAN

A custom scope requires the following configuration.

- An EL expression specifying a map, which is a Map<String,Object> object, for the custom scope
- Configuration of the EL expression for the custom scope in faces-config.xml or the @ManagedScoped annotation
- An EL resolver (extends ELResolver) to resolve the custom scope and the beans in the map
- Registration of the EL resolver in faces-config.xml

You will use the EL expression #{customScope} to specify the map for a custom scope. Configure the custom scope on the catalog2 managed bean class Catalog2.java using the @CustomScoped annotation:

```
@ManagedBean(name = "catalog2")
@CustomScoped(value="#{customScope}")
public class Catalog2 {
}
```

The managed bean in custom scope is shown in Figure 9.16.

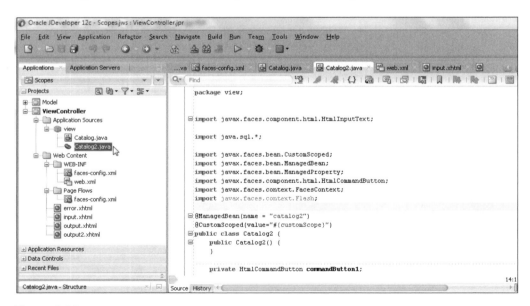

Figure 9.16
The managed bean in custom scope.
Source: Oracle Corporation.

You can also configure the custom scope in faces-config.xml with the EL expression for the custom scope map:

```
<managed-bean>
    <managed-bean-name>catalog2</managed-bean-name>
    <managed-bean-class>view.Catalog2</managed-bean-class>
    <managed-bean-scope>#{customScope}</managed-bean-scope>
</managed-bean>
```

Also, you can specify the outcome from the command action method in catalog2 bean class Catalog2.java as follows:

```
return "output2";
```

Comment out the following section, which was used for the flash scope example, in Catalog2.java:

```
Flash flash =FacesContext.getCurrentInstance().getExternalContext().getFlash();
flash.put("catalog2", this);
return "output2?faces-redirect=true";
```

Modify output2.xhtml, which was used in the flash scope example, to use the custom scoped bean catalog2 rather than the EL implicit object flash to access the resultSet object:

```
<h:dataTable id="dataTable1" value="#{catalog2.resultSet}" var="resultset"
                border="1" rows="4">
```

Create an EL resolver, a Java class (CustomScopeELResolver) that extends the javax.el.ELResolver class in the view package, as shown in Figure 9.17.

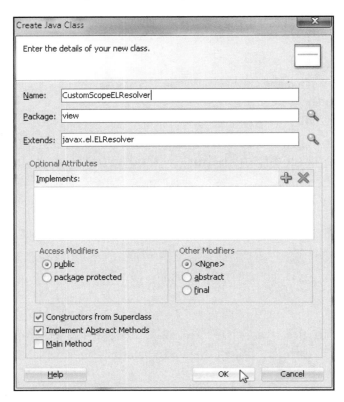

Figure 9.17
Creating an EL resolver class.
Source: Oracle Corporation.

Override the `ELResolver` methods. The `getValue` method is used to resolve the value of a custom-scoped EL expression. The `getScope` method returns a custom scope, which is just a `ConcurrentHashMap` object. The EL resolver class appears in Listing 9.9.

Listing 9.9   The `CustomScopeELResolver` Class

```
package view;
import javax.el.ELResolver;
import javax.el.ELContext;
import javax.el.PropertyNotFoundException;
import javax.faces.context.FacesContext;
import javax.faces.application.Application;
import javax.faces.event.ScopeContext;
import javax.faces.event.PostConstructCustomScopeEvent;
import javax.faces.event.PreDestroyCustomScopeEvent;
import java.util.Iterator;
```

```java
import java.util.Map;
import java.util.Collections;
import java.util.concurrent.ConcurrentHashMap;
import java.beans.FeatureDescriptor;
public class CustomScopeELResolver extends ELResolver {
    private static final String SCOPE_NAME = "customScope";
    // Overridden Methods From ELResolver
    public Object getValue(ELContext elContext, Object base, Object property) {
        if (property == null) {
            throw new PropertyNotFoundException();
        }
        if (base == null && SCOPE_NAME.equals(property.toString())) {
            // explicit scope lookup request
            CustomScope customScope = getScope(elContext);
            elContext.setPropertyResolved(true);
            return customScope;
        } else if (base != null && base instanceof CustomScope) {
            // We're dealing with the custom scope that has been explictly referenced
            // by an expression. 'property' will be the name of some entity
            // within the scope.
            return lookup(elContext, (CustomScope) base, property.toString());
        } else if (base == null) {
            // bean may have already been created and is in scope.
            // check to see if the bean is present
            return lookup(elContext, getScope(elContext), property.toString());
        }
        return null;
    }
    public Class<?> getType(ELContext elContext, Object base, Object property)
{
        return Object.class;
    }
    public void setValue(ELContext elContext, Object base, Object property,
Object value) {
        // this scope isn't writable in the strict sense, so do nothing.
    }
    public boolean isReadOnly(ELContext elContext, Object base,
Object property) {
        return true;
    }
    public Iterator<FeatureDescriptor> getFeatureDescriptors(ELContext elContext,
Object base) {
        return Collections.<FeatureDescriptor>emptyList().iterator();
```

```
    }
    public Class<?> getCommonPropertyType(ELContext elContext, Object base) {
        if (base != null) {
            return null;
        }
        return String.class;
    }
    // Methods to get scope, remove scope, and lookup scope
    public static void destroyScope(FacesContext ctx) {
        Map<String,Object> sessionMap =
ctx.getExternalContext().getSessionMap();
        CustomScope customScope = (CustomScope) sessionMap.remove(SCOPE_NAME);
    }
    private CustomScope getScope(ELContext elContext) {
        FacesContext ctx = (FacesContext)
elContext.getContext(FacesContext.class);
        Map<String,Object> sessionMap =
ctx.getExternalContext().getSessionMap();
        CustomScope customScope = (CustomScope) sessionMap.get(SCOPE_NAME);
        if (customScope == null) {
            customScope = new CustomScope(ctx.getApplication());
            sessionMap.put(SCOPE_NAME, customScope);
        }
        return customScope;
    }
    private Object lookup(ELContext elContext,
                          CustomScope scope,
                          String key) {
        Object value = scope.get(key);
        elContext.setPropertyResolved(value != null);
        return value;
    }
    private static final class CustomScope extends
ConcurrentHashMap<String,Object> {
        private Application application;
        private CustomScope(Application application) {
            this.application = application;
        }
    }
}
```

Next, register the EL resolver in faces-config.xml with the `el-resolver` tag:

```xml
<?xml version="1.0" encoding="windows-1252"?>
<faces-config version="2.0" xmlns="http://java.sun.com/xml/ns/javaee">
 <application>
  <el-resolver>view.CustomScopeELResolver</el-resolver>
 </application>
</faces-config>
```

The faces-config.xml file with the EL resolver configured and the directory structure of the Scopes application are shown in Figure 9.18.

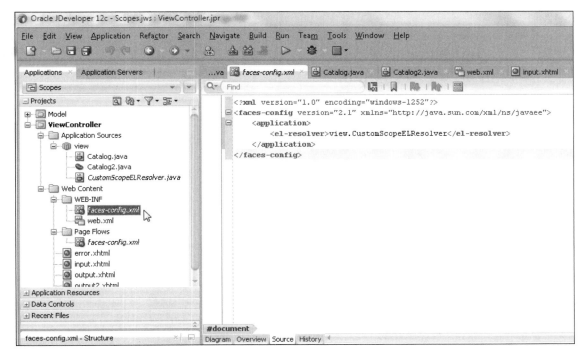

Figure 9.18
The faces-config.xml file with the EL resolver.
Source: Oracle Corporation.

Registration of the EL resolver is required. Without it, the custom scope evaluates to `null` and the custom-scoped managed bean is not added to the custom scope. Redeploy the application and run input.xhtml with the following URL: http://localhost:7101/webapp1/faces/input.xhtml. Submit an SQL query, as shown in Figure 9.19. A data table is rendered, as shown in Figure 9.20.

Figure 9.19
Submitting an SQL query to demonstrate custom scope.

Google and the Google logo are registered trademarks of Google Inc., used with permission.

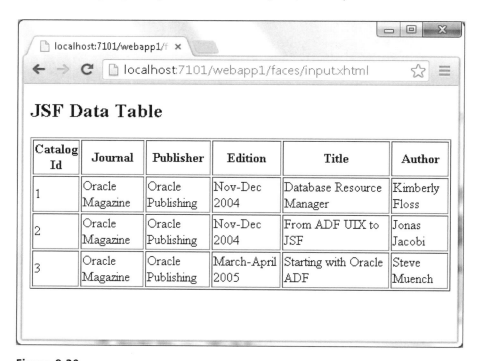

Figure 9.20
A data table rendered with custom scope.

Google and the Google logo are registered trademarks of Google Inc., used with permission.

You can also use the custom scope with the PRG pattern. Modify the outcome of the action method to include a `faces-redirect`:

```
return "output2?faces-redirect=true";
```

Redeploy and rerun input.xhtml. Submit an SQL query. A data table is generated even with a `faces-redirect`, as shown in Figure 9.21. You did not need to use the flash scope. Because the view is redirected to output2.xhtml, output2.xhtml is displayed in the browser instead of input.xhtml without the redirect.

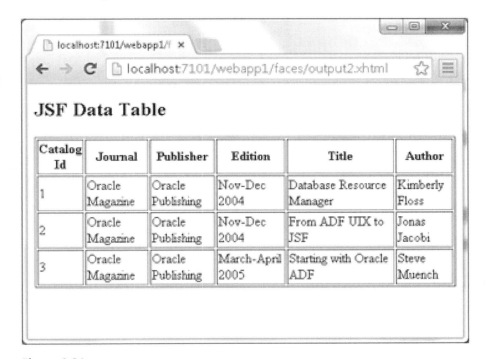

Figure 9.21
Custom scope with redirect.
Google and the Google logo are registered trademarks of Google Inc., used with permission.

The view and flash scopes are greater in scope than request, but lesser in scope than session.

SUMMARY

This chapter introduced three new scopes: view, custom, and flash. It also discussed the `@ViewScoped` and `@CustomScoped` annotations. It discussed using each of the new scopes with an example. It also discussed the new configuration option called project stage. The next chapter discusses the resource-handling feature introduced in JSF 2.0.

CHAPTER 10

RESOURCE HANDLING

A Web application commonly requires resources to run—associated files such as Java-Script, CSS, images, or other Facelets pages. JSF 2.0 has introduced the ResourceHandler API to serve resources. ResourceHandler defines a path-based packaging convention for resources. After ViewHandler has rendered a view and the browser has parsed the completely rendered page, the browser requests for the resources are included in the page. The Faces servlet invokes the ResourceHandler.isResourceRequest() method to determine if the request is for a resource. If the method returns true, the Faces servlet invokes the ResourceHandler.handleResourceRequest() method to handle the resource request. A resource is represented with the Resource class.

OVERVIEW OF THE RESOURCE HANDLER API

The tag library for JSF component tags has introduced the tags discussed in Table 10.1 in the 2.0 version to facilitate resource handling.

Table 10.1 New Annotations

Tag	Description
h:head	Renders the markup for the `<head>` element
h:body	Renders the markup for a `<body>` element
h:outputScript	Renders the markup for the `<script>` element that renders the resource script
h:outputStylesheet	Renders the markup for the `<link>` element that renders the resource style

This chapter discusses the encoding methodology of these new tags to handle resources. The `h:head` element renders the starting `<head>` tag and the attributes of the element, if any. Next, the resources targeted to the `<head/>` element are rendered.

Rendering the resources involves the following steps:

1. You obtain a `UIViewRoot` instance.

2. You invoke the `UIViewRoot.getComponentResources()` with `"head"` as the argument to obtain a list of component resources targeted to the head.

3. The list of `UIComponent` resources is iterated over and encoded. All methods are invoked on each of the component resources. The `<head/>` element is rendered.

The `h:body` tag is encoded similarly to the `h:head` tag. The only difference is that the `UIViewRoot.getComponentResources` is invoked with `"body"` as the argument.

The `h:outputScript` tag is encoded as follows.

1. If the `UIComponent`'s attribute map has a `target` attribute, you invoke the `UIViewRoot.addComponentResource()` method to add the component as a resource to the view.

2. You create a `Resource` object using the `ResourceHandler`'s `createResource()` method, like so:

   ```
   Resource resource=Application.getResourceHandler.createResource(name, library);
   ```

   name and *library* are obtained from the attribute map for the component. *library* may be *null*.

3. The `<script/>` element to be rendered requires the `src` attribute and the `type` attribute. You obtain the `src` attribute value from the resource as follows:

   ```
   String src=resource.getResourcePath();
   ```

You obtain the `type` attribute value as follows.

```
String type=resource.getContentType();
```

4. You render the `<script/>` element at the specified target. If the `target` attribute is not in the component attribute map, the script is rendered inline and a `<script/>` element is not added.

The `h:outputStyleSheet` tag is always rendered in the `<head/>` element as a `<link/>` element. The encoding procedure is as follows:

1. You invoke the `UIViewRoot.addComponentResource(FacesContext, UIComponent, target)` method with "head" as the last argument.

2. A `Resource` object is created using the `ResourceHandler`'s `createResource()` method, like so:

```
Resource resource=Application.getResourceHandler.createResource(name, library);
```

`name` and `library` are obtained from the attribute map for the component. `library` may be `null`.

3. The `<link>` element to be rendered requires the `href` attribute, the `type` attribute, the `rel` attribute, and the `media` attribute. You obtain the href attribute value from the resource like so:

```
String href=resource.getResourcePath();
```

4. You obtain the `type` attribute value as follows:

```
String type=resource.getContentType();
```

You specify the `stylesheet` value in the `rel` attribute and the `screen` value in the `media` attribute.

5. The `<link>` attribute is rendered in the `<head>` element.

Setting the Environment

As a first step, download and install the following software:

- Oracle JDeveloper 12c (12.1.2.0.0) (www.oracle.com/technetwork/developer-tools/jdev/downloads/index.html)

- Oracle WebLogic Server 12c (included with JDeveloper 12c)

- Oracle Database Express Edition (XE) 11g (www.oracle.com/technetwork/database/database-technologies/express-edition/downloads/index.html)

To generate a JSF data table, you need a data source from which to create a database table in Oracle Database 11g XE. Use the SQL script in Listing 10.1. (The database table is the same as the one used in previous chapters. If you have already created it, you don't have to create it again.)

Listing 10.1　SQL Script to Create an Oracle Database Table

```
CREATE USER OE IDENTIFIED BY OE;
GRANT CONNECT, RESOURCE to OE;
CREATE TABLE OE.Catalog(CatalogId INTEGER
PRIMARY KEY, Journal VARCHAR(25), Publisher VARCHAR(25),
 Edition VARCHAR(25), Title Varchar(45), Author Varchar(25));
INSERT INTO OE.Catalog VALUES('1', 'Oracle Magazine',
 'Oracle Publishing', 'Nov-Dec 2004', 'Database Resource
Manager', 'Kimberly Floss');
INSERT INTO OE.Catalog VALUES('2', 'Oracle Magazine',
 'Oracle Publishing', 'Nov-Dec 2004', 'From ADF UIX to JSF',
'Jonas Jacobi');
INSERT INTO OE.Catalog VALUES('3', 'Oracle Magazine',
 'Oracle Publishing', 'March-April 2005', 'Starting with
Oracle ADF ', 'Steve Muench');
COMMIT;
```

If the OE.Catalog table was already created for an earlier chapter, you can reuse it. If not, run the SQL script in SQL Command Line to create a database table OE.CATALOG. As in Chapter 2, "Templating with Facelets," configure and start the IntegratedWebLogicServer.

CREATING A JAVA EE WEB APPLICATION

To grasp resource handling in JSF 2.0, you will use the same example as in previous chapters. You will create a Java EE Web application consisting of an input.xhtml page and an output.xhtml page. The input.xhtml page has an input field for an SQL query and a Submit button to submit the SQL query. The output.xhtml JSF page consists of a JSF data table generated from the SQL query specified in input.xhtml. Follow these steps:

1. Select File > New > From Gallery.

2. In the New Gallery dialog box, choose General > Applications in the Categories pane and choose Java EE Web Application in the Items pane. Then click OK.

3. In the Name Your Application screen, type ResourceHandling in the Application Name field and click Next, as shown in Figure 10.1.

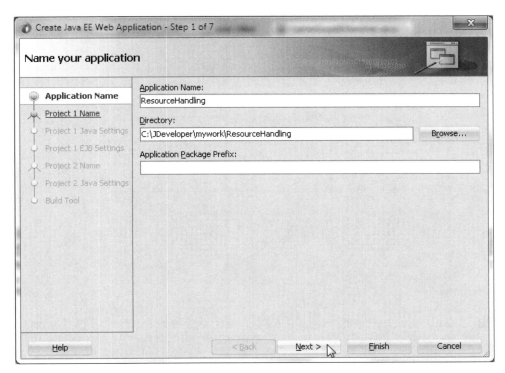

Figure 10.1
Creating a Java EE Web application named "ResourceHandling."
Source: Oracle Corporation.

4. Select the default settings for the Model project name and click Next.

5. Select the default Java settings for the Model project and click Next.

6. Select the default EJB settings for the Model project and click Next.

7. For the ViewController project, select JavaServer Faces under Project Features and click Next, as shown in Figure 10.2.

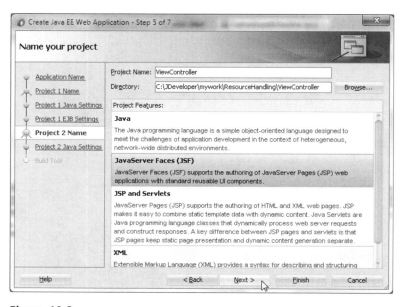

Figure 10.2
Select JavaServer Faces under Project Features.
Source: Oracle Corporation.

8. Select the default Java settings for the ViewController project and click Next.

9. In the Select Build Environment screen, select the defaults settings and click Finish.
   The ResourceHandling application is added to the Applications navigator, as shown
   in Figure 10.3.

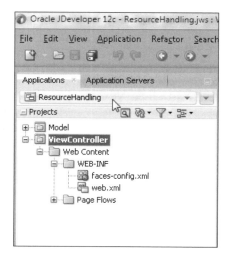

Figure 10.3
The ResourceHandling Java EE Web application is created.
Source: Oracle Corporation.

10. The application consists of a Model and a ViewController project; you will use only the ViewController project. Because you are using the default view definition language in JSF 2.0, Facelets, you will create XHTML pages for the JSF pages. As explained in detail in earlier chapters, such as Chapter 2, add an XHTML page named input.xhtml. (We will use the same input.xhtml file with different code examples to demonstrate resource handling.)

11. Add a managed bean catalog with a managed bean class Catalog.java, as explained in Chapter 2. The directory structure of the ResourceHandling application is shown in Figure 10.4.

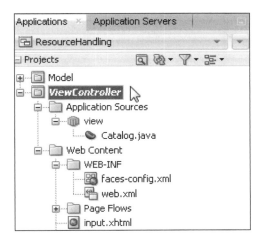

Figure 10.4
The directory structure of the ResourceHandling application.
Source: Oracle Corporation.

12. In the managed bean, which is a POJO, specify the properties inputText1 and resultSet.

13. Add accessor methods for the managed bean properties.

14. Add an action method, commandButton_action. (Note that the name of this action method is the same as in earlier chapters, but could be made different.) A command button is used to invoke the method. In the action method, the SQL query specified in the input text field is retrieved and run in the Oracle Database to generate a ResultSet, whose value is set on the resultSet managed bean property. The resultSet property has a value binding with the data table in the input.xhtml Facelets page.

`Catalog.java` appears in Listing 10.2.

Listing 10.2 `Catalog.java`

```java
package view;
import java.sql.Connection;
import java.sql.DriverManager;
import java.sql.ResultSet;
import java.sql.SQLException;
import java.sql.Statement;
import javax.faces.application.ResourceDependency;
import javax.faces.bean.ManagedBean;
import javax.faces.bean.RequestScoped;
import javax.faces.component.html.HtmlCommandButton;
import javax.faces.component.html.HtmlInputText;

@ManagedBean(name = "catalog")
@RequestScoped
public class Catalog {
    public Catalog() {
    }
    private HtmlCommandButton commandButton1;
    private Statement stmt;
    private Connection connection;
    private ResultSet resultSet;
    private HtmlInputText inputText1;
    private HtmlInputText inputText2;
    private Long maxValue;
    private String sqlQuery;

    public String getSqlQuery() {
        return sqlQuery;
    }
    public void setSqlQuery(String sqlQuery) {
        this.sqlQuery = sqlQuery;
    }
    private int catalogId;
    public int getCatalogId() {
        return catalogId;
    }
    public void setCatalogId(int catalogId) {
        this.catalogId = catalogId;
    }
    public void setInputText2(HtmlInputText inputText2) {
        this.inputText2 = inputText2;
    }
```

```java
    public HtmlInputText getInputText2() {
        return inputText2;
    }
    public void setMaxValue(Long maxValue) {
        this.maxValue = maxValue;
    }
    public Long getMaxValue() {
        return maxValue;
    }
    public void setInputText1(HtmlInputText inputText1) {
        this.inputText1 = inputText1;
    }
    public HtmlInputText getInputText1() {
        return inputText1;
    }
    public void setCommandButton1(HtmlCommandButton commandButton1) {
        this.commandButton1 = commandButton1;
    }
    public HtmlCommandButton getCommandButton1() {
        return commandButton1;
    }
    public void setResultSet(ResultSet resultSet) {
        this.resultSet = resultSet;
    }
    public ResultSet getResultSet() {
        return resultSet;
    }
    public void commandButton_action() {
        try {
            Class.forName("oracle.jdbc.OracleDriver");
            String url = "jdbc:oracle:thin:@localhost:1521:XE";
            connection = DriverManager.getConnection(url, "OE", "OE");
            stmt =
connection.createStatement(ResultSet.TYPE_SCROLL_INSENSITIVE,
ResultSet.CONCUR_READ_ONLY);
            String sqlQuery = (String)(inputText1.getValue());
            resultSet = stmt.executeQuery((sqlQuery));
            if (resultSet != null) {
                this.setResultSet(resultSet);
            }
        }
        catch (SQLException e) {
            System.out.println(e.getMessage());
```

```
    } catch (ClassNotFoundException e) {
        System.out.println(e.getMessage());
    } catch (Exception e) {
        System.out.println(e.getMessage());
    } finally {
    }
  }
}
```

The web.xml page consists of the Faces servlet because you selected the JSF project technology. The web.xml page appears in Listing 10.3.

Listing 10.3   The web.xml Page

```
<?xml version = '1.0' encoding = 'windows-1252'?>
<web-app xmlns="http://java.sun.com/xml/ns/javaee"
xmlns:xsi="http://www.w3.org/2001/XMLSchema-instance"
         xsi:schemaLocation="http://java.sun.com/xml/ns/javaee
http://java.sun.com/xml/ns/javaee/web-app_3_0.xsd"
         version="3.0">
  <servlet>
    <servlet-name>Faces Servlet</servlet-name>
    <servlet-class>javax.faces.webapp.FacesServlet</servlet-class>
    <load-on-startup>1</load-on-startup>
  </servlet>
  <servlet-mapping>
    <servlet-name>Faces Servlet</servlet-name>
    <url-pattern>/faces/*</url-pattern>
  </servlet-mapping>
</web-app>
```

Because you have configured the `Catalog.java` class as a managed bean using the `@ManagedBean` annotation, faces-config.xml is an empty file.

```
<?xml version="1.0" encoding="windows-1252"?>
<faces-config version="2.1" xmlns="http://java.sun.com/xml/ns/javaee">
</faces-config>
```

PACKAGING AND RENDERING RESOURCES

The input.xhtml JSF page consists of an `h:outputLabel` for a label for the input field and an `h:inputText` for an input text field to specify an SQL query. `h:inputText` binds to a managed bean property, `inputText1`. The input.xhtml page also consists of an `h:dataTable` element with value binding to a managed bean property, `resultSet`, which is the JDBC `ResultSet` for an SQL query specified in the input field. The `var` attribute of `h:dataTable` specifies the iteration variable to be used to iterate over the data model and is set to `"resultset"`. The `h:column` elements within `h:dataTable` have value binding to the `ResultSet` columns accessed using the iteration variable specified in the `var` attribute.

The `ResourceHandler` API uses path-based packaging conventions with the default implementation being to package resources in the Web application root in the `resources/<resourceIdentifier>` resource path. You use `ResourceHandler` support for serving resources from the resources folder, which is in the Web application root.

To see how this works, follow these steps:

1. Create a resources folder in the Web application root of the ResourceHandling application, which is in the public_html folder.

2. Create an images folder in the resources folder. The images folder represents a resource library.

3. Copy an image—logo.jpg is used in this chapter—to the images folder.

4. Choose View > Refresh to refresh the directory structure in JDeveloper.

5. In input.xhtml, add an `h:graphicImage` tag:

```
<h:graphicImage library="images" name="logo.jpg"></h:graphicImage>
```

The variation of input.xhtml used to demonstrate the use of a graphics image appears in Listing 10.4.

Listing 10.4   The input.xhtml Page with `h:graphicImage`

```
<!DOCTYPE html PUBLIC "-//W3C//DTD XHTML 1.0 Transitional//EN"
    "http://www.w3.org/TR/xhtml1/DTD/xhtml1-transitional.dtd">
<html xmlns="http://www.w3.org/1999/xhtml"
    xmlns:ui="http://java.sun.com/jsf/facelets"
    xmlns:h="http://java.sun.com/jsf/html"
    xmlns:f="http://java.sun.com/jsf/core">
<f:view>
 <h:head>
  <title></title>
 </h:head>
  <h:body>
<h:graphicImage library="images" name="logo.jpg"></h:graphicImage>
  <h:form id="form1">
```

```
<h2>JSF Data Table</h2>
 <h:panelGrid columns="2">
    <h:outputLabel for="inputText1"
                   value="SQL Query: "/>
  <h:inputText id="inputText1" binding="#{catalog.inputText1}"
required="true"/>
  <h:commandButton binding="#{catalog.commandButton1}"
action="#{catalog.commandButton_action}" value="Submit"/>
  </h:panelGrid>
  </h:form>
</h:body>
</f:view>
</html>
```

In the h:graphicImage tag, the library attribute specifies the images library, which you created earlier. The name attribute specifies the image, logo.jpg. The directory structure of the JSF application with the graphics image is shown in Figure 10.5.

Figure 10.5
The directory structure with the images resource library.
Source: Oracle Corporation.

6. Start the IntegratedWebLogicServer if not already started.

7. Create a WAR file deployment profile, webapp1, for the ViewController project as explained in Chapter 2.

8. Right-click the ViewController project and select Deploy > webapp1, as shown in Figure 10.6.

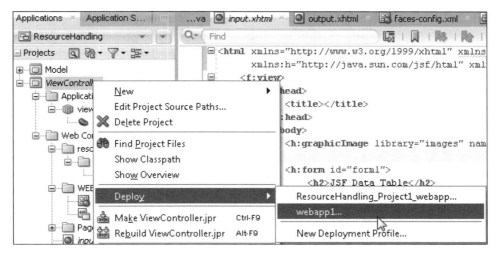

Figure 10.6
Deploying webapp1 to IntegratedWebLogicServer.
Source: Oracle Corporation.

9. Use the Deploy webapp1 wizard to deploy the webapp1 application to the IntegratedWebLogicServer, as explained in Chapter 2. The Java EE Web application is deployed to IntegratedWebLogicServer.

10. Run the input.xhtml JSF page with the following URL http://localhost:7101/webapp1/faces/input.xhtml. The JPEG in `h:imageGraphic` is rendered, as shown in Figure 10.7.

Figure 10.7
Rendering graphics from a resource library.
Google and the Google logo are registered trademarks of Google Inc., used with permission.

An alternative method to packaging resources into the classpath is also provided. The resources to be served by ResourceHandler must be packaged into a JAR file and the JAR file added to the runtime classpath. The resources in the JAR file must be packaged using path-based conventions in the META-INF/resources/<resourceIdentifier> path. To use this method, follow these steps:

1. Create a folder structure outside the ResourceHandling application, as shown in Figure 10.8.

Figure 10.8
Creating a folder structure for packaging resources.
Source: Oracle Corporation.

2. Copy the logo.jpg file to the images folder.

3. In Command Line, change directories to the folder preceding the META-INF folder.

4. Create a JAR file using the following command:

```
>jar cf resources.jar META-INF
```

5. Add the resources.jar file to the CLASSPATH variable in the \\DefaultDomain\bin\startWebLogic batch script.

6. Restart the IntegratedWebLogicServer. The resources.jar file is added to the runtime classpath of the IntegratedWebLogicServer and becomes available to Java EE Web applications running on the server.

Next, let's discuss the use of multiple libraries in the ResourceHandling application. You can create multiple resource libraries in the resources folder for other types of resources such as CSS files, JavaScript files, and Facelets pages (XHTML pages). As a further example, follow these steps:

1. Create a folder, css, in the resources folder.

2. Copy the following listing to a file named style.css and copy the style.css file to the css folder as shown. The directory structure of the resources folder with two libraries, images and css, is shown in Figure 10.9.

```
h1 {
    font-family: Helvetica, Geneva, Arial,
        SunSans-Regular, sans-serif }
```

```
body {
    font-family: Georgia, "Times New Roman",
            Times, serif;
    color: purple;
    background-color: #d8da3d
}
```

Figure 10.9
The resources folder.
Source: Oracle Corporation.

3. Add an h:outputStylesheet tag to input.xhtml from the JSF > HTML Components palette, as shown in Figure 10.10.

Figure 10.10
Adding an h:outputStylesheet tag.
Source: Oracle Corporation.

4. Set the library attribute value as "css" and the name as "style.css", as shown. If you prefer, you can add the attributes added using Code Assist in JDeveloper, as shown in Figure 10.11.

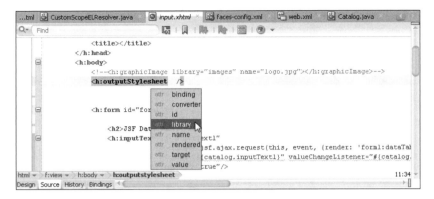

Figure 10.11
Adding attributes with Code Assist.

Source: Oracle Corporation.

```
<h:outputStylesheet library="css" name="style.css"/>
```

5. Add the `h:graphicImage` tag with the resource specified using the EL expression `#{resource['images:logo.jpg']}`:

```
<h:graphicImage value="#{resource['images:logo.jpg']}"/>
```

The EL expression for an image resource can also be used in other elements, such as the `</a>` element:

```
<a href="#{resource['images:logo.jpg']}" >Logo</a>
```

The `h:graphicImage`, `h:outputStylesheet`, and `<a/>` tags in input.xhtml are shown in Figure 10.12.

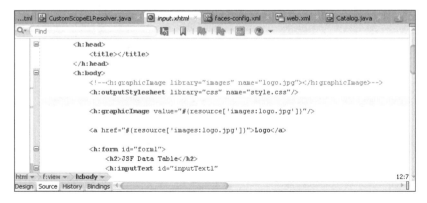

Figure 10.12
The different tags to add resources to input.xhtml.

Source: Oracle Corporation.

The input.xhtml Facelets page appears in Listing 10.5.

Listing 10.5   The input.xhtml Page with CSS and Image

```
<!DOCTYPE html PUBLIC "-//W3C//DTD XHTML 1.0 Transitional//EN"
    "http://www.w3.org/TR/xhtml1/DTD/xhtml1-transitional.dtd">
<html xmlns="http://www.w3.org/1999/xhtml"
xmlns:ui="http://java.sun.com/jsf/facelets"
      xmlns:h="http://java.sun.com/jsf/html"
xmlns:f="http://java.sun.com/jsf/core">
    <f:view>
        <h:head>
            <title></title>
        </h:head>
        <h:body>
            <!--<h:graphicImage library="images"
name="logo.jpg"></h:graphicImage>-->
            <h:outputStylesheet library="css" name="style.css"/>
            <h:graphicImage value="#{resource['images:logo.jpg']}"/>
            <a href="#{resource['images:logo.jpg']}">Logo</a>
            <h:form id="form1">
                <h2>JSF Data Table</h2>
                <h:outputLabel for="inputText1" value="SQL Query: "/>
                <h:inputText id="inputText1" binding="#{catalog.inputText1}"/>
                <h:dataTable id="dataTable1" value="#{catalog.resultSet}"
var="resultset" border="1" rows="4">
                    <h:column id="column1">
                        <f:facet name="header">
                            <h:outputText value="Catalog Id"/>
                        </f:facet>
                        <h:outputText id="outputText1"
value="#{resultset.catalogid}"/>
                    </h:column>
                    <h:column id="column2">
                        <f:facet name="header">
                            <h:outputText value="Journal"/>
                        </f:facet>
                        <h:outputText id="outputText2"
value="#{resultset.journal}"/>
                    </h:column>
                    <h:column id="column3">
                        <f:facet name="header">
                            <h:outputText value="Publisher"/>
                        </f:facet>
                        <h:outputText id="outputText3"
```

```
value="#{resultset.publisher}"/>
                        </h:column>
                        <h:column id="column4">
                            <f:facet name="header">
                                <h:outputText value="Edition"/>
                            </f:facet>
                            <h:outputText id="outputText4"
value="#{resultset.edition}"/>
                        </h:column>
                        <h:column id="column5">
                            <f:facet name="header">
                                <h:outputText value="Title"/>
                            </f:facet>
                            <h:outputText id="outputText5"
value="#{resultset.title}"/>
                        </h:column>
                        <h:column id="column6">
                            <f:facet name="header">
                                <h:outputText value="Author"/>
                            </f:facet>
                            <h:outputText id="outputText6"
value="#{resultset.author}"/>
                        </h:column>
                    </h:dataTable>
                    <h:commandButton binding="#{catalog.commandButton1}"
                     action="#{catalog.commandButton_action}"
                                    value="Submit"/>
                </h:form>
            </h:body>
        </f:view>
</html>
```

6. Right-click ViewController and select Deploy > webapp1 to
   IntegratedWebLogicServer, as shown in Figure 10.13. Because you previously
   deployed the webapp1 application to IntegratedWebLogicServer, the integrated
   server is listed as an option in the Deploy submenu.

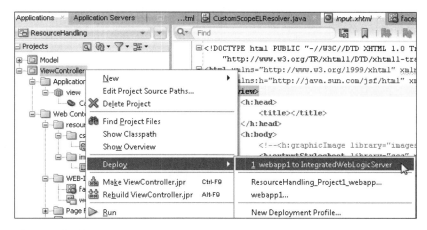

Figure 10.13
Deploying webapp1 to IntegratedWebLogicServer.
Source: Oracle Corporation.

7. Run the input.xhtml page with the following URL: http://localhost:7101/webapp1/ faces/input.xhtml. The graphic image and style.css resources are rendered.

8. Specify an SQL query (SELECT * FROM OE.CATALOG) and click Submit, as shown in Figure 10.14. A data table is rendered, as shown in Figure 10.15. The Logo link is also rendered in input.xhtml.

Figure 10.14
Submitting an SQL query.
Google and the Google logo are registered trademarks of Google Inc., used with permission.

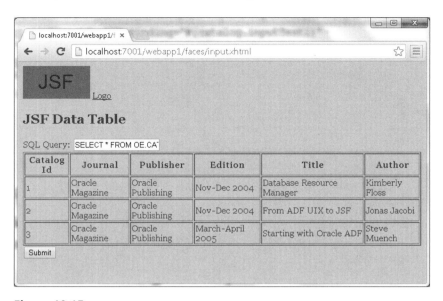

Figure 10.15
Rendering a JSF data table.

Google and the Google logo are registered trademarks of Google Inc., used with permission.

9. Click the Logo link, as shown in Figure 10.16. The logo.jpg image is rendered, as shown in Figure 10.17.

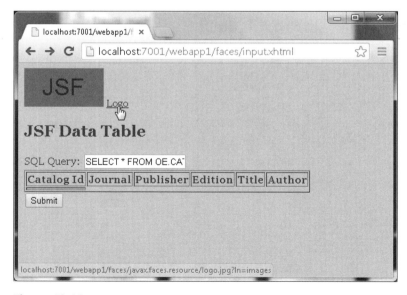

Figure 10.16
Clicking the Logo link.

Google and the Google logo are registered trademarks of Google Inc., used with permission.

Figure 10.17
Rendering an image resource.

Google and the Google logo are registered trademarks of Google Inc., used with permission.

You have only used the simplest form of convention for a resource in the resources folder: a library and the resource file. The resource identifier may consist of other components, however. The complete format of the resource identifier can include a locale prefix, a library version, and the resource version, adding support for localization and versioning.

```
[localePrefix/][libraryName/][libraryVersion/]resourceName[/resourceVersion]
```

`resourceName` is the only required component of a resource identifier. The localization, versioning, and grouping into libraries is implemented using `ResourceHandler`.

Custom components and renderers may require resources that are not available in a JSF page in which the components/renderers are included. You can annotate components and renderers with the `@ResourceDependency` annotation, which may be grouped using the `@ResourceDependencies` annotation, to specify resources that are required by the component/renderer.

RELOCATING RESOURCES

Some resources, such as JavaScript scripts, can be rendered in a location other than the location of the resource tag. For example, using resource relocation, you can render a JavaScript library in the `<head/>` element using the `target` attribute in an `h:ouputScript` tag, which renders the `<script>` element in the `<head>` element:

```
<h:outputScript library="js" name="jsf.js" target="head"/>
```

If you omit the `target` attribute, jsf.js would have rendered inline. `h:outputStylesheet` renders only in the `<head>` element and is not required to be targeted to the `<head/>` element explicitly. The `<h:head>` tag is required in the JSF 2.0 page if a script is to be targeted to the `<head>` element or a stylesheet is to be rendered. As an example, remove the `h:head` tag by commenting it out in input.xhtml, as shown in Figure 10.18.

Figure 10.18
Commenting out the h:head tag.
Source: Oracle Corporation.

Redeploy the ResourceHandling application and run the input.xhtml page. h:graphicImage is rendered but style.css is not, as shown in Figure 10.19.

Figure 10.19
The CSS stylesheet resource does not get rendered.
Google and the Google logo are registered trademarks of Google Inc., used with permission.

The target for a resource may also be specified in @ResourceDependency with the target element.

ORDERING OF APPLICATION CONFIGURATION RESOURCES

You can specify multiple application-configuration resources in a Facelets application. The JSF implementation searches for application-configuration resources in the following order and makes a list:

1. All resources that match META-INF/faces-config.xml or end with .facesconfig in the META-INF directory

2. The `javax.faces.CONFIG_FILES` context initialization parameter resource paths

3. The application configuration resources in the /WEB-INF directory, except faces-config.xml

JSF 2.0 has added the provision to order the application-configuration resources. A JSF 2.0 application with multiple view handlers may be required to configure the view handler delegation chain in a specific order. Or, with multiple phase listeners registered, an application may be required to process the phase listeners in a particular order.

The faces-config.xml file in JSF 2.0 has introduced new elements, `<ordering/>` and `<absolute-ordering/>`, to order named application-configuration resources. The `<ordering/>` element specifies the relative ordering of application-configuration resources. The `<absolute-ordering/>` element specifies the absolute ordering. <absolute-ordering/> may have zero or more `<name/>` sub-elements, which represent named application-configuration resources, and optionally an `<others/>` element, which represents all the other application-configuration resources, named or unnamed. The `<ordering/>` element may contain the sub-elements discussed in Table 10.2.

Table 10.2   Sub-Elements of `<ordering/>`

Sub-Element	Description
`<before></before>`	The resource must be ordered before the named resource.
`<after></after>`	The resource must be ordered after the named resource.

Next, we will discuss an example of using multiple faces-config<n>.xml files with a different `PhaseListener` element configured in each to demonstrate the ordering of faces-config<n>.xml. (Note that <n> specifies the resource number.) The faces-config.xml file is always last in the ordering of multiple faces-config<n>.xml application-configuration resources. To see this in action follow these steps:

1. Specify a `PhaseListenerA` in WEB-INF/faces-config.xml:

```
<?xml version="1.0" encoding="windows-1252"?>
<faces-config version="2.0" xmlns="http://java.sun.com/xml/ns/javaee">
    <name>A</name>
    <lifecycle>
<phase-listener>view.PhaseListenerA</phase-listener>
</lifecycle>
</faces-config>
```

2. Create a `PhaseListenerA` Java class (a class that extends the `PhaseListener` class) in the view package.

3. Add a `System.out.println` message in the `beforePhase` and `afterPhase` methods to indicate the phase. The `PhaseListenerA` class appears in Listing 10.6.

Listing 10.6   The `PhaseListenerA` Class

```
package view;
import javax.faces.event.PhaseEvent;
import javax.faces.event.PhaseId;
import javax.faces.event.PhaseListener;
public class PhaseListenerA implements PhaseListener {
    public PhaseListenerA() {
        super();
    }
    public void afterPhase(PhaseEvent event) {
        System.out.println("After PhaseListener A");
    }
    public void beforePhase(PhaseEvent event) {
        System.out.println("Before PhaseListener A");
    }
    public PhaseId getPhaseId() {
        return PhaseId.ANY_PHASE;
    }
}
}
```

4. Add three more faces-config<n>.xml files (faces-config1.xml, faces-config2.xml, and faces-config3.xml). To begin, choose File > New > From Gallery.

5. In the New Gallery dialog box, select Web Tier > JSF/Facelets in the Categories pane and select the faces-config.xml option in the Items pane. Then click OK. (See Figure 10.20.)

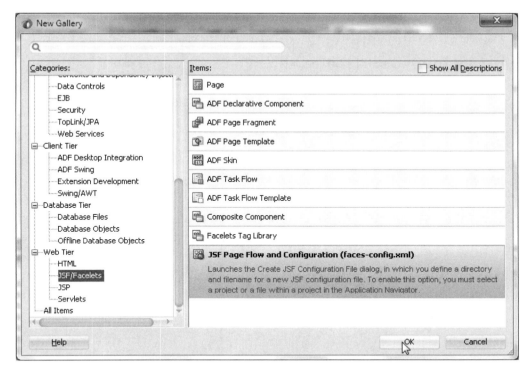

Figure 10.20
Adding a faces-config.xml file.

Source: Oracle Corporation.

6. In the Create JSF Configuration File dialog box, type `faces-config1.xml` in the File Name field and click OK, as shown in Figure 10.21.

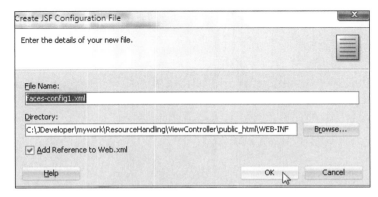

Figure 10.21
Creating a JSF configuration file.

Source: Oracle Corporation.

7. In faces-config1.xml, add a `<name>B</name>` element and a `phase-listener` class, `view.PhaseListenerB`:

```xml
<?xml version="1.0" encoding="windows-1252"?>
<faces-config version="2.1" xmlns="http://java.sun.com/xml/ns/javaee">
   <name>B</name>
    <lifecycle>
        <phase-listener>view.PhaseListenerB</phase-listener>
    </lifecycle>
</faces-config>
```

8. In faces-config1.xml, add an `<ordering/>` element after the `<name/>` element.

9. Add a less-than symbol (`<`). A Code Assist for the elements that may be added appears. Select the `ordering` element from the list, as shown in Figure 10.22.

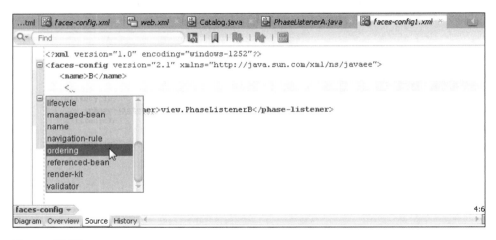

Figure 10.22
Adding an `<ordering>` element.
Source: Oracle Corporation.

10. Use Code Assist to select the `after` element to add within the `<ordering/>` element, as shown in Figure 10.23.

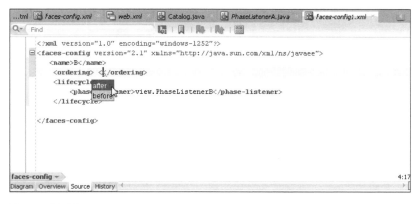

Figure 10.23
Adding the ⟨after⟩ element.
Source: Oracle Corporation.

11. Use Code Assist to select the name sub-element to add to the ⟨after/⟩ element, as shown in Figure 10.24.

Figure 10.24
Adding the ⟨name/⟩ element.
Source: Oracle Corporation.

12. Add name as C. Faces-config1.xml has an ⟨after/⟩ element to order the faces-config1.xml configuration file after the named resource C. The faces-config1.xml file appears in Listing 10.7.

Listing 10.7   The faces-config1.xml File

```
<?xml version="1.0" encoding="windows-1252"?>
<faces-config version="2.0" xmlns="http://java.sun.com/xml/ns/javaee">
   <name>B</name>
```

```
<ordering><after><name>C</name></after></ordering>
  <lifecycle>
      <phase-listener>view.PhaseListenerB</phase-listener>
  </lifecycle>
</faces-config>
```

13. Create a `PhaseListenerB` class. The `PhaseListenerB` class appears in Listing 10.8.

Listing 10.8   The `PhaseListenerB` Class

```java
package view;
import javax.faces.event.PhaseEvent;
import javax.faces.event.PhaseId;
import javax.faces.event.PhaseListener;
public class PhaseListenerB implements PhaseListener {
    public PhaseListenerB() {
        super();
    }
    public void afterPhase(PhaseEvent event) {
        System.out.println("After PhaseListener B");
    }
    public void beforePhase(PhaseEvent event) {
System.out.println("Before PhaseListener B");
    }
    public PhaseId getPhaseId() {
        return PhaseId.ANY_PHASE;
    }
}
```

The faces-config1.xml file is shown in Figure 10.25.

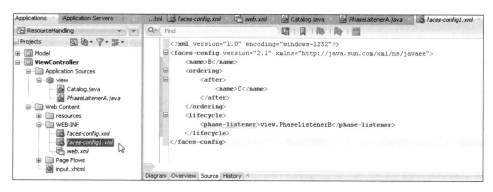

Figure 10.25
The faces-config1.xml file.

Source: Oracle Corporation.

14. Add absolute ordering using the `<absolute-ordering/>` element to `faces-config2.xml`. To begin, add a less-than symbol (`<`). A Code Assist for the elements that may be added appears. Select `absolute-ordering`, as shown in Figure 10.26.

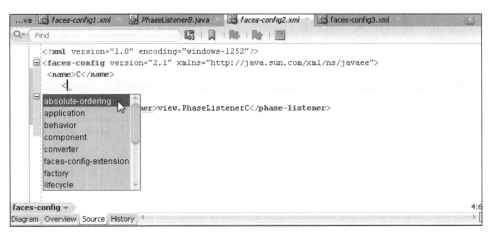

Figure 10.26
Adding the `<absolute-ordering/>` element.
Source: Oracle Corporation.

15. Add named resources within the `<absolute-ordering/>` element using the `<name/>` elements selected with Code Assist. You can also add the `<others/>` element to the `<absolute-ordering/>` element, as shown in Figure 10.27.

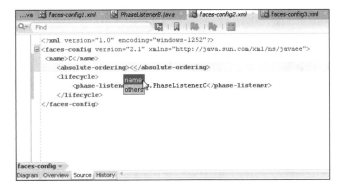

Figure 10.27
Adding the `<others/>` element.
Source: Oracle Corporation.

The `<resource-ordering/>` element lists the order of named resources as B, C, D. The faces-config2.xml file appears in Listing 10.9.

Listing 10.9   The faces-config2.xml File

```xml
<?xml version="1.0" encoding="windows-1252"?>
<faces-config version="2.0" xmlns="http://java.sun.com/xml/ns/javaee">
    <name>C</name>
    <absolute-ordering>
        <name>B</name>
        <name>C</name>
        <name>D</name>
    </absolute-ordering>
    <lifecycle>
        <phase-listener>view.PhaseListenerC</phase-listener>
    </lifecycle>
</faces-config>
```

16. Add the `PhaseListenerC` class specified in faces-config2.xml. (See Listing 10.10.)

Listing 10.10   The PhaseListenerC Class

```java
package view;
import javax.faces.event.PhaseEvent;
import javax.faces.event.PhaseId;
import javax.faces.event.PhaseListener;
public class PhaseListenerC implements PhaseListener {
    public PhaseListenerC() {
        super();
    }
    public void afterPhase(PhaseEvent event) {
        System.out.println("After PhaseListener C");
    }
    public void beforePhase(PhaseEvent event) {
        System.out.println("Before PhaseListener C");
    }
    public PhaseId getPhaseId() {
        return PhaseId.ANY_PHASE;
    }
}
```

17. In faces-config3.xml, add an `<ordering/>` element with a `<before/>` sub-element to specify an ordering of D before `<others/>`. The faces-config3.xml file has a PhaseListenerD configured. (See Listing 10.11.)

Listing 10.11   The faces-config3.xml File

```
<?xml version="1.0" encoding="windows-1252"?>
<faces-config version="2.0" xmlns="http://java.sun.com/xml/ns/javaee">
    <name>D</name>
    <ordering><before><others /></before></ordering>
    <lifecycle>
        <phase-listener>view.PhaseListenerD</phase-listener>
    </lifecycle>
</faces-config>
```

18. Add the PhaseListenerD class. (See Listing 10.12.)

Listing 10.12   The PhaseListenerD Class

```
package view;
import javax.faces.event.PhaseEvent;
import javax.faces.event.PhaseId;
import javax.faces.event.PhaseListener;
public class PhaseListenerD implements PhaseListener {
    public PhaseListenerD() {
        super();
    }
    public void afterPhase(PhaseEvent event) {
        System.out.println("After PhaseListener D");
    }
    public void beforePhase(PhaseEvent event) {
        System.out.println("Before PhaseListener D");
    }
    public PhaseId getPhaseId() {
        return PhaseId.ANY_PHASE;
    }
}
```

The different faces-config<n>.xml files and phase listener classes are shown in Figure 10.28.

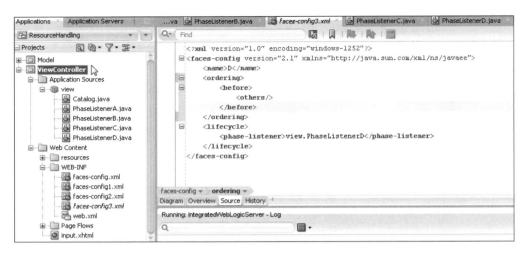

Figure 10.28
Multiple faces-config.xml files.
Source: Oracle Corporation.

19. To process the phase listeners, redeploy the ResourceHandling application and run input.xhtml. The output on the IntegratedWebLogicServer shows the order in which the phase listeners are processed: D, C, B, A. (See Figure 10.29.)

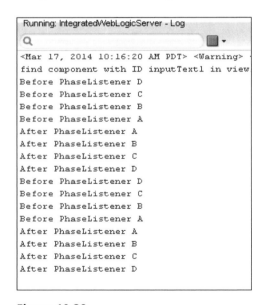

Figure 10.29
The order in which phase listeners are processed.
Source: Oracle Corporation.

A is faces-config.xml, which is always ordered last. D is ordered first because you specified D to be ordered before others using the `<before/>` and `<others/>` elements. C is ordered after B, because you specified an `<after/>` element in faces-config1.xml (B) with ordering of B after C. The absolute ordering of B, C, D is overridden by the relative ordering. First, the relative ordering is implemented. Any ordering not ascertained is implemented using absolute ordering.

20. As another example, comment out the `<ordering/>` element in faces-config1.xml, as shown in Figure 10.30.

Figure 10.30
Commenting out the `<ordering>` element.
Source: Oracle Corporation.

21. Redeploy and rerun the application. The ordering of phase listeners, which indicates the ordering of the faces-config\<n>.xml files, is D, B, C, A, as shown in Figure 10.31. D and A are ordered as before. Because you removed the relative ordering in B, the absolute ordering for B and C is implemented.

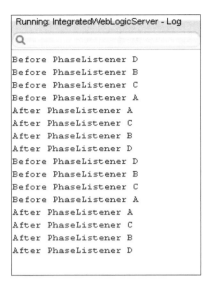

Figure 10.31
Implementing absolute ordering for B and C.
Source: Oracle Corporation.

22. Remove the relative ordering of D in faces-config3.xml. Then redeploy and rerun input.xhtml. With no relative ordering, absolute ordering of B, C, D is implemented, as shown in Figure 10.32. A (faces-config.xml) is always last.

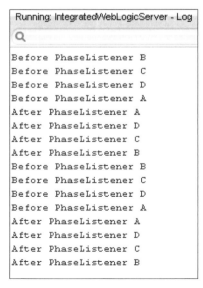

Figure 10.32
Implementing absolute ordering of B, C, and D.
Source: Oracle Corporation.

SUMMARY

This chapter introduced the `ResourceHandler` API and the new tags in JSF 2.0 for resource handling. It discussed packaging and rendering of resources using the `ResourceHandler` with an example consisting of a JSF page to create a data table from an SQL query. For resources, you used a JPEG image and a CSS stylesheet. This chapter also discussed the ordering of application-configuration resources using phase listeners. The next chapter discusses exception handling features introduced in JSF 2.0.

CHAPTER 11

EVENT HANDLING AND EXCEPTION HANDLING

Events are broadcast by JSF components, the different phases of a Java request lifecycle, and the application, and are received by registered event listeners. JSF 1.2 provides phase events, which are broadcast before and after every phase, and application events, which are generated by the JSF components.

Phase events in JSF 2.0 are the same as in JSF 1.2. The only difference is a new method in `UIViewRoot`: `getPhaseListeners()`. It returns a `List<PhaseListener>`. JSF 1.2 provided two application events: `ValueChangeEvent` and `ActionEvent`. JSF 2.0 added two behavior events: `BehaviorEvent` and `AjaxBehaviorEvent`. These add behavior to components and were discussed in Chapter 8, "Client Behaviors." JSF 2.0 has also added a new type of event, system events, which are non–application specific events that may be broadcast by arbitrary objects.

SYSTEM EVENTS

System events represent specific stages in time for a JSF application. Phase events also represent specific stages in time for a JSF application, but the granularity of the system events is more precise. System events are represented by the `javax.faces.event.SystemEvent` class, which provides the two methods discussed in Table 11.1.

Table 11.1   SystemEvent Class Methods

Method	Description
`isAppropriateListener(FacesListener listener)`	Returns a Boolean to indicate if `FacesListener` is an appropriate listener for an event
`processListener(FacesListener listener)`	Broadcasts an event to a `FacesListener`

Two types of system events are provided: application system events and component system events. Table 11.2 discusses the application-scoped system events.

Table 11.2   Application-Scoped System Events

Event	Description
`ExceptionQueuedEvent`	Represents an exception instance that has been queued by calls to `Application().publishEvent(ExceptionQueuedEvent.class, eventContext)`. `eventContext` is an `ExceptionQueuedEventContext` object.
`PostConstructApplicationEvent`	The event is broadcast by the runtime after all the configuration resources have been parsed and processed. Listeners that are required to perform post-configuration processing may register with the event.
`PostConstructCustomScopeEvent`	Broadcast by custom scopes after the beginning of a custom scope.
`PreDestroyApplicationEvent`	The event broadcast by the runtime before the factories associated with an application are released. Listeners that are required to perform custom shutdown processing may register with the event.
`PreDestroyCustomScopeEvent`	Broadcast by custom scopes before a scope ends.

Just as `FacesEvent` (`ActionEvent` and `ValueChangeEvent`) from JSF 1.2 are broadcast to `FacesListener` (`ActionListener`, `ValueChangeListener`) and `PhaseEvent` to `PhaseListener`, JSF 2.0 provides `SystemEventListener` (which extends the `FacesListener` interface) for `SystemEvent`. Listener classes that are required to listen to system events must implement the interface. The `SystemEventListener` class provides the methods discussed in Table 11.3.

Table 11.3   SystemEventListener Class Methods

Method	Description
isListenerForSource(java.lang.Object source)	Returns a Boolean to indicate if the listener is a listener for the specified source
processEvent(SystemEvent event)	Processes the specified system event

System events provide a publish/subscribe model to broadcast and listen to events. For the application-scoped system events, the sequence of the publish/subscribe is as follows:

1. The application registers listeners represented by the SystemEventListener class with the system events.

2. The application broadcasts system events represented by the SystemEvent class.

3. The listeners that are registered for the system events broadcast are invoked and the processEvent method of the SystemEventListener is called.

You can generate system events, application-scoped events, and component system events using the methods from the javax.faces.application.Application class discussed in Table 11.4.

Table 11.4   Application Class Methods to Generate Events

Method	Description
publishEvent(FacesContext context,Class <? extends SystemEvent> systemEventClass,Object source)	Broadcasts a system event of type systemEventClass and includes the source of the event. Any listeners subscribing to the event of type systemEventClass are called.
publishEvent(FacesContext context, Class <? extends SystemEvent> systemEventClass,Class<?> sourceBaseType,Object source)	The same as the other variant except that the class of the sourceBaseType is used to find listeners instead of the class of the source.

Listeners for application-scoped system events can subscribe (register with) and unsubscribe (unregister with) to the system events using the `javax.faces.application.Application` methods discussed in Table 11.5.

Table 11.5 Application Class Methods to Register/Unregister Listeners

Method	Description
subscribeToEvent(Class<? extends SystemEvent> systemEventClass,SystemEventListener listener)	Registers the listener with the systemEventClass. When an event of type systemEventClass is generated, the listener is notified and the processEvent method of the listener is invoked.
subscribeToEvent(Class<? extends SystemEvent> systemEventClass, Class<?> sourceClass, SystemEventListener listener)	Registers the listener with the event of type systemEventClass originating from the source of type sourceClass.
unsubscribeFromEvent(Class<? extends SystemEvent> systemEventClass,SystemEventListener listener)	Unregisters the listener from the event of type systemEventClass.
unsubscribeFromEvent(Class<? extends SystemEvent> systemEventClass,Class<?> sourceClass, SystemEventListener listener)	Unregisters the listener from the event of type systemEventClass originating from the source of type sourceClass.

The `SystemEventListenerHolder` interface is provided for implementing classes to keep a list of `SystemEventListener` instances for each type of `SystemEvent` that the classes generate. The `UIComponent` and `ExceptionQueuedEventContext` classes implement the `SystemEventListenerHolder` interface. `SystemEventListenerHolder` provides only the method discussed in Table 11.6.

Table 11.6 `SystemEventListenerHolder` Method

Method	Description
getListenersForEventClass(java.lang.Class <? extends SystemEvent> facesEventClass)	Returns a list of SystemEventListener instances that are registered with the class implementing the interface

Component system events, which are specific to a `UIComponent`, are represented with the `ComponentSystemEvent` class. Table 11.7 discusses the different types of component system events.

Table 11.7 ComponentSystemEvent Class Methods

Event	Description
PostAddToViewEvent	Broadcast when a `UIComponent` instance or a containing `UIComponent` instance is added to the view
PostConstructViewMapEvent	Broadcast by `UIViewRoot` when a view map is first created
PostRestoreStateEvent	Broadcast by a `UIComponent` instance that is in a UI component tree whose state has been just restored
PostValidateEvent	Broadcast by a `UIComponent` that has just been validated
PreDestroyViewMapEvent	Broadcast by `UIViewRoot` before a view map is cleared
PreRemoveFromViewEvent	Broadcast by a `UIComponent` that is about to be removed from the view
PreRenderComponentEvent	Broadcast by a `UIComponent` that is about to be rendered
PreRenderViewEvent	Broadcast by a `UIViewRoot` instance that is about to be rendered
PreValidateEvent	Broadcast by a `UIComponent` that is about to be validated

Listeners that must be registered to listen to `ComponentSystemEvents` must implement the `ComponentSystemEventListener` interface, which provides the method discussed in Table 11.8.

Table 11.8 ComponentSystemEventListener Method

Method	Description
processEvent(ComponentSystemEvent event)	Processes the `ComponentSystemEvent`, which is always associated with a `UIComponent`

An `isListenerForSource()` method is not provided and is implicit because the `ComponentSystemEventListener` listener is specific to a `UIComponent`. The publish/subscribe model for `ComponentSystemEvent` is similar to the application-scoped system events. For application-scoped system events, the sequence of the publish/subscribe is as follows:

1. A `UIComponent` instance registers `ComponentSystemEventListener` listeners to listen to a `ComponentSystemEvent` system event.

2. A `ComponentSystemEvent` system event is broadcast using a `publishEvent` method of `javax.faces.application.Application`, which was discussed in Table 11.4.

3. The listeners that are registered for the `ComponentSystemEvent` system event broadcast are invoked and the `processEvent` method of the `ComponentSystemEventListener` is called.

The `UIComponent` class provides the methods discussed in Table 11.9 to subscribe and unsubscribe to component system events.

Table 11.9 `UIComponent` Class Methods to Subscribe/Unsubscribe

Method	Description
`subscribeToEvent(Class<? extends SystemEvent> eventClass, ComponentSystemEventListener componentListener)`	Registers a component system event listener for an event of type `eventClass`
`unsubscribeFromEvent(Class<? extends SystemEvent> eventClass,ComponentSystemEventListener componentListener)`	Unregisters a component system event listener for an event of type `eventClass`

Setting the Environment

As a first step, download and install the following software.

- Oracle JDeveloper 12c (12.1.2.0.0) (www.oracle.com/technetwork/developer-tools/jdev/downloads/index.html)

- Oracle WebLogic Server 12c (included with JDeveloper 12c)

- Oracle Database Express Edition (XE) 11g (www.oracle.com/technetwork/database/database-technologies/express-edition/downloads/index.html)

- Bean validations API JAR (validation-api-1.0.0.GA.jar) (http://mvnrepository.com/artifact/javax.validation/validation-api/1.0.0.GA)

- Hibernate's bean validation reference implementation (hibernate-validator-4.0.0.GA.jar) (http://mvnrepository.com/artifact/org.hibernate/hibernate-validator/4.0.0.GA)

- Simple Logging Facade for Java (slf4j-1.7.6.zip) (www.slf4j.org/download.html)

To generate a JSF data table, you need a data source from which to create a database table in Oracle Database 11g XE. Use the SQL script in Listing 11.1. (The database table is the same as the one used in previous chapters. If you have already created it, you don't have to create it again.

Listing 11.1   SQL Script for Creating an Oracle Database Table

```
CREATE USER OE IDENTIFIED BY OE;
GRANT CONNECT, RESOURCE to OE;
CREATE TABLE OE.Catalog(CatalogId INTEGER
PRIMARY KEY, Journal VARCHAR(25), Publisher VARCHAR(25),
 Edition VARCHAR(25), Title Varchar(45), Author Varchar(25));
INSERT INTO OE.Catalog VALUES('1', 'Oracle Magazine',
 'Oracle Publishing', 'Nov-Dec 2004', 'Database Resource
Manager', 'Kimberly Floss');
INSERT INTO OE.Catalog VALUES('2', 'Oracle Magazine',
 'Oracle Publishing', 'Nov-Dec 2004', 'From ADF UIX to JSF',
'Jonas Jacobi');
INSERT INTO OE.Catalog VALUES('3', 'Oracle Magazine',
 'Oracle Publishing', 'March-April 2005', 'Starting with
Oracle ADF ', 'Steve Muench');
COMMIT;
```

Run the SQL script in SQL Command Line to create a database table OE.CATALOG. Then add the hibernate validator, validation API, and slf4j-1.7.6.zip files to the CLASSPATH variable in the \\DefaultDomain\bin\startWebLogic script like so:

```
set CLASSPATH=%SAVE_CLASSPATH%;C:\JSF2.0\hibernate-validator-4.0.0.GA.jar;C:\JSF2.0\
validation-api-1.0.0.GA.jar;C:\JSF2.0\slf4j-1.7.6\slf4j-api-1.7.6.jar;C:\JSF2.0\
slf4j-1.7.6\slf4j-log4j12-1.7.6.jar;C:\JSF2.0\slf4j-1.7.6\slf4j-simple-1.7.6.jar
```

As in Chapter 2, "Templating with Facelets," configure and start the IntegratedWebLogic Server.

CREATING A JAVA EE WEB APPLICATION

To demonstrate the new event handling features in JSF 2.0, you will create a JSF application consisting of an input.xhtml page and an output.xhtml page. The input.xhtml page has an input field for an SQL query and a Submit button to submit the SQL query.

The output.xhtml JSF page consists of a JSF data table generated from the SQL query specified in input.xhtml. An error.xhtml page is also included in case an error is generated. Follow these steps:

1. Select File > New.

2. In the New Gallery dialog box, select General > Applications in the Categories pane and select Java EE Web Application in the Items pane. Then click OK.

3. In the Application Name field, type `EventHandling` and click Next, as shown in Figure 11.1.

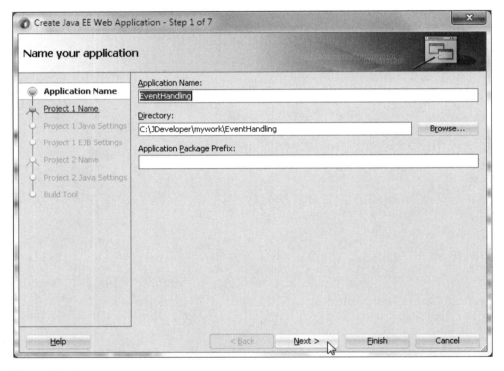

Figure 11.1
Creating a Java EE Web application called "EventHandling."
Source: Oracle Corporation.

4. Select the default settings for the Model project.

5. For the ViewController project, select the JavaServer Faces project feature and click Finish. A Java EE Web application consisting of a Model and a ViewController project is created, as shown in Figure 11.2.

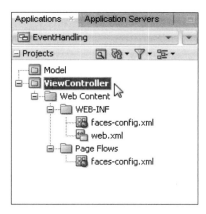

Figure 11.2
The EventHandling Java EE Web application.
Source: Oracle Corporation.

6. Right-click the ViewController project and select Project Properties.

7. Select Libraries and Classpath in the pane on the left.

8. Click the Add JAR/Directory button to add the validation API JAR file, as shown in Figure 11.3.

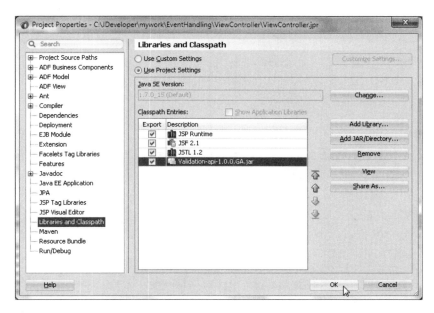

Figure 11.3
Adding the validation API JAR file to the Java build path.
Source: Oracle Corporation.

9. For the JSF pages, create a managed bean, `catalog`, and a managed bean class, `Catalog.java`, as explained in Chapter 2.

10. Add the following JSF pages: input.xhtml, input2.xhtml (for the Ajax event handling example), output.xhtml (for output from input.xhtml), and error.xhtml. The directory structure of the EventHandling application is shown in Figure 11.4.

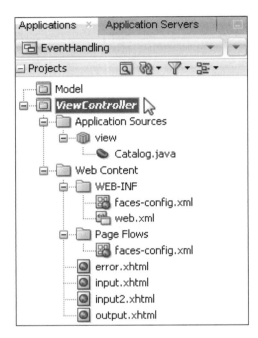

Figure 11.4
Directory structure of the EventHandling application.
Source: Oracle Corporation.

The web.xml page consists of the Faces servlet because we selected the JSF project technology. The web.xml page appears in Listing 11.2.

Listing 11.2   The web.xml Page

```
<?xml version = '1.0' encoding = 'windows-1252'?>
<web-app xmlns="http://java.sun.com/xml/ns/javaee"
xmlns:xsi="http://www.w3.org/2001/XMLSchema-instance"
        xsi:schemaLocation="http://java.sun.com/xml/ns/javaee
http://java.sun.com/xml/ns/javaee/web-app_3_0.xsd"
        version="3.0">
  <servlet>
    <servlet-name>Faces Servlet</servlet-name>
```

```
    <servlet-class>javax.faces.webapp.FacesServlet</servlet-class>
    <load-on-startup>1</load-on-startup>
  </servlet>
  <servlet-mapping>
    <servlet-name>Faces Servlet</servlet-name>
    <url-pattern>/faces/*</url-pattern>
  </servlet-mapping>
</web-app>
```

Because you are using JSF 2.0 annotations to configure a managed bean and the request scope and are using implicit navigation, faces-config.xml is an empty file.

```
<?xml version="1.0" encoding="windows-1252"?>
<faces-config version="2.1" xmlns="http://java.sun.com/xml/ns/javaee">
</faces-config>
```

11. The input.xhtml JSF page consists of an `h:outputLabel` for a label for the input field, an `h:inputText` for an input text field to specify an SQL query, and an `h:commandButton` to submit the SQL query. The `h:inputText` field binds to a managed bean property `inputText1`. Add an `h:message` element to output a validation error message. The `h:commandButton` binds to a managed bean property `commandButton1`, and has action binding to a managed bean method `commandButton_action`. The input.xhtml page appears in Listing 11.3.

Listing 11.3 The input.xhtml Page

```
<!DOCTYPE html PUBLIC "-//W3C//DTD XHTML 1.0 Transitional//EN"
    "http://www.w3.org/TR/xhtml1/DTD/xhtml1-transitional.dtd">
<html xmlns="http://www.w3.org/1999/xhtml"
xmlns:ui="http://java.sun.com/jsf/facelets"
    xmlns:h="http://java.sun.com/jsf/html"
xmlns:f="http://java.sun.com/jsf/core">
    <f:view>
        <h:head>
            <title></title>
        </h:head>
        <h:body>
            <h:form id="form1">
                <h2>JSF Data Table</h2>
                <h:panelGrid columns="3">
                    <h:outputLabel for="inputText1" value="SQL Query: "/>
```

```
                    <h:inputText id="inputText1"
binding="#{catalog.inputText1}"
                                validatorMessage="SELECT Query not valid">
                <!-- <h:inputText id="inputText1"
binding="#{catalog.inputText1}">-->
                    <f:validateRegex
pattern="SELECT+[\s]+[*]+[\s]+FROM+[\s]+[a-zA-Z]+"/>
                        <f:event type="postValidate"
listener="#{catalog.postValidationEvent}"/>
                </h:inputText>
                <h:message for="inputText1" style="color:red"/>
                <h:commandButton binding="#{catalog.commandButton1}"
action="#{catalog.commandButton_action}"
                                value="Submit"/>
            </h:panelGrid>
        </h:form>
      </h:body>
    </f:view>
</html>
```

The output.xhtml page consists of an h:Data Table element with value binding to a managed bean property resultSet, which is the JDBC ResultSet for an SQL query specified in the input field and submitted using the Submit button. The var attribute of h:Data Table specifies the iteration variable to be used to iterate over the data model and is set to "resultset". The h:column elements within the h:Data Table have value binding to the ResultSet columns accessed using the iteration variable specified in the var attribute. The output.xhtml page appears in Listing 11.4.

Listing 11.4   The output.xhtml Page

```
<!DOCTYPE html PUBLIC "-//W3C//DTD XHTML 1.0 Transitional//EN"
    "http://www.w3.org/TR/xhtml1/DTD/xhtml1-transitional.dtd">
<html xmlns="http://www.w3.org/1999/xhtml"
      xmlns:ui="http://java.sun.com/jsf/facelets"
      xmlns:h="http://java.sun.com/jsf/html"
      xmlns:f="http://java.sun.com/jsf/core">
<f:view>
 <h:head>
  <title></title>
</h:head>
  <h:body>
  <h:form id="form1">
```

```
    <h2>JSF Data Table</h2>
    <h:dataTable id="DataTable1" value="#{catalog.resultSet}" var="resultset"
                 border="1" rows="4">
     <h:column id="column1">
      <f:facet name="header">
       <h:outputText value="Catalog Id"/>
      </f:facet>
      <h:outputText id="outputText1" value="#{resultset.catalogid}"/>
     </h:column>
     <h:column id="column2">
      <f:facet name="header">
       <h:outputText value="Journal"/>
      </f:facet>
      <h:outputText id="outputText2" value="#{resultset.journal}"/>
     </h:column>
     <h:column id="column3">
      <f:facet name="header">
       <h:outputText value="Publisher"/>
      </f:facet>
      <h:outputText id="outputText3" value="#{resultset.publisher}"/>
     </h:column>
     <h:column id="column4">
      <f:facet name="header">
       <h:outputText value="Edition"/>
      </f:facet>
      <h:outputText id="outputText4" value="#{resultset.edition}"/>
     </h:column>
     <h:column id="column5">
      <f:facet name="header">
       <h:outputText value="Title"/>
      </f:facet>
      <h:outputText id="outputText5" value="#{resultset.title}"/>
     </h:column>
     <h:column id="column6">
      <f:facet name="header">
       <h:outputText value="Author"/>
      </f:facet>
      <h:outputText id="outputText6" value="#{resultset.author}"/>
     </h:column>
    </h:dataTable>
   </h:form>
 </h:body>
</f:view>
</html>
```

The error.xhtml page consists of an error message, and appears in Listing 11.5.

Listing 11.5   The error.xhtml Page

```
<!DOCTYPE html PUBLIC "-//W3C//DTD XHTML 1.0 Transitional//EN"
    "http://www.w3.org/TR/xhtml1/DTD/xhtml1-transitional.dtd">
<html xmlns="http://www.w3.org/1999/xhtml"
    xmlns:ui="http://java.sun.com/jsf/facelets"
    xmlns:h="http://java.sun.com/jsf/html"
    xmlns:f="http://java.sun.com/jsf/core">
<f:view>
 <h:head>
  <title></title>
 </h:head>
  <h:body>Error Page</h:body>
</f:view>
</html>
```

12. In the managed bean, which is a POJO, specify the properties `inputText1`, `commandButton1`, and `resultSet`.

13. Add accessor methods for the managed bean properties.

14. Add an action method, `commandButton_action`, which has action binding to the Submit button in input.xhtml. In the action method the SQL query specified in the input text field is retrieved and run in the Oracle Database to generate a `ResultSet`, whose value is set on the `ResultSet` managed bean property. The action method has a return value of `"output"` and a return value of `"error"` if an error is generated. Implicit navigation is implemented using the return value (outcome).

`Catalog.java` appears in Listing 11.6. Some of the code sections have been commented, which you will uncomment based on the event handling example discussed in later sections.

Listing 11.6   Managed Bean Class Catalog.java

```
package view;

import javax.faces.bean.ManagedBean;
import javax.faces.bean.RequestScoped;
import javax.faces.component.html.HtmlInputText;
import javax.faces.event.ComponentSystemEventListener;
```

```java
import java.sql.*;
import javax.annotation.PostConstruct;
import javax.el.ValueExpression;
import javax.faces.application.Application;
import javax.faces.application.ConfigurableNavigationHandler;
import javax.faces.application.NavigationCase;
import javax.faces.component.UIComponent;
import javax.faces.component.UIViewRoot;
import javax.faces.component.html.HtmlCommandButton;
import javax.faces.context.FacesContext;
import javax.faces.event.AbortProcessingException;
import javax.faces.event.AjaxBehaviorEvent;
import javax.faces.event.ComponentSystemEvent;
import javax.faces.event.ComponentSystemEventListener;
import javax.faces.event.ExceptionQueuedEvent;
import javax.faces.event.PostAddToViewEvent;
import javax.faces.event.PostConstructApplicationEvent;
import javax.faces.event.PostValidateEvent;
import javax.faces.event.PreDestroyApplicationEvent;
import javax.faces.event.PreRenderViewEvent;
@ManagedBean(name = "catalog")
@RequestScoped
public class Catalog {
    public Catalog() {
    }
    private HtmlInputText inputText1;
    private HtmlCommandButton commandButton1;
    private Statement stmt;
    private Connection connection;
    private ResultSet resultSet;
    /** @PostConstruct
    public void registerApplicationListeners(){
        Application application =
FacesContext.getCurrentInstance().getApplication();
        //application.subscribeToEvent(PostConstructApplicationEvent.class, new
ApplicationConfigurationListener());

        // application.subscribeToEvent(PreDestroyApplicationEvent.class, new
ApplicationConfigurationListener());
    }
     */
  /*
```

```
@PostConstruct
    public void subscribe() {
        FacesContext ctx = FacesContext.getCurrentInstance();
        inputText1 = (HtmlInputText)
ctx.getApplication().createComponent("javax.faces.HtmlInputText");
        UIViewRoot viewRoot = ctx.getViewRoot();
        inputText1.subscribeToEvent(PostAddToViewEvent.class, new
InputTextComponentListener());
      viewRoot.getChildren().add(inputText1);
    }
*/
/**    public void inputTextListener(AjaxBehaviorEvent event) {
      try {
            Class.forName("oracle.jdbc.OracleDriver");
            String url = "jdbc:oracle:thin:@localhost:1521:XE";
            connection = DriverManager.getConnection(url, "OE", "OE");
            stmt = connection.createStatement(ResultSet.TYPE_SCROLL_INSENSITIVE,
ResultSet.CONCUR_READ_ONLY);
            resultSet = stmt.executeQuery((String)inputText1.getValue());
            if (resultSet != null) {
                this.setResultSet(resultSet);
            }
        } catch (SQLException e) {
            System.out.println(e.getMessage());
        } catch (ClassNotFoundException e) {
            System.out.println(e.getMessage());
        } catch (Exception e) {
            System.out.println(e.getMessage());
        } finally {
        }
    }*/
/**    public void inputTextListener() {
      try {
            Class.forName("oracle.jdbc.OracleDriver");
            String url = "jdbc:oracle:thin:@localhost:1521:XE";
            connection = DriverManager.getConnection(url, "OE", "OE");
            stmt = connection.createStatement(ResultSet.TYPE_SCROLL_INSENSITIVE,
ResultSet.CONCUR_READ_ONLY);
```

```java
            resultSet = stmt.executeQuery((String)inputText1.getValue());
            if (resultSet != null) {
                this.setResultSet(resultSet);
            }
        } catch (SQLException e) {
            System.out.println(e.getMessage());
        } catch (ClassNotFoundException e) {
            System.out.println(e.getMessage());
        } catch (Exception e) {
            System.out.println(e.getMessage());
        } finally {
        }
    }*/
    public void setInputText1(HtmlInputText inputText1) {
        this.inputText1 = inputText1;
    }
    public HtmlInputText getInputText1() {
        return inputText1;
    }
    public void setCommandButton1(HtmlCommandButton commandButton1) {
        this.commandButton1 = commandButton1;
    }
    public HtmlCommandButton getCommandButton1() {
        return commandButton1;
    }
    public void setResultSet(ResultSet resultSet) {
        this.resultSet = resultSet;
    }
    public ResultSet getResultSet() {
        return resultSet;
    }
/**     public void postValidationEvent(javax.faces.event.ComponentSystemEvent
componentSystemEvent) {

        System.out.println("PostValidateEvent event");
        FacesContext ctx = FacesContext.getCurrentInstance();
        System.out.println("Component System Event generated by:" +
componentSystemEvent.getSource().getClass().getName());
        System.out.println("Component Client Id: " +
componentSystemEvent.getComponent().getClientId());
    }*/
```

```
public String commandButton_action() {
    try {
        Class.forName("oracle.jdbc.OracleDriver");
        String url = "jdbc:oracle:thin:@localhost:1521:XE";
        connection = DriverManager.getConnection(url, "OE", "OE");
        stmt = connection.createStatement(ResultSet.TYPE_SCROLL_INSENSITIVE,
ResultSet.CONCUR_READ_ONLY);
        resultSet = stmt.executeQuery((String)inputText1.getValue());
        if (resultSet != null) {
            this.setResultSet(resultSet);
        }
    }
    catch (SQLException e) {
        System.out.println(e.getMessage());
        return "error";
    } catch (ClassNotFoundException e) {
        System.out.println(e.getMessage());
        return "error";
    } catch (Exception e) {
        System.out.println(e.getMessage());
        return "error";
    } finally {
    }
    return "output";
}
}
```

REGISTERING AN APPLICATION-SCOPED SYSTEM EVENT LISTENER

The SystemEventListener interface is the listener for application-scoped system events. In this section, you will create an application-scoped listener class. You will register the listener class in faces-config.xml to listen to some application-scoped events. Subsequently, you will run the JSF application in IntegratedWebLogicServer to generate application-scoped events and demonstrate that the listener gets notification of the events. First, you need to create an implementation class for SystemEventListener. Follow these steps:

1. Select File > New.

2. In the New Gallery dialog box, select General > Java in the Categories pane and select Class in the Items pane. Then click OK.

3. In the Create Java Class dialog box, type `ApplicationConfigurationListener` in the Name field. Then click the Add Interface button to add an interface, as shown in Figure 11.5.

Figure 11.5
Adding an interface in the `ApplicationConfigurationListener` class.
Source: Oracle Corporation.

4. In the Class Browser dialog box, select the `javax.faces.event.SystemEventListener` interface and click OK, as shown in Figure 11.6.

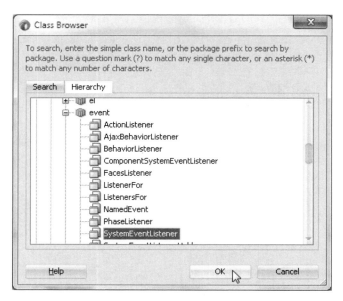

Figure 11.6
Adding the `SystemEventListener` interface.
Source: Oracle Corporation.

5. As shown in Figure 11.7, the `SystemEventListener` interface is added in the
    Implements field. Click OK. A class that implements the `SystemEventListener`
    interface is created. The class implements the `processEvent(SystemEvent)` method
    that throws an `AbortProcessingException`, which is a new exception in JSF 2.0.
    The `SystemEventListener` implementation class is shown in Figure 11.8.

Figure 11.7
Creating the `ApplicationConfigurationListener` class.
Source: Oracle Corporation.

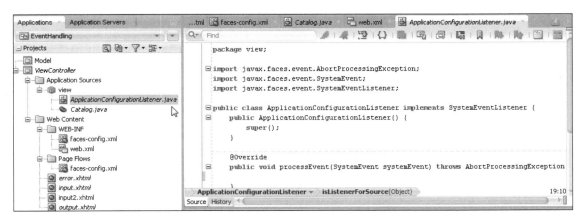

Figure 11.8
The `ApplicationConfigurationListener` class in JDeveloper.
Source: Oracle Corporation.

6. Register the listener class to listen to the `PostConstructApplicationEvent` and `PreDestroyApplicationEvent` application-scoped system events. In the implementation class's `processEvent` method, determine whether the `SystemEvent` is an instance of one of these system events and output a message indicating the same:

```
if(systemEvent instanceof PostConstructApplicationEvent){
                    System.out.println("PostConstructApplicationEvent is
generated");
            }
```

7. Override the `isListenerForSource(Object object)` method and return `true` if the source object is an instance of `Application`. The implementation listener class for the `SystemEventListener` appears in Listing 11.7.

Listing 11.7 `ApplicationConfigurationListener.java`

```java
package view;

import javax.faces.application.Application;
import javax.faces.event.AbortProcessingException;
import javax.faces.event.ExceptionQueuedEvent;
import javax.faces.event.PostConstructApplicationEvent;
import javax.faces.event.PreDestroyApplicationEvent;
import javax.faces.event.SystemEvent;
import javax.faces.event.SystemEventListener;
public class ApplicationConfigurationListener implements SystemEventListener {
    public ApplicationConfigurationListener() {
        super();
    }
    @Override
    public void processEvent(SystemEvent systemEvent) throws
AbortProcessingException {
        if(systemEvent instanceof PostConstructApplicationEvent){
                    System.out.println("PostConstructApplicationEvent is
generated");
            }
                if(systemEvent instanceof PreDestroyApplicationEvent){
                    System.out.println("PreDestroyApplicationEvent is
generated");
            }
```

```
        System.out.println("System Event generated by:"+
systemEvent.getSource().getClass().getName());
    }
    @Override
    public boolean isListenerForSource(Object object) {
        return (object instanceof Application);
    }
}
}
```

8. Next, you will register the listener with the PostConstructApplicationEvent and PreDestroyApplicationEvent application-scoped system events. In faces-config.xml, add an <application> </application> tag. Within the <application> tag, add a < tag. A list of elements that may be added appears. Select the system-event-listener element, as shown in Figure 11.9.

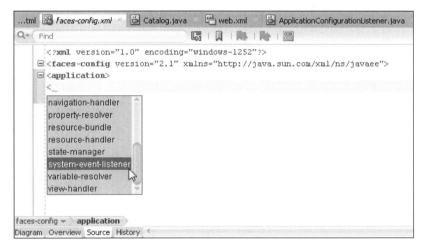

Figure 11.9
Selecting the <system-event-listener> tag.
Source: Oracle Corporation.

9. In the <system-event-listener> tag you just added, add a <system-event-listener-class> tag, as shown in Figure 11.10.

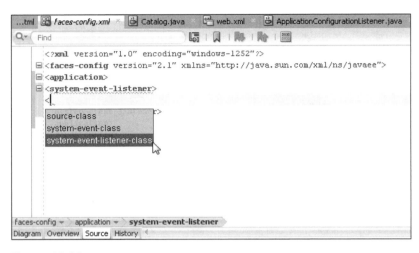

Figure 11.10
Selecting the `<system-event-listener-class>` tag.
Source: Oracle Corporation.

10. Add a `<system-event-class>` tag within the `<system-event-listener>` element you just added, as shown in Figure 11.11.

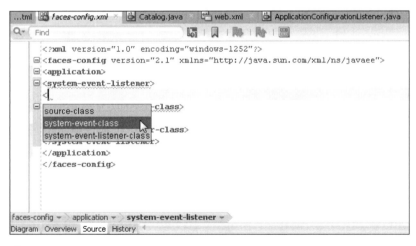

Figure 11.11
Selecting the `<system-event-class>` tag.
Source: Oracle Corporation.

11. Add another `<system-event-listener>` tag. Then, in the two `<system-event-listener-class>` tags, add the `view.ApplicationConfigurationListener` class.

12. In the `<system-event-class>` tags, add the `javax.faces.event.PostConstructApplicationEvent` class and the `javax.faces.event.PreDestroyApplicationEvent` class.
The faces-config.xml file appears in Listing 11.8.

Listing 11.8   The faces-config.xml File

```xml
<?xml version="1.0" encoding="windows-1252"?>
<faces-config version="2.0" xmlns="http://java.sun.com/xml/ns/javaee">
    <application>
        <system-event-listener>
            <system-event-listener-
class>view.ApplicationConfigurationListener</system-event-listener-class>
            <system-event-
class>javax.faces.event.PostConstructApplicationEvent</system-event-class>
        </system-event-listener>
        <system-event-listener>
            <system-event-listener-
class>view.ApplicationConfigurationListener</system-event-listener-class>
            <system-event-
class>javax.faces.event.PreDestroyApplicationEvent</system-event-class>
        </system-event-listener>
    </application>
</faces-config>
```

13. Uncomment the `postValidationEvent` method in the `Catalog` class if it is commented out. Create a deployment profile, webapp1, for the ViewController project. To begin, start the IntegratedWebLogicServer. Then right-click the ViewController project and select Deploy > webapp1 to deploy the deployment profile to the IntegratedWebLogicServer, as shown in Figure 11.12.

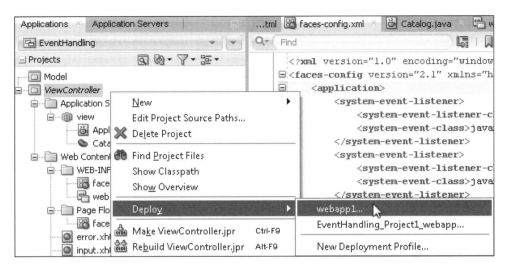

Figure 11.12
Deploying the application to IntegratedWebLogicServer.
Source: Oracle Corporation.

After the application starts, the `PostConstructApplicationEvent` event is generated and broadcast to the registered listener, which outputs a message indicating that the event has occurred. (See Figure 11.13.)

Figure 11.13
PostConstructApplicationEvent
Source: Oracle Corporation.

When the server is shut down or the application is redeployed, the `javax.faces.event.PreDestroyApplicationEvent` event is generated, the listener is notified about the event, and a message indicating that the event has been generated is output, as shown in Figure 11.14.

Figure 11.14
The PreDestroyApplicationEvent event.
Source: Oracle Corporation.

Faces-config.xml may be used only to register listeners for application-scoped events. In the next section, you will learn how to register a component system event listener.

REGISTERING A COMPONENT SYSTEM EVENT LISTENER

The ComponentSystemEventListener interface represents a listener for a component system event. To see it in action, follow these steps:

1. Create a Java class. To begin, choose File > New.

2. In the New Gallery dialog box, choose General > Java in the Categories pane and choose Class in the Items pane. Then click OK.

3. In the Create Java Class dialog box, type InputTextComponentListener in the Name field and click the Add Interface button, as shown in Figure 11.15.

Figure 11.15
Adding an interface to `InputTextComponentListener`.
Source: Oracle Corporation.

4. Select the `javax.faces.event.ComponentSystemEventListener` interface in the Class Browser dialog box, as shown in Figure 11.16. Click OK.

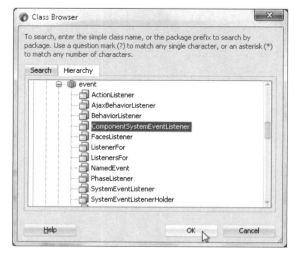

Figure 11.16
Selecting the `ComponentSystemEventListener` interface.
Source: Oracle Corporation.

5. The `ComponentSystemEventListener` interface is added to the Implements field for the implementation class. Click OK to close the Create Java Class dialog box. (See Figure 11.17.)

Figure 11.17
Creating the `InputTextComponentListener` class.
Source: Oracle Corporation.

The implementation class implements the `ComponentSystemEventListener` interface, as shown here:

```
public class InputTextComponentListener implements ComponentSystemEventListener
{
}
```

6. Override the `processEvent` method to process the event for which the listener is registered. You will be registering the listener for the `PostAddToViewEvent` event.

7. In the `processEvent` method, determine whether the system event is an instance of `PostAddToViewEvent` and output a message indicating the same. Also output the source class name for the component system event. The `ComponentSystemEventListener` implementation class appears in Listing 11.9.

Listing 11.9   InputTextComponentListener.java

```
package view;
import javax.faces.event.AbortProcessingException;
import javax.faces.event.ComponentSystemEvent;
import javax.faces.event.ComponentSystemEventListener;
import javax.faces.event.PostAddToViewEvent;

public class InputTextComponentListener implements ComponentSystemEventListener
{
    public InputTextComponentListener() {
        super();
    }
    @Override
    public void processEvent(ComponentSystemEvent systemEvent) throws
AbortProcessingException {
        if (systemEvent instanceof PostAddToViewEvent) {
        System.out.println("PostAddToViewEvent event");
        System.out.println("System Event generated by:"+
systemEvent.getSource().getClass().getName());
        }
    }
}
```

8. Having created the listener for component system events, you need to register the listener with a `UIComponent`. The input.xhtml page includes an `h:inputText` field and a command button. You will register the listener with the `h:inputText` component, which binds to `inputText1` in the managed bean class `view.Catalog.java`. Add a `@PostConstruct` method, which is invoked after a managed bean has been constructed, to register the listener with `inputText1`.

9. Annotate the method `subscribe` with the `@PostConstruct` annotation.

10. Obtain a `FacesContext` instance.

11. Create a `UIComponent` of type `javax.faces.HtmlInputText` using the `createComponent` method.

12. Obtain an instance of `UIViewRoot` from `FacesContext` using the `getViewRoot` method.

13. Register the `inputText1` `UIComponent` with the `PostAddToViewEvent` using the `subscribeToEvent` method:

    ```
    inputText1.subscribeToEvent(PostAddToViewEvent.class, new
    InputTextComponentListener());
    ```

14. Add the `inputText1` to `UIViewRoot` using the `getChildren` method to obtain the component tree and invoking the `add` method to add `inputText1` to the component tree.

```
viewRoot.getChildren().add(inputText1);
```

The `@PostConstruct` method `subscribe` appears in Listing 11.10.

Listing 11.10   `@PostConstruct` Method `subscribe()`

```
@PostConstruct
    public void subscribe() {
        FacesContext ctx = FacesContext.getCurrentInstance();
            inputText1 =
(HtmlInputText)ctx.getApplication().createComponent("javax.faces.HtmlInputText")
;
        UIViewRoot viewRoot = ctx.getViewRoot();
  inputText1.subscribeToEvent(PostAddToViewEvent.class, new
InputTextComponentListener());
        viewRoot.getChildren().add(inputText1);
    }
```

15. Right-click the ViewController project and select Deploy > webapp1 to redeploy the project to the IntegratedWebLogicServer.

16. Run input.xhtml with the following URL: http://localhost:7101/webapp1/faces/input .xhtml. You need not submit the SQL query to demonstrate that the component system event has been generated and received by the listener. The output shows that `PostAddToViewEvent` was generated and the source of the event is the `HtmlInputText` component. The `PostAddToViewEvent` is generated twice—once for the `inputText1` component and once for the containing component `h:panelGrid`. (See Figure 11.18.)

Figure 11.18
The `PostAddToViewEvent` event.
Source: Oracle Corporation.

Declaratively Registering a ComponentSystemEventListener with the f:event Tag

JSF 2.0 has added the provision to declaratively register a ComponentSystemEventListener using the f:event tag. Chapter 7, "View Parameters," demonstrated the use of the f:event tag with PreRenderViewEvent to invoke a managed bean method prior to rendering a view. And, in the managed bean method we navigated to another view. In this section, you will declaratively register the ComponentSystemEventListener using the f:event tag on the h:inputText component that has a validator configured to validate the SQL query with a regular expression. The event type in f:event is postValidate, which is the PostValidateEvent. Follow these steps:

1. Register a listener using the listener attribute. To do so, uncomment the following section from the input.xhtml page.

```
<h:inputText id="inputText1" binding="#{catalog.inputText1}"
                        validatorMessage="SELECT Query not valid">
                <f:validateRegex
pattern="SELECT+[\s]+[*]+[\s]+FROM+[\s]+[a-zA-Z]+"/>
                        <f:event type="postValidate"
listener="#{catalog.postValidationEvent}"/>
                </h:inputText>
```

2. Comment out the @PostConstruct method subscribe.

3. Add a listener method, postValidationEvent(javax.faces.event.ComponentSystemEvent componentSystemEvent), to the managed bean class. The listener method has ComponentSystemEvent as the parameter.

4. In the listener method, output a message indicating that a PostValidateEvent has been generated. Also, output the source class name, obtained using the getSource method, and the client ID of the component generating the event, obtained using the getComponent().getClientId() methods. The postValidationEvent method in the managed bean class is shown in Listing 11.11.

Listing 11.11 The postValidationEvent Method

```
public void postValidationEvent(javax.faces.event.ComponentSystemEvent
componentSystemEvent) {
        System.out.println("PostValidateEvent event");
        FacesContext ctx = FacesContext.getCurrentInstance();
```

```
      System.out.println("Component System Event generated by:" +
            componentSystemEvent.getSource().getClass().getName());
      System.out.println("Component Client Id: " +
componentSystemEvent.getComponent().getClientId());
   }
```

5. Redeploy the JSF application and run the input.xhtml page.

6. Specify an SQL query that does not conform to the regular expression in the validator and click Submit, as shown in Figure 11.19.

Figure 11.19
Submitting an SQL query that does not conform to the regular expression.

Google and the Google logo are registered trademarks of Google Inc., used with permission.

A validation error message is output, indicating that the SQL query is not valid according to the regular expression in the validator. (See Figure 11.20.)

Figure 11.20
Validation Error Message

Google and the Google logo are registered trademarks of Google Inc., used with permission.

In addition, the listener method registered declaratively using the f:event tag is invoked, and a message is output on the server indicating that the PostValidationEvent has been generated, as shown in Figure 11.21. The UIComponent generating the event and the client ID of the component are output.

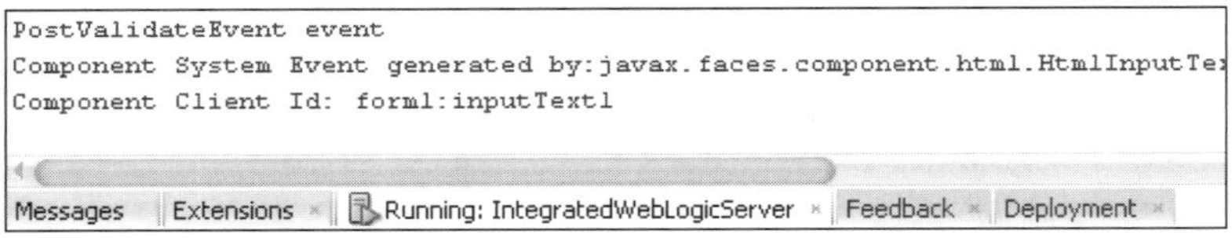

```
PostValidateEvent event
Component System Event generated by: javax.faces.component.html.HtmlInputTe
Component Client Id: form1:inputText1
```

Messages │ Extensions × │ Running: IntegratedWebLogicServer × │ Feedback × │ Deployment ×

Figure 11.21
PostValidationEvent.
Source: Oracle Corporation.

JSF 2.0 has added the @NamedEvent annotation to create a custom ComponentSystemEvent that may be declaratively registered with the f:event. For example, a custom event is created as follows:

```
@NamedEvent(name="userLogin")
public class UserLoginEvent extends ComponentSystemEvent {
}
```

You can declaratively register a listener with the custom event using the f:event tag as follows:

```
<f:event type="userLogin" listener="#{catalog.UserLoginListener}"/>
```

Registering a System Event Listener with the @ListenerFor Annotation

You can register a listener with a UIComponent using one of the following provisions:

- Programmatically using the subscribeToEvent method in UIComponent, as discussed in an earlier section
- Declaratively using the f:event tag, as discussed in the previous section
- With annotations using the @ListenerFor annotation, discussed in this section

To register a listener using the @ListenerFor annotation, follow these steps:

1. Create a custom component using the @FacesComponent annotation.
2. Create a Java class, UIInputComponent, that extends HtmlInputText and annotate it with @FacesComponent. Also annotate the class with the @ListenerFor annotation, which

registers the class as a listener with the system event specified in the systemEventClass element.

3. Specify the systemEventClass element as PostRestoreStateEvent. HtmlInputText implements the ComponentSystemEventListener interface.

4. Override the processEvent method and, in the processEvent method, determine whether the system event is an instance of PostRestoreStateEvent. If it is, output a message indicating this. Also output the source class name. The UIInputComponent class appears in Listing 11.12.

Listing 11.12   The UIInputComponent Class

```
package view;

import javax.faces.component.FacesComponent;
import javax.faces.component.html.HtmlInputText;
import javax.faces.event.AbortProcessingException;
import javax.faces.event.ComponentSystemEvent;
import javax.faces.event.ListenerFor;
import javax.faces.event.PostRestoreStateEvent;
@FacesComponent("UIInputComponent")
@ListenerFor(systemEventClass = PostRestoreStateEvent.class)
public class UIInputComponent extends HtmlInputText {
    @Override
    public void processEvent(ComponentSystemEvent systemEvent) throws
AbortProcessingException {
        if (systemEvent instanceof PostRestoreStateEvent) {
            System.out.println("PostRestoreStateEvent event");
            System.out.println("System Event generated by:"+
systemEvent.getSource().getClass().getName());
        }
        super.processEvent(systemEvent);
    }
}
```

5. You have registered a listener to a component system event. Next, you will create a UIInputComponent instance and add it to the UIViewRoot. In the @PostConstruct annotated method subscribe, create a UIViewRoot instance, create a UIInputComponent instance, and add the component to the view root. You don't need to subscribe to an event because the UIInputComponent is registered as a listener with PostRestoreStateEvent. The subscribe method appears in Listing 11.13.

Listing 11.13 @PostConstruct Method subscribe()

```
@PostConstruct
  public void subscribe() {
        FacesContext ctx = FacesContext.getCurrentInstance();
        UIViewRoot viewRoot = ctx.getViewRoot();
        inputText1 = new UIInputComponent();
        viewRoot.getChildren().add(inputText1);
    }
```

6. Redeploy and run input.xhtml with the following URL: http://localhost:7101/ webapp1/faces/input.xhtml. Then specify an SQL query and click Submit, as shown in Figure 11.22. A data table is generated, as shown in Figure 11.23.

Figure 11.22
Submitting a valid SQL query.

Google and the Google logo are registered trademarks of Google Inc., used with permission.

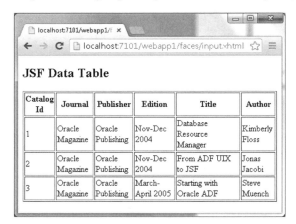

Figure 11.23
Rendering a JSF data table.

Google and the Google logo are registered trademarks of Google Inc., used with permission.

In the postback, the PostRestoreStateEvent gets generated and the registered listener is invoked. A message is output to indicate that the PostRestoreStateEvent has been generated and identifying the component that generated it.

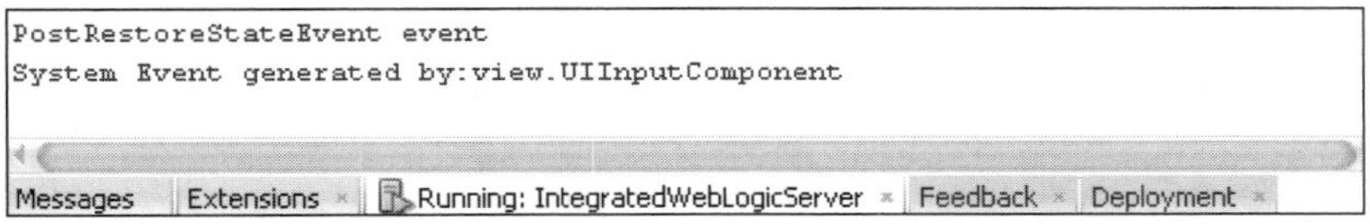

Figure 11.24
PostRestoreStateEvent.
Source: Oracle Corporation.

You can use the @ListenerFor annotation to annotate a class that implements ComponentSystemEventListener (for component system events) or SystemEventListener (for application-scoped system events). In addition, you can use the @ListenersFor annotation (note the "s") to register a listener for multiple events. In the section on registering application-scoped listeners, you registered the listener in faces-config.xml. Alternatively, you can register the listener with the PostConstructApplicationEvent and PreDestroyApplicationEvent events as follows:

```
@ListenersFor({
@ListenerFor(systemEventClass=PostConstructApplicationEvent.class),
@ListenerFor(systemEventClass=PreDestroyApplicationEvent.class)})

public class ApplicationConfigurationListener implements SystemEventListener {
}
```

CREATING AN EVENT HANDLER FOR AN AJAX REQUEST

We discussed using the f:ajax tag to send an Ajax request to the server. You can also register a callback function using the onevent attribute. The callback method is invoked on an Ajax event. An Ajax request generates the events discussed in Table 11.10.

Table 11.10   Ajax Request Events

Event	Description
begin	Generated before the Ajax request is sent.
complete	Generated immediately before the request has completed. For successful requests, this is generated immediately before the javax.faces.response is called. For unsuccessful requests, this is generated immediately before the error handler callback is invoked.
success	Generated immediately after the jsf.ajax.response has completed.

To see this in action, follow these steps:

1. In input2.xhtml, add an f:ajax tag to the h:inputText tag and add a onevent attribute to the f:ajax tag. You will generate a data table from the SQL query specified in h:inputText and output the events generated by the Ajax request.

2. To add an event attribute, click within the f:ajax tag and select event from the list that appears, as shown in Figure 11.25.

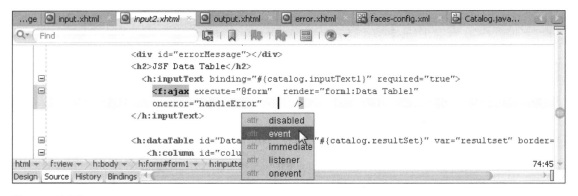

Figure 11.25
Adding the event attribute to f:ajax.
Source: Oracle Corporation.

3. Specify the event as valueChange and select the listener attribute from the list, as shown in Figure 11.26.

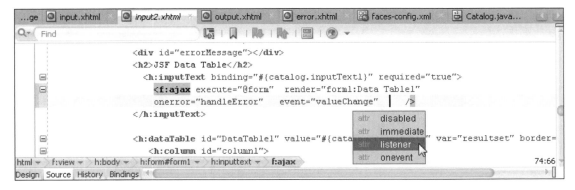

Figure 11.26
Adding the `listener` attribute to `f:ajax`.
Source: Oracle Corporation.

4. Specify the listener as #{catalog.inputTextListener} and select the onevent attribute from the list, as shown in Figure 11.27.

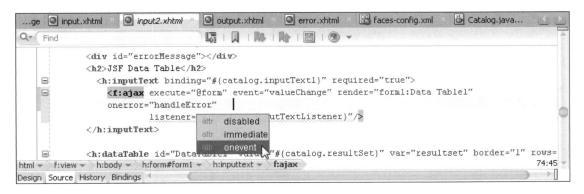

Figure 11.27
Adding the `onevent` attribute to `f:ajax`.
Source: Oracle Corporation.

5. Specify the value for the onevent attribute as handleEvent, which is the callback JavaScript function. The h:inputText component with the f:ajax tag including the onevent attribute is as follows:

```
<h:inputText binding="#{catalog.inputText1}" required="true">
                <f:ajax execute="@form" event="valueChange"
render="form1:Data Table1"   onevent="handleEvent"
                        listener="#{catalog.inputTextListener}"/>
        </h:inputText>
```

6. Create a callback function, `handleEvent`, with `eventData` as the parameter:

```
function handleEvent(eventData) {
}
```

The event data consists of the attributes discussed in Table 11.11.

Table 11.11   Event Data Attributes

Property	Description
type	Type is "event"
status	One of the events discussed in the previous table
source	The DOM element that generated the event
responseCode	The Ajax request object `XMLHttpRequest.status`
responseXML	The XML response `XMLHttpRequest.responseXML`
responseText	The response text `XMLHttpResponse.responseText`

The `responseCode`, `responseXML`, and `responseText` properties are not included for the `begin` event.

7. To monitor an Ajax request, add `<div/>` elements and output the different attributes of the event data within them.

```
<div id="type"></div>
<div id="status"></div>
<div id="source"></div>
<div id="responseCode"></div>
<div id="responseXML"></div>
<div id="responseText"></div>
```

8. In the `handleEvent` function, retrieve the elements for the event data and set the `innerHTML` to the `eventData` properties:

```
function handleEvent(eventData) {
                var type = document.getElementById("type");
                type.innerHTML = "Type: " + eventData.type;
                var status = document.getElementById("status");
                status.innerHTML = "Status: " + eventData.status;
```

```
        var source = document.getElementById("source");
        source.innerHTML = "Source:" + eventData.source;
        var responseCode = document.getElementById("responseCode");
        responseCode.innerHTML = "Response Code: " +
eventData.responseCode;
        var xmlMessage = eventData.responseXML;
        var textMessage = eventData.responseText;
        var responseText = document.getElementById("responseText");
            responseText.innerHTML = "Response Text: " + textMessage;
    }
```

9. Add a listener method for an Ajax request in the managed bean. The listener method has an AjaxBehaviorEvent, which was discussed in Chapter 3, "Ajax."

```
public void inputTextListener(AjaxBehaviorEvent event) {
        try {
            Class.forName("oracle.jdbc.OracleDriver");
            String url = "jdbc:oracle:thin:@localhost:1521:XE";
            connection = DriverManager.getConnection(url, "OE", "OE");
            stmt = connection.createStatement(ResultSet.TYPE_SCROLL_INSENSITIVE,
ResultSet.CONCUR_READ_ONLY);
            resultSet = stmt.executeQuery((String)inputText1.getValue());
            if (resultSet != null) {
                this.setResultSet(resultSet);
            }
        } catch (SQLException e) {
            System.out.println(e.getMessage());
        } catch (ClassNotFoundException e) {
            System.out.println(e.getMessage());
        } catch (Exception e) {
            System.out.println(e.getMessage());
        } finally {
        }
    }
```

The input2.xhtml page, which includes an inputText for an SQL query and an h:data Table for a data table generated from the SQL query, appears in Listing 11.14. An error handler callback function handleError is also included, which we will discuss in a later section.

Listing 11.14   The input2.xhtml Page

```
<!DOCTYPE html PUBLIC "-//W3C//DTD XHTML 1.0 Transitional//EN"
    "http://www.w3.org/TR/xhtml1/DTD/xhtml1-transitional.dtd">
<html xmlns="http://www.w3.org/1999/xhtml"
xmlns:ui="http://java.sun.com/jsf/facelets"
     xmlns:h="http://java.sun.com/jsf/html"
xmlns:f="http://java.sun.com/jsf/core">
    <f:view>
        <h:head>
            <script type="text/javascript">
                function handleEvent(eventData) {
                    var type = document.getElementById("type");
                    type.innerHTML = "Type: " + eventData.type;
                    var status = document.getElementById("status");
                    status.innerHTML = "Status: " + eventData.status;
                    var source = document.getElementById("source");
                    source.innerHTML = "Source:" + eventData.source;
                    var responseCode = document.getElementById("responseCode");+
                    responseCode.innerHTML = "Response Code: "
eventData.responseCode;
                    var xmlMessage = eventData.responseXML;
                    var textMessage = eventData.responseText;
                    // var responseText = document.getElementById("responseText");
                    // responseText.innerHTML = "Response Text: " + textMessage;
                }
                function handleError(errorData) {
                    var type = document.getElementById("errorType");
                    type.innerHTML = "Error Type: " + errorData.type;
                    var status = document.getElementById("errorStatus");
                    status.innerHTML = "Status: " + errorData.status;
                    var source = document.getElementById("errorSource");
                    source.innerHTML = "Source:" + errorData.source;
                    var responseCode =
document.getElementById("errorResponseCode");
                    responseCode.innerHTML = "Error Response Code: " +
errorData.responseCode;
                    var errorName = document.getElementById("errorName");
                    errorName.innerHTML = "Error Name: " + errorData.errorName;
                    var errorMessage = document.getElementById("errorMessage");
                    errorMessage.innerHTML = "Error Message: " +
errorData.errorMessage;
```

```
                    var xmlMessage = errorData.responseXML;
                    var textMessage = errorData.responseText;
                }
            </script>
            <title></title>
        </h:head>
        <h:body>
            <h:form id="form1">

                    <div id="type"></div>
                    <div id="status"></div>
                    <div id="source"></div>
                    <div id="responseCode"></div>
                    <div id="responseXML"></div>
                    <div id="responseText"></div>
                    <div id="errorType"></div>
                    <div id="errorStatus"></div>
                    <div id="errorSource"></div>
                    <div id="errorResponseCode"></div>
                    <div id="errorName"></div>
                    <div id="errorMessage"></div>
                    <h2>JSF Data Table</h2>
                      <h:inputText binding="#{catalog.inputText1}" required="true">
                         <f:ajax execute="@form" event="valueChange"
render="form1:DataTable1" onerror="handleError" onevent="handleEvent"
                             listener="#{catalog.inputTextListener}"/>
                    </h:inputText>
                    <h:dataTable id="DataTable1" value="#{catalog.resultSet}"
var="resultset" border="1" rows="4">
                        <h:column id="column1">
                            <f:facet name="header">
                                <h:outputText value="Catalog Id"/>
                            </f:facet>
                            <h:outputText id="outputText1"
value="#{resultset.catalogid}"/>
                        </h:column>
                        <h:column id="column2">
                            <f:facet name="header">
                                <h:outputText value="Journal"/>
                            </f:facet>
                            <h:outputText id="outputText2"
value="#{resultset.journal}"/>
```

```
                        </h:column>
                        <h:column id="column3">
                            <f:facet name="header">
                                <h:outputText value="Publisher"/>
                            </f:facet>
                            <h:outputText id="outputText3"
value="#{resultset.publisher}"/>
                        </h:column>
                        <h:column id="column4">
                            <f:facet name="header">
                                <h:outputText value="Edition"/>
                            </f:facet>
                            <h:outputText id="outputText4"
value="#{resultset.edition}"/>
                        </h:column>
                        <h:column id="column5">
                            <f:facet name="header">
                                <h:outputText value="Title"/>
                            </f:facet>
                            <h:outputText id="outputText5"
value="#{resultset.title}"/>
                        </h:column>
                        <h:column id="column6">
                            <f:facet name="header">
                                <h:outputText value="Author"/>
                            </f:facet>
                            <h:outputText id="outputText6"
value="#{resultset.author}"/>
                        </h:column>
                    </h:dataTable>
                </h:form>
            </h:body>
        </f:view>
</html>
```

10. Comment out the @PostConstruct subscribe method from the previous example, if enabled.

11. Redeploy the ViewController project and run input2.xhtml with the following URL: http://localhost:7101/webapp1/faces/input2.xhtml. Then specify an SQL query and click outside the input field, as shown in Figure 11.28.

Figure 11.28
Submitting an SQL query with Ajax.

Google and the Google logo are registered trademarks of Google Inc., used with permission.

A `valueChange` event is generated and an Ajax request is sent. The callback function `handleEvent` monitors the Ajax events and outputs the type, status, source, and response code properties. Just before the Ajax request is sent, the type is `event`, the status is `begin`, the source is the `HtmlInputElement`, and the response code is `undefined`. When the response is complete, a data table is generated. The type is `event`, the status is `success`, the source is the `HtmlInputElement`, and the response code is `200`, as shown in Figure 11.29.

Figure 11.29
Generating a JSF data table with Ajax.

Google and the Google logo are registered trademarks of Google Inc., used with permission.

CREATING A CUSTOM EXCEPTION HANDLER

JSF 2.0 has introduced a new mechanism for handling unexpected exceptions that may occur during a Faces lifecycle. The ExceptionHandler is not notified of any exceptions that may occur during application startup or shutdown. Exceptions are sent to the ExceptionHandler by one of the two methods:

- By not catching exceptions, or by catching and re-throwing exceptions
- By broadcasting an ExceptionQueuedEvent, which wraps an exception with the system event mechanism as listed:

```
catch (Exception e) {
    FacesContext facesContext= FacesContext.getCurrentInstance();
    ExceptionQueuedEventContext eventContext = new
ExceptionQueuedEventContext(ctx, e);
    facesContext.getApplication().publishEvent(ExceptionQueuedEvent.class,
eventContext);
  }
```

ExceptionQueuedEvent represents an exception instance that has been queued by calls to Application.publishEvent(ExceptionQueuedEvent.class, eventContext). At the end of the Faces lifecycle, any ExceptionQueuedEvent broadcasts are handled using the handle() method. The ExceptionHandler provides the methods in Table 11.12.

Table 11.12 ExceptionHandler Methods

Method	Description
getHandledExceptionQueuedEvent()	Returns the first ExceptionQueuedEvent handled with the exception handler
getHandledExceptionQueuedEvents()	Returns an iterable over all the ExceptionQueuedEvents handled by the exception handler
getRootCause(java.lang.Throwable t)	Returns the root cause of the throwable
getUnhandledExceptionQueuedEvents()	Returns an iterable over all the unhandled ExceptionQueuedEvents not yet handled by the exception handler
handle()	Handles the queued ExceptionQueuedEvents
isListenerForSource(java.lang.Object source)	Returns a Boolean indicating if the listener instance is a listener for the source
processEvent(SystemEvent exceptionQueuedEvent)	Processes a SystemEvent

The ExceptionHandlerWrapper class is a simple implementation of ExceptionHandler. The getWrapped method returns the ExceptionHandler wrapped by the ExceptionHandlerWrapper. ExceptionHandlerFactory is a factory that returns a new ExceptionHandler object. JSF 2.0 has introduced a new property, EXCEPTION_HANDLER_FACTORY, in FactoryFinder to return an ExceptionHandlerFactory:

```
ExceptionHandlerFactory factory = (ExceptionHandlerFactory)
FactoryFinder.getFactory(FactoryFinder.EXCEPTION_HANDLER_FACTORY);
```

An ExceptionHandler is obtained from a factory as follows:

```
ExceptionHandler exceptionHandler= factory.getExceptionHandler();
```

This section discusses the procedure to handle an unexpected exception such as the `javax.faces.application.ViewExpiredException`, which occurs when a view has timed out—for example, if you have set the `session-timeout` to 1 minute in web.xml like so:

```
<session-config>
      <session-timeout>1</session-timeout>
   </session-config>
```

If a JSF application is being run and the session times out, the `ViewExpiredException` is generated, as shown in Figure 11.30.

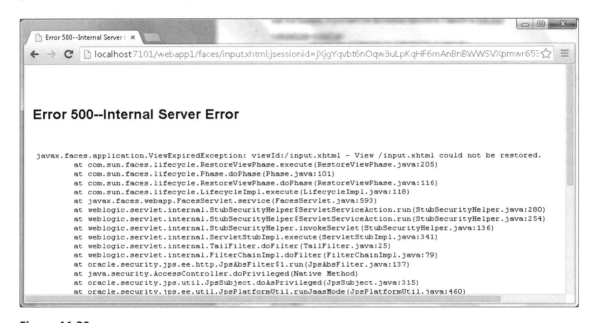

Figure 11.30
`ViewExpiredException`.
Google and the Google logo are registered trademarks of Google Inc., used with permission.

To handle the `ViewExpiredException` (and any other exceptions to be handled), follow these steps:

1. Create an error page for each of the exceptions in web.xml as follows:

```
<error-page>

      <exception-type>javax.faces.application.ViewExpiredException</exception-
   type>
```

```
            <location>/faces/viewExpired.xhtml</location>
        </error-page>
        <error-page>

            <exception-type>javax.faces.event.AbortProcessingException</exception-
type>
            <location>/faces/abortProcess.xhtml</location>
        </error-page>
        <error-page>
            <exception-
type>java.lang.reflect.UndeclaredThrowableException</exception-type>
            <location>/faces/UndeclaredThrowable.xhtml</location>
        </error-page>
```

2. Add three error pages—viewExpired.xhtml, abortProcess.xhtml, and
   UndeclaredThrowable.xhtml—as shown in Figure 11.31.

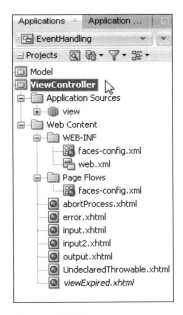

Figure 11.31
Directory structure with JSF pages to handle exceptions.
Source: Oracle Corporation.

As an example, viewExpired.xhtml appears in Listing 11.15.

Listing 11.15   The viewExpired.xhtml Page

```
<html xmlns="http://www.w3.org/1999/xhtml">
    <head>
        <meta http-equiv="Content-Type" content="text/html; charset=windows-
1252"></meta>
    </head>
    <body>javax.faces.application.ViewExpiredException: viewId:/input.xhtml -
View /input.xhtml could not be restored.</body>
</html>
```

3. Create a custom exception handler factory class `CustomExceptionHandlerFactory`, which extends the `ExceptionHandlerFactory` class, as shown in Figure 11.32.

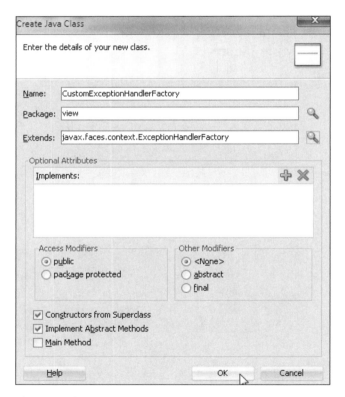

Figure 11.32
Creating the CustomExceptionHandlerFactory class.
Source: Oracle Corporation.

4. Override the `getExceptionHandler` method to return a new `CustomExceptionHandler`, which you will define later in the section. The `CustomExceptionHandlerFactory` appears in Listing 11.16.

Listing 11.16 The `CustomExceptionHandlerFactory` Class

```
package view;

import javax.faces.context.ExceptionHandler;
import javax.faces.context.ExceptionHandlerFactory;
public class CustomExceptionHandlerFactory extends ExceptionHandlerFactory {
    private ExceptionHandlerFactory factory;
    public CustomExceptionHandlerFactory(ExceptionHandlerFactory factory) {
        this.factory = factory;
    }
    @Override
    public ExceptionHandler getExceptionHandler() {
        ExceptionHandler result = factory.getExceptionHandler();
        result = new CustomExceptionHandler(result);
        return result;
    }
}
```

5. Register the `CustomExceptionHandlerFactory` in faces-config.xml with the following tag:

```
<factory>
        <exception-handler-
factory>view.CustomExceptionHandlerFactory</exception-handler-factory>
    </factory>
```

6. Create the `CustomExceptionHandler` class, which extends the `ExceptionHandlerWrapper` class, as shown in Figure 11.33.

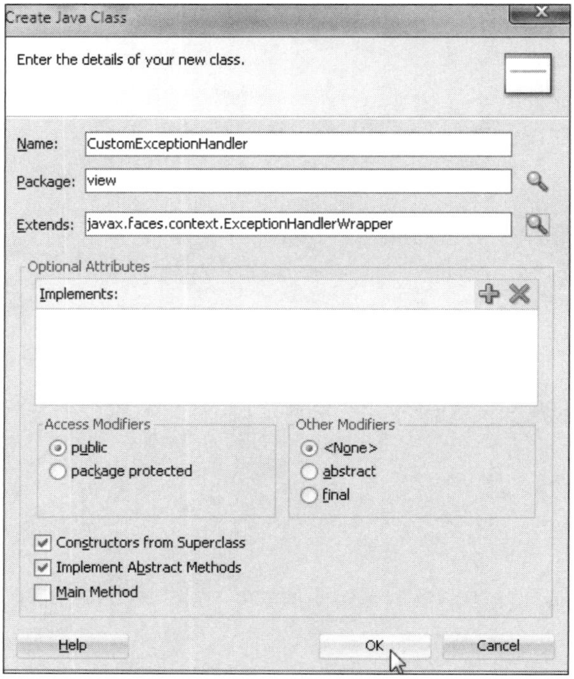

Figure 11.33
Creating the `CustomExceptionHandler` class.
Source: Oracle Corporation.

7. Override the handle method in the `CustomExceptionHandler` class. Obtain the iterator over the unhandled `ExceptionQueuedEvent`s using the `getUnhandledExceptionQueuedEvents().iterator()` method. Then, using a `for` loop, iterate over the unhandled `ExceptionQueuedEvent`s:

```
for (Iterator<ExceptionQueuedEvent> iter =
getUnhandledExceptionQueuedEvents().iterator(); iter.hasNext(); ) {
}
```

8. Obtain an `ExceptionQueuedEvent` using the `next()` method:

```
ExceptionQueuedEvent event = iter.next();
```

9. Obtain the `ExceptionQueuedEventContext` from the `ExceptionQueuedEvent` using the `getSource()` method and obtain the Throwable from the `ExceptionQueuedEventContext` using the `getException` method:

```
ExceptionQueuedEventContext context =
(ExceptionQueuedEventContext)event.getSource();
            Throwable throwable = context.getException();
```

10. The Throwable is the exception to handle. First, determine if the Throwable is an instance of the unexpected exceptions configured in web.xml. For example, determine whether the Throwable is an instance of `ViewExpiredException` as follows:

```
if (throwable instanceof ViewExpiredException) {
}
```

11. If the Throwable is an instance of one of the unexpected exceptions, output the root cause of the Throwable:

```
System.out.println("Root Cause: "+this.getRootCause(throwable));
```

12. Cast the Throwable to the type it is. For example, if the Throwable is an instance of `ViewExpiredException`, cast the Throwable to `ViewExpiredException`:

```
ViewExpiredException viewExpiredException = (ViewExpiredException)throwable;
```

13. Handle the Exception. For example, navigate to a specified view configured in the `error-page` element in web.xml using a `NavigationHandler` instance. Obtain a **NavigationHandler** as follows:

```
FacesContext facesContext = FacesContext.getCurrentInstance();
 NavigationHandler navigationHandler
=facesContext.getApplication().getNavigationHandler();
navigationHandler.handleNavigation(facesContext, null, "viewExpired");
```

14. Remove the `ExceptionQueuedEvent` from the iterator:

```
iter.remove();
```

15. Similarly handle other unexpected exceptions:

```
else if (throwable instanceof AbortProcessingException) {}
else if (throwable instanceof UndeclaredThrowableException) {}
```

The `CustomExceptionHandler` class appears in Listing 11.17.

Listing 11.17   The `CustomExceptionHandler` Class

```
package view;

import java.lang.reflect.UndeclaredThrowableException;
import java.util.Iterator;
import java.util.Map;
import javax.faces.FacesException;
import javax.faces.application.NavigationHandler;
import javax.faces.application.ViewExpiredException;
```

```java
import javax.faces.component.UIViewRoot;
import javax.faces.context.ExceptionHandler;
import javax.faces.context.ExceptionHandlerWrapper;
import javax.faces.context.FacesContext;
import javax.faces.event.AbortProcessingException;
import javax.faces.event.ExceptionQueuedEvent;
import javax.faces.event.ExceptionQueuedEventContext;
public class CustomExceptionHandler extends ExceptionHandlerWrapper {
    private ExceptionHandler wrapped;
    public CustomExceptionHandler(ExceptionHandler wrapped) {
        this.wrapped = wrapped;
    }
    @Override
    public ExceptionHandler getWrapped() {
        return this.wrapped;
    }
    @Override
    public void handle() throws FacesException {
        for (Iterator<ExceptionQueuedEvent> iter =
getUnhandledExceptionQueuedEvents().iterator(); iter.hasNext(); ) {
            ExceptionQueuedEvent event = iter.next();
            ExceptionQueuedEventContext context =
(ExceptionQueuedEventContext)event.getSource();
            Throwable throwable = context.getException();
            if (throwable instanceof ViewExpiredException) {
                System.out.println("Root Cause: "+this.getRootCause(throwable));
                ViewExpiredException viewExpiredException =
(ViewExpiredException)throwable;
                FacesContext facesContext = FacesContext.getCurrentInstance();

                NavigationHandler navigationHandler =
facesContext.getApplication().getNavigationHandler();
                try {
                    navigationHandler.handleNavigation(facesContext, null,
"viewExpired");
                    facesContext.renderResponse();
                } finally {
                    iter.remove();
                }
            } else if (throwable instanceof AbortProcessingException) {
                System.out.println("Root Cause: "+this.getRootCause(throwable));
                System.out.println(this.getRootCause(throwable));
```

```
                    AbortProcessingException abortProcessingException =
(AbortProcessingException)throwable;
                FacesContext facesContext = FacesContext.getCurrentInstance();
            // Map<String, Object> requestMap =
facesContext.getExternalContext().getRequestMap();
                NavigationHandler navigationHandler =
facesContext.getApplication().getNavigationHandler();
                try {
                    // requestMap.put("currentViewId",
abortProcessingException.getViewId());
                        navigationHandler.handleNavigation(facesContext, null,
"abortProcess");
                        facesContext.renderResponse();
                } finally {
                    iter.remove();
                }
            } else if (throwable instanceof UndeclaredThrowableException) {
                System.out.println("Root Cause: "+this.getRootCause(throwable));
                UndeclaredThrowableException undeclaredThrowableException =
(UndeclaredThrowableException)throwable;
                FacesContext facesContext = FacesContext.getCurrentInstance();
            // Map<String, Object> requestMap =
facesContext.getExternalContext().getRequestMap();
                NavigationHandler navigationHandler =
facesContext.getApplication().getNavigationHandler();
                try {
                 // requestMap.put("currentViewId",
undeclaredThrowableException.getViewId());
                        navigationHandler.handleNavigation(facesContext, null,
"undeclaredThrowable");
                        facesContext.renderResponse();
                } finally {
                    iter.remove();
                }
            }
        }
    }
    getWrapped().handle();
    }
    public Throwable getRootCause(Throwable t) {
        return t.getCause();
    }
}
```

The directory structure of the EventHandling application is shown in Figure 11.34.

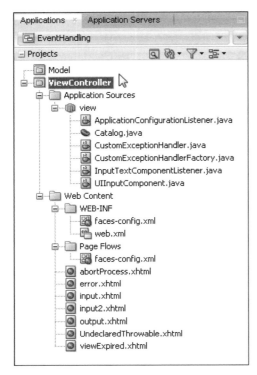

Figure 11.34
The directory structure of the EventHandling application.
Source: Oracle Corporation.

16. Redeploy the ViewHandler project to IntegratedWebLogicServer.

17. Run input.xhtml with the following URL: http:/localhost:7101/webapp1/faces/input. xhtml.

18. After the session timeout (1 minute) specified in web.xml, rerun input.xhtml. The ViewExpiredException is generated and the error page viewExpired.xhtml is rendered, as shown in Figure 11.35.

Figure 11.35
Rendering viewExpired.xhtml.

Google and the Google logo are registered trademarks of Google Inc., used with permission.

ERROR HANDLER FOR AN AJAX REQUEST

The `f:ajax` tag supports error handling, which was discussed in the "Creating an Event Handler for an Ajax Request" section earlier in this chapter. The `f:ajax` tag provides the `onerror` attribute to specify an error handler callback function. To see it in action, follow these steps:

1. Add the `onerror` handler. To do so, click within the `f:ajax` tag, click the spacebar, and select `onerror` from the list that appears.

2. Specify the `handleError` callback function in the `onerror` attribute. The `f:ajax` tag with the `onevent` and `onerror` attributes is listed here:

```
<h:inputText binding="#{catalog.inputText1}" required="true">
                <f:ajax execute="@form" event="valueChange"
render="form1:Data Table1" onerror="handleError" onevent="handleEvent"
listener="#{catalog.inputTextListener}"/>
                </h:inputText>
```

3. Add a callback JavaScript function `handleError(errorData)`:

```
function handleError(errorData) {
}
```

The types of errors that an Ajax request can generate are discussed in Table 11.13.

Table 11.13   Ajax Request Error Types

Error	Description
httpError	The request.status is one of the following: null undefined <200 >=300
serverError	The Ajax response contains an error element.
malformedXML	The Ajax response does not conform to the proper format.
emptyResponse	The Ajax response is empty or there is no Ajax response.

The errorData consists of the properties discussed in Table 11.14.

Table 11.14   Ajax Request errorData Properties

Property	Description
type	"error"
status	One of the types discussed in the previous table
description	Description of the error
source	The DOM element that generated the Ajax request
responseCode	Ajax request object status XMLHttpRequest.status
responseXML	The response XML XMLHttpRequest.responseXML
responseText	The response text XMLHttpResponse.responseTxt
errorName	The error name specified within the "error" element.
errorMessage	The error message specified within the "error" message.

4. To monitor and output error data, add <div/> elements to input2.xhtml:

```
<div id="errorType"></div>
            <div id="errorStatus"></div>
            <div id="errorSource"></div>
```

```
<div id="errorResponseCode"></div>
<div id="errorName"></div>
<div id="errorMessage"></div>
```

5. In the `handleError` function, retrieve the elements for error data and set their `innerHTML` to the `errorData` properties. The `handleError` function appears in Listing 11.18.

Listing 11.18   The `handleError` Function

```
function handleError(errorData) {
                var type = document.getElementById("errorType");
                type.innerHTML = "Error Type: " + errorData.type;
                var status = document.getElementById("errorStatus");
                status.innerHTML = "Status: " + errorData.status;
                var source = document.getElementById("errorSource");
                source.innerHTML = "Source" + errorData.source;
                var responseCode =
document.getElementById("errorResponseCode");
                responseCode.innerHTML = "Error Response Code: " +
errorData.responseCode;
                var errorName = document.getElementById("errorName");
                errorName.innerHTML = "Error Name: " + errorData.errorName;
                var errorMessage = document.getElementById("errorMessage");
                errorMessage.innerHTML = "Error Message: "
+ errorData.errorMessage;
                var xmlMessage = errorData.responseXML;
                var textMessage = errorData.responseText;

        }
```

COMMENTED OUT JSF

Prior to JSF 2.0 XML, comments, in the form `<!--` and `-->`, could be used to comment out JSF code sections. Here's an example:

```
<!-- <h:commandButton action="#{catalogBean.deleteRow}" value="Delete"/>-->
```

In JSF 2.0 and later, JSF parses EL expressions that are commented out, and the preceding commented out UI component would generate an error such as the following:

```
The class 'view.Catalog' does not have the property 'deleteRow'.
```

Several options are available to comment out JSF code sections in JSF 2.0. These include the following:

- Adding the `javax.faces.FACELETS_SKIP_COMMENTS` or `facelets.SKIP_COMMENTS` context parameter in web.xml, like so:

```
<context-param>
    <param-name>javax.faces.FACELETS_SKIP_COMMENTS</param-name>
    <param-value>true</param-value>
</context-param>
```

- Adding the JSF code section within `ui:remove`, like so:

```
<ui:remove>
<h:commandButton action="#{catalogBean.deleteRow}" value="Delete"/>
</ui:remove>
```

- Adding the - character in the EL expression, like so:

```
<!-- <h:commandButton action="#-{catalogBean.deleteRow}" value="Delete"/>-->
```

Summary

This chapter discussed the new event handling and exception handling features in JSF 2.0. It covered system event listeners and component event listeners, as well as registering them with an application. It also discussed event handling in combination with Ajax. Finally, it covered creating a custom exception handler.

INDEX

A

AbortProcessingException, 358
absolute ordering, 336
element, adding, 331
accessing flash scopes, 266
ActionController::Flash module, 266
action event, 64
action method, 25, 161
actions, deployment, 39
adding
   element, 331
  <after> element, 329
  Ajax functionality, 60–67
  attributes (Code Assist), 318
  behaviors, 253
  comments, 324, 335
  event attribute, 62, 376
  execute attribute, 62, 64
  facets, 97
  h:link tag, 217, 218
  h:outputStylesheet tag, 317
  h:outputText tag, 212
  hyperlinks, 218
  includeViewParams attribute, 219
  interfaces, 357
  Java classes, 256
  less-than (<) symbol, 331
  listener attribute, 63
  listener methods, 215
  managed beans, 23, 54, 90, 119, 243
  <name/> element, 329
  navigation case, 147
  <ordering> elements, 328
  <others/> element, 331
  outcome attribute, 218
  render attribute, 61
  resources, 318
  <system-event-listener>, 361, 362
  tags, 161
  validation, 347
    APIs, 197
    view parameters, 210–213
  validators, 211
  view parameters, 217, 228
<after> element, 329
Ajax, 5, 47
  applications, deployment, 67–73
  classpaths, 52
  components, rendering, 76–81
  directories, 59
  environment configuration, 47–48
  Facelets, formatting, 49–53
  formatting, 58–59
  functionality, adding, 60–67
  libraries, 52
  managed beans, formatting, 53–58

Ajax (*Continued*)
partial page rendering, 73–76
requests, 71
error handlers for, 395–397
formatting event handlers for, 375–384
AjaxBehavior class, 236
AjaxBehaviorEvent, 235
AjaxJSF2.0 Java EE Web application, 51
annotations
constraints, validation, 164–173
formatting, 186
implementation, 188
@ListenerFor, 372–375
@ManagedBean, 244
@Pattern, 172
managed beans, 55
ResourceHandler API, 304
scopes, 267
@Size, 166
SQL (Structured Query Language) queries, 187
APIs (application programming interfaces)
Behavior API, 236–238
packaging/rendering, 312–323
ResourceHandler, 303–305
validation, adding, 197
**ApplicationConfigurationListener class,
357, 359**
applications
Ajax
deployment, 67–73
JSF2.0 Java EE Web, 51
ClientBehaviors, 240, 242. *See also* clients
composite components, running, 102–106
configuration, 215
EventHandling, 346, 348
events, generating, 341
Facelets
deployment, 34–44
running, 44–46
Java EE Web
formatting, 15, 21
naming, 16

JDeveloper, formatting, 116–126
loading, 215
naming, 49
Navigation Web, 129
resource configuration, 325–336
ResourceHandling, 307–312
Scopes, 270. *See also* scopes
system events, 340
ViewParams, 196. *See also* view parameters
@ApplicationScoped annotation, 267
application-scoped event listeners, 356–365
Application Servers, 11
applying
client behaviors, 259–262
listener methods, 216
ManagedBean annotation, 284–285
validation, 212
attributes
Code Assist, adding, 318
definition pages, 96
event, adding, 62, 376
events, 378
execute, adding, 62
includeViewParams, adding, 219
library, 314
listener, adding, 63
name, 314
onevent, 375
outcome, 218
render, adding, 61
tags, composite components, 88
templates, 32

B
BasicTemplate.xhtml, 30
beans
managed, 22–27. *See also* managed beans
validation
custom validators with, 185–191
integration, 177–181
Behavior API, overview of, 236–238
BehaviorBase class, 236

Behavior class, 236
behaviors
  adding, 253
  classes, specifying, 253
  clients, 6, 235–236
    applying, 259–262
    Behavior API, 236–238
    configuration, 253–259
    environments, 238–239
    Facelets taglibs, 249–253
    Java EE Web applications, 239–249
    testing, 262–264
  defining, 254
  ID, specifying, 253
behavior tag, 254
binding
  composite components, 107–114
  EL expressions, 98
bookmarking
  component parameters, 222
  view parameters, 216–221
Boolean, configuration, 132
Browse Classes button, 257
build environments, 19
buttons, rendering, 216

C
cascading style sheets. *See* **CSSs**
case, adding navigation, 147
Catalog class, 24, 55
  ConfigurableNavigationHandler, 147
  managed beans, 56, 92
catalogId property, 205
<cc:attribute> tag, 96
Class Browser dialog box, 257, 357
classes
  AjaxBehavior, 236
  ApplicationConfigurationListener,
    357, 359
  Behavior, 236
  BehaviorBase, 236
  Catalog, 55

  ConfigurableNavigationHandler, 147
  Java, 24
  managed beans, 56, 92
  ComponentSystemEvent, 343
  ComponentSystemEventListener,
    343, 365, 366, 370–372
  ConfigurableNavigationHandler, 140–150
  CustomExceptionHandler, 390, 391–393
  CustomExceptionHandlerFactory, 388, 389
  CustomScopeELResolver, 296
  EL resolver, 296
  ExceptionHandler, 385
  @FacesBehavior, 237
  InputTextComponentListener, 366
  Java, adding, 256
  javax.faces.application.ViewHandler, 53
  PhaseListenerA, 326
  PhaseListenerB, 330
  PhaseListenerC, 332–333
  SystemEvent, 340
  SystemEventListener, 341, 358
  SystemEventListenerHolder, 342
  UIComponent, 344
  UIInputComponent, 373
  UIViewParameter, 206
  validation, 188
classpaths
  Ajax, 52
  validation, 155
ClientBehaviorBase class, 236, 257, 258
ClientBehavior class, 236
ClientBehaviorContext class, 237
ClientBehaviorHolder interface, 235, 236–237
client behaviors, 6, 235–236
  applying, 259–262
  Behavior API, 236–238
  configuration, 253–259
  environments, 238–239
  Facelets taglibs, 249–253
  Java EE Web applications, 239–249
  testing, 262–264
ClientBehaviors application, 240, 242

Code Assist, adding attributes, 318

collections, 6. *See also* composites

commandButton_action() method, 25, 91, 207, 215

commands, SQL, 10

comments, 397–398
  adding, 324, 335
  <ordering> element, 335

components
  Ajax, rendering, 76–81
  composite, 6
  events, registering, 365–369
  hierarchies, 2, 105
  parameters, 221–222

ComponentSystemEvent class, 343

ComponentSystemEventListener class, 343, 365, 366, 370–372

composite components, 6. *See also* components
  applications, running, 102–106
  definition page attributes, 96
  environment configuration, 84–85
  formatting, 83–84, 94–102
  Java EE Web applications, 85
  managed beans
    binding to unique properties, 107–114
    formatting, 89–93
  tags, attributes, 88
  using pages, formatting, 86–89

composition pages, formatting Facelets, 30–33

conditional navigation, 131–140
  output, 135
  rendering, 135, 137

ConfigurableNavigationHandler class, 140–150
  methods, 141
  rendering, 146

configuration, 5
  Ajax
    environments, 47–48
    managed beans, 53–58
  applications, 215, 325–336
  Boolean, 132

client behaviors, 253–259
  environments, 238–239
  Facelets taglibs, 249–253
  Java EE Web applications, 239–249

composite components, 83–84, 94–102
  environments, 84–85
  Java EE Web applications, 85
  managed beans, 89–93
  using pages, 86–89

converters, 210

EL resolver classes, 296

enhanced navigation
  conditional navigation, 131–140
  customization, 181–191
  environments, 115–116
  implicit navigation, 126–131
  Java EE Web applications, 116–126
  preemptive navigation, 140–150

enhanced validations
  bean validation integration, 177–181
  environments, 151–152
  Java EE Web applications, 152–164
  new validators, 174–176
  validation constraint annotations, 164–173

events
  environments, 344–345
  Java EE Web applications, 345–356

Facelets, 9
  composition pages, 30–33
  environments, 9–10
  managed beans, 22–27
  navigation, 34
  projects, 15–22
  templates, 27–30

files, formatting, 327

File web.xml, 121

integrated WebLogic Servers, Facelets, 11–14

managed beans, 55

scopes, 267–269, 284–287
  environments, 269–270
  Java EE Web applications, 270–284
  managed beans, 294–302

redirects, 290–293

same view with view scope, 288–290

validators, 210

view parameters

adding validation, 210–213

bookmarking, 216–221

component parameters, 221–222

environments, 194–195

GET request, 208

Java EE Web applications, 195–205

in JSF 2.0, 206–210

POST requests, 205–206

preemptive navigation, 216–221

preRenderView event, 214–216

redirects, 223–234

confirmation dialog boxes, 263

confirm tag, 261

constants, ProjectStage enum, 268

constraints

annotation validation, 164–173

bean validation, 177

@Max, 170

@Min, 170

multiple, errors, 181

converters, configuration, 210

create, read, update, and delete. *See* **CRUD**

Create Annotation dialog box, 186

Create DataTable button, 225

Create DataTable link, 227

Create Default Domain dialog box, 12

Create Deployment Profile wizard, 103

Create HTML File dialog box, 28, 94

Create Java Class dialog box, 256, 258

Create Java EE Web Application wizard, 49

Create JSF Configuration File dialog box, 327

Create Managed Bean dialog box, 23, 55, 120

createStatement method, 25

Create XML File dialog box, 250

creating. *See* **configuration; formatting**

CRUD (create, read, update, and delete), 266

CSS (cascading style sheets), 324

CustomExceptionHandler class, 390

CustomExceptionHandlerFactory class, 388

customization

bean validation, 177

enhanced navigation, 181–191

exception handlers, 384–395

scopes, 267

managed beans, 294–302

redirects, 301

validation classes, 191

WebLogic Servers, 68

@CustomScoped annotation, 267

CustomScopeELResolver class, 296

D

databases, formatting, 48

datatable:, 260

data tables

composite components, 106

custom scopes, 300

empty, 291

generating, 10, 72

grouping, 81

headers, 74

rendering, 71, 112, 173, 216

SQL queries, 45

view parameters, rendering, 208, 213

default domains, 13

DefaultServer, deployment, 129

default settings, Java, 18

defining behaviors, 254

definition pages

attributes, 96

compositeDataTable1.xhtml, 98

compositeDataTable2.xhtml, 101

formatting, 95

Delete links, 289

deleteRow method, 289

deleting rows, 290

deployment

actions, 39

Ajax applications, 67–73

composite component applications, 102–106

deployment (*Continued*)
DefaultServer, 129
Facelets, applications, 34–44
faces-config.xml deployment descriptor, 23
implicit navigation, 128
integrated WebLogic Servers, 40
profiles, naming, 35
summaries, 42
webapp1, 134
WebLogic Servers, 110
web.xml deployment descriptors, 21, 22
Deploy webapp1 dialog box, 38
Deploy webapp1 wizard, 128
dialog boxes
Class Browser, 257, 357
confirmation, 263
Create Annotation, 186
Create Default Domain, 12
Create HTML File, 28, 94
Create Java Class, 256, 258
Create JSF Configuration File, 327
Create Managed Bean, 23, 55, 120
Create XML File, 250
Deploy webapp1, 38
Edit WAR Deployment Profile Properties, 36
Insert Behavior, 253
Insert Outcome Target Hyperlink target, 217
New Gallery, 15, 34, 49
directories
Ajax, 59
conditional navigation, 139
definition pages, 95
EventHandling application, 348, 394
exception handlers, 387
image resource libraries, 314
ResourceHandling application, 309
scopes, 274
validations, 157, 190
view parameters, 201
Web Content root, 29
WEB-INF, 250
disabling validation, 168

Document Object Model. *See* **DOM**
documents, XML, 250
DOM (Document Object Model), 64
domains
formatting, 11
parameters, 13

E
EditableValueHolder, 206, 210
Edit WAR Deployment Profile Properties
dialog box, 36
elements
, 331
<after>, 329
h:dataTable, 88
, 329
, 325
<ordering>, 335
, 331
EL expressions, 87, 98, 294–301
empty data tables, 291
empty fields
preventing validation of, 168
validation, 185
empty values, 181–185
enhanced navigation, 115. *See also* **navigation**
conditional navigation, 131–140
customization, 181–191
environment configuration, 115–116
implicit navigation, 126–131
Java EE Web applications, formatting,
116–126
preemptive navigation, 140–150
enhanced validations, 151
bean validation integration, 177–181
environment configuration, 151–152
Java EE Web applications, formatting, 152–164
managed beans, 161
new validators, 174–176
validation constraint annotations, 164–173
enums, ProjectStage, 268, 285

environments
Ajax configuration, 47–48
build, 19
client behaviors, 238–239
configuration
composite components, 84–85
enhanced navigation, 115–116
enhanced validations, 151–152
events, 344–345
Facelets, 9–10
scopes, 269–270
view parameters, 194–195
resources, handling, 305–306
errors
conditional navigation, rendering, 137
handlers for Ajax requests, 395–397
messages, 167, 287, 371
multiple constraints, 181
validations, 161
error.xhtml page, 124
event attribute, adding, 62, 376
EventHandling application, 346, 348, 394
events
action, 64
AjaxBehaviorEvent, 235
application-scoped listeners, 356–365
attributes, 378
comments, 397–398
components, registering, 365–369
environments, configuration, 344–345
generating, 341
handlers, formatting for Ajax requests, 375–384
handling, 6
Java EE Web applications, 345–356
listeners, registering, 372–375
managed beans, 352
PostAddToViewEvent, 367, 369
PostConstructApplicationEvent, 364
PostRestoreStateEvent, 375
PreDestroyApplicationEvent, 365
preRenderView, 214–216
system, 339–344
valueChange, 64, 77, 81

ExceptionHandler class, 385
exceptions
AbortProcessingException, 358
comments, 397–398
handlers, customization, 384–395
handling, 6
ViewExpiredException, 386
execute attribute, adding, 62, 64
expressions
EL, 87, 98, 294–301
regular, 287, 371
extending ClientBehaviorBase class, 257

F
Facelets, 3, 7
Ajax, formatting, 49–53
applications
deployment, 34–44
running, 44–46
composition pages, formatting, 30–33
configuration, 9
environments, 9–10
integrated WebLogic Servers, 11–14
managed beans, 22–27
formatting
navigation, 34
projects, 15–22
templates, 27–30
overview of, 8–9
templates, 9
**Facelets taglibs, client behaviors,
249–253**
@FacesBehavior annotation, 268
@FacesBehavior class, 237
@FacesComponent annotation, 267
faces-config.xml deployment descriptor, 23
@FacesConverter annotation, 268
@FacesRenderer annotation, 268
@FacesValidator annotation, 268
facets, adding, 97
f:ajax tag, 76, 375
f:event tag, 370–372

fields, empty
preventing validation of, 168
validation, 185
files
Create XML File dialog box, 250
formatting
configuration, 327
HTML (Hypertext Markup Language), 87
HTML (Hypertext Markup Language), 28
templates, 9. *See also* templates
File web.xml configuration, 121
filtering SQL (Structured Query Language)
queries, 73
flash scope, 266, 290–293
folders
formatting, 316
resources, 313, 317
footers, 45
formatting. *See also* **configuration**
Ajax, managed beans, 53–58
annotations, 186
ApplicationConfigurationListener
class, 359
client behaviors, 253–259
environments, 238–239
Facelets taglibs, 249–253
Java EE Web applications, 239–249
composite components, 83–84, 94–102
environments, 84–85
Java EE Web applications, 85
managed beans, 89–93
using pages, 86–89
configuration files, 327
CustomExceptionHandler class, 390–393
databases, 48
definition pages, 95
domains, 11, 13
EL resolver classes, 296
enhanced navigation
conditional navigation, 131–140
customization, 181–191
implicit navigation, 126–131

Java EE Web applications, 116–126
preemptive navigation, 140–150
enhanced validations
bean validation integration, 177–181
environments, 151–152
Java EE Web applications, 152–164
new validators, 174–176
validation constraint annotations, 164–173
event handlers for Ajax requests, 375–384
exception handlers, 384–395
Facelets
Ajax, 49–53
composition pages, 30–33
navigation, 34
projects, 15–22
templates, 27–30
folders, 316
HTML (Hypertext Markup Language)
files, 28, 87
Java EE Web applications, 15, 21, 85
JDeveloper applications, 116–126
JSF (JavaServer Faces) pages, 58–59
managed beans, 91, 120
passwords, 12
resources, folders, 313
scopes, 267–269, 284–287
Java EE Web applications, 270–284
managed beans, 294–302
redirects, 290–293
same view with view scope, 288–290
view parameters
adding validation, 210–213
bookmarking, 216–221
component parameters, 221–222
GET request, 208
Java EE Web applications, 195–205
in JSF 2.0, 206–210
POST requests, 205–206
preemptive navigation, 216–221
preRenderView event, 214–216
redirects, 223–234
XML documents, 250

forms
    redirection, submitting, 226, 227
    view parameters, submitting, 210, 213
functionality, adding Ajax, 60–67
functions, handleError, 397
f:validateLength validator, 211
f:validateRegex validator, 174–176
f:validateRequired validator, 174–176
f:viewParam tag, 206, 229

G

generating
    data tables, 10, 72
    events, 341
getFlash() method, 266
GET request, 6
    request parameters, sending, 206
    view parameters, 208
getScript() method, 235
getter/setter methods, 161
graphics, rendering, 315
grouping
    data tables, 81
    validation, 179

H

handleError function, 397
handlers
    errors for Ajax requests, 395–397
    events, formatting for Ajax requests, 375–384
    exceptions, customization, 384–395
handling
    events, 6. *See also* events
    exceptions, 6
    resources, 5, 303
        environments, 305–306
        Java EE Web applications, 306–312
        ordering application configuration, 325–336
        packaging/rendering, 312–323
        relocating, 323–324
        rendering, 304
        ResourceHandler API, 303–305

h:body tag, 304
h:button, 216
h:commandButton tag, 260
h:dataTable elements, 88
headers, 45, 74
<head> tag, 304
h:head tag, 304
hierarchies, components, 2, 105
h:link tag, 216, 217, 218
h:outputLabel tag, 312
h:outputScript tag, 304
h:outputStylesheet tag, 304, 317
h:outputText tag, 212
HTML (Hypertext Markup Language), 28
    files, formatting, 87
    pages, 86
hyperlinks. *See also* **bookmarking**
    adding, 218
    Create DataTable link, 227
    Delete links, 289
    rendering, 216
Hypertext Markup Language. *See* **HTML**

I

images
    rendering, 323
    resource libraries, 314
implementation
    absolute ordering, 336
    annotations, 188
implicit navigation, 126–131
includeViewParams attribute, 219
input
    buttons, rendering, 111
    values, 171
InputTextComponentListener class, 366
Insert Behavior dialog box, 253
Insert Outcome Target Hyperlink target dialog box, 217, 218
integrated WebLogic Servers
    deployment, 40
    Facelets, configuration, 11–14
    redeployment, 110

integration, bean validation, 177–181
interfaces, 1. *See also* UIs
    ClientBehaviorHolder, 235
    InputTextComponentListener class, 366
    PartialStateHolder, 2
    SystemEventListener, 358

J
Java
    classes, adding, 256
    default settings, 18
Java EE Web applications
    client behaviors, 239–249
    events, 345–356
    formatting, 15, 21, 85
        enhanced navigation, 116–126
        enhanced validations, 152–164
    handling resources, 306–312
    naming, 16
    scopes, 270–284
    view parameters, 195–205
JavaServer Faces. *See* JSF
JavaServer Pages Standard Tag Library. *See* JSTL
javax.faces.application.ViewHandler
        class, 53
JDeveloper
    ApplicationConfigurationListener
        class, 359
    applications, formatting, 116–126
    pages, viewing, 89
JSF (JavaServer Faces), 1, 58–59
JSF Configuration Elements Components
        palette, 253
JSTL (JavaServer Pages Standard Tag Library), 7

L
labels, h:outputLabel tag, 312
languages
    HTML (Hypertext Markup Language), 28
    VDL (View Declaration Language), 7

less-than (<) symbol, 229, 260, 331
libraries
    Ajax, 52
    Facelets taglibs, client behaviors, 249–253
    graphics, rendering, 315
    images, 314
    JSTL (JavaServer Pages Standard Tag Library), 7
    multiple, 316
    resources, 110
    validation, 155
library attribute, 314
links, 322. *See also* hyperlinks
listener attribute, adding, 63
@ListenerFor annotation, 372–375
listeners
    methods
        adding, 215
        applying, 216
    registering, 342
        application-scoped event, 356–365
        events, 372–375
Listen Ports, 12
lists, Project Feature, 50
loading applications, 215
locations, moving resources, 323–324
logos, 322

M
ManagedBean annotation, 284–285
@ManagedBean annotation, 121, 244, 267
managed beans
    adding, 23, 54, 90, 119
    Ajax, formatting, 53–58
    annotations, 55
    Catalog class, 56, 92
    client behaviors, 243, 247
    component hierarchies, 111
    composite components
        binding to unique properties, 107–114
        formatting, 89–93
    configuration, 55
    enhanced validations, 161

events, 352
Facelets, configuration, 22–27
formatting, 91, 120
scopes, 280, 294–302
validation, 156
views
  parameters, 198–200
  scopes, 273
@ManagedProperty annotation, 267
management, application configuration,
   325–336
maps, request parameter, 205
@Max constraints, 170
memory, saving state, 2
messages
errors, 167, 287
validation, 171, 191
value validation, 166
methods
action, 25, 161
commandButton_action, 25, 91, 207, 215
ConfigurableNavigationHandler, 141
createStatement, 25
deleteRow, 289
events, generating, 341
ExceptionHandler class, 385
getFlash(), 266
getScript(), 235
getter/setter, 161
listeners
  adding, 215
  registering, 342
  unregistering, 342
NavigationCase object, 142
PartialStateHolder interfaces, 2
@PostConstruct, 369, 374
postValidationEvent, 370–372
processEvent, 367
SystemEvent class, 340
SystemEventListener class, 341
@Min constraints, 170
modules, ActionController::Flash, 266

moving resources, 323–324
multiple constraints, errors, 181
multiple libraries, 316

N

name attribute, 314
<name/> element, adding, 329
namespace tags, 9
naming
applications, 49
deployment profiles, 35
Java EE Web applications, 16
projects, 50
templates, 32
navigation, 4
case, adding, 147
Facelets, formatting, 34
preemptive, 216–221
rules, 140
views, 215
NavigationCase object, 142
Navigation Web application, 129
new features, 1–6
Ajax, 5
client behaviors, 6
composite components, 6
configuration, 5
event handling, 6
exception handling, 6
Facelets, 3
h:button, 216
h:link, 216
navigation, 4
preRenderView event, 214–216
resource handling, 5
scopes, 5, 265
state saving, 2–3
validation, 4–5
validators, 174–176
view parameters, 6
New Gallery dialog box, 15, 34, 49

none scope, 273
null outcomes, specifying, 138
null values, 181–185

O
objects, NavigationCase, 142
onevent attribute, 375
options, WebLogic Servers, 68
Oracle Database Express Edition (XE), 9. *See also*
      databases
Oracle JDeveloper 12c, 9
Oracle WebLogic Server 12c, 9
ordering
   absolute, implementation, 336
   application configuration resources, 325–336
tag, 325, 335
element, adding, 331
outcome attribute, 218
outcomes, specifying null, 138
output
   conditional navigation, 135
   implicit navigation, 131
overriding
   parameters, 221
   view parameters, 226, 232–234

P
packaging resource handling, 312–323
pages
   error.xhtml, 124
   HTML (Hypertext Markup Language), 86
   JDeveloper, viewing, 89
   JSF (JavaServer Faces), formatting, 58–59
   XHTML, 118
palettes, 253
parameters
   components, 221–222
   domains, 13
   overriding, 221
   views, 6. *See also* view parameters
partial page rendering, Ajax, 73–76
PartialStateHolder interface, 2
passwords, formatting, 12

@Pattern annotation, 172
patterns, POST/REDIRECT/GET(PRG), 290
performance, state, 2
PhaseListenerA class, 326
PhaseListenerB class, 330
PhaseListenerC class, 332–333
phase listeners, processing, 334
POJOs (plain old Java objects), 22, 24
ports, Listen Ports, 12
PostAddToViewEvent event, 367, 369
PostConstructApplicationEvent event, 364
@PostConstruct method, 369, 374
POST/REDIRECT/GET(PRG) pattern, 290
POST requests, 6, 205–206
PostRestoreStateEvent event, 375
postValidationEvent method, 370–372
PreDestroyApplicationEvent event, 365
preemptive navigation, 140–150, 216–221
preRenderView event, 214–216
processEvent method, 367
profiles
   deployment, naming, 35
   WAR Deployment, 35
Project Feature lists, 50
projects
   Facelets, formatting, 15–22
   naming, 50
   properties, 20
   selecting, 241
   ViewController, 17
ProjectStage enum, 268, 285
properties
   catalogId, 205
   projects, 20
   resultSet, 92, 278
   sqlQuery, 166
property tags, 255

Q
queries, SQL (Structured Query Language), 45
   Ajax requests, 71
   annotations, 187
   custom scopes, 300

filtering, 73
handling resources, 321
regular expressions, 371
simplified configuration of scopes, 286
submitting, 1–6, 130, 134, 291
testing client behaviors, 263

R

redeployment, integrated WebLogic Servers, 110
redirects
custom scopes, 301
flash scope, 290–293
view parameters, 223–234
redirect tag, 226
tag, 229
registering
application-scoped event listeners, 356–365
components, events, 365–369
ComponentSystemEventListener class, 370–372
events, 372–375
listeners, 342
regular expressions, 287, 371
relocating resources, 323–324
removing tags, 161
render attribute, 61
rendering
Ajax components, 76–81
buttons, 216
conditional navigation, 135, 137
ConfigurableNavigationHandler class, 146
CSS (cascading style sheets), 324
data tables, 71, 112, 173, 216
adding view parameters in redirects, 228
view parameters, 208, 213
graphics, 315
hyperlinks, 216
images, 323
input buttons, 111
partial page rendering (Ajax), 73–76
resources, 304, 312–323
view parameters, 214–216

requests
Ajax, 71
error handlers for, 395–397
formatting event handlers for, 375–384
GET, 6, 206
POST, 6, 205–206
scopes, 265
@RequestScoped annotation, 121, 267
requirements, value validation messages, 166
resolvers, EL expressions, 294–301
ResourceHandler API, 303–305, 312–323
ResourceHandling application, 307–312
resources
adding, 318
folders, 317
graphics, rendering, 315
handling, 5, 303
environments, 305–306
Java EE Web applications, 306–312
ordering application configuration, 325–336
packaging/rendering, 312–323
relocating, 323–324
ResourceHandler API, 303–305
images
libraries, 314
rendering, 323
libraries, 110
rendering, 304
restoring state, 2
resultSet property, 92, 278
rows, deleting, 290
rules, navigation, 4, 140
running
Ajax applications, 67–73
applications
composite components, 102–106
Facelets, 44–46

S

same view with view scope, 288–290
saving state, 2–3

scopes, 5, 265
  customization, 267
  directories, 274
  environment configuration, 269–270
  flash, 266
  flash, redirects, 290–293
  Java EE Web applications, 270–284
  managed beans, 280, 294–302
  none, 273
  redirects, customization, 301
  requests, 265
  same view with view scope, 288–290
  sessions, 265
  simplified configuration, 267–269, 284–287
  views, 265–266, 273
scripts, SQL, 10
selection
  datatable:, 260
  projects, 241
  <system-event-listener> tag, 361, 362
servers
  Application Servers, 11
  deployment
    DefaultServer, 129
    integrated WebLogic Servers, 40, 110
  WebLogic Servers
    configuration, 11–14
    options, 68
server-side UIs, 1. *See also* **UIs**
sessions, scopes, 265
@SessionScoped annotation, 267
simplified configuration, 267–269, 284–287
@Size annotation, 166
Source view, component hierarchies, 105
specifying
  behavior class/ID, 253
  null outcomes, 138
SQL (Structured Query Language)
  databases. *See* databases
  queries, 45
    Ajax requests, 71
    annotations, 187

  custom scopes, 300
  filtering, 73
  handling resources, 321
  regular expressions, 371
  simplified configuration of scopes, 286
  submitting, 1–6, 130, 134, 291
  testing client behaviors, 263
  scripts, 10
sqlQuery property, 166
starting
  conditional navigation, 132
  integrated WebLogic Servers, 14
state
  restoring, 2
  saving, 2–3
sub-elements, <ordering/> tag, 325
submitting
  forms
    redirection, 226, 227
    view parameters, 210, 213
  SQL queries, 1–6, 130, 134, 291
summaries, deployment, 42
symbol, less-than (<), 229, 260, 331
SystemEvent class, 340
SystemEventListener class, 341, 358
SystemEventListenerHolder class, 342
<system-event-listener> tag, 361, 362
system events, 6, 339–344, 340. *See also* **events**

T
tables, data
  generating, 10
  SQL queries, 45
tags
  adding, 161
  attributes, composite components, 88
  behavior, 254
  <cc:attribute>, 96
  confirm, 261
  Facelets, 8–9, 249–253
  f:ajax, 76, 375

f:event, 370–372
f:viewParam, 206, 229
h:body, 304
h:commandButton, 260
<head>, 304
h:head, 304
h:outputLabel, 312
h:outputScript, 304
h:outputStylesheet, 304, 317
h:outputText, 212
JSTL (JavaServer Pages Standard Tag Library), 7
namespaces, 9
, 325
property, 255
redirect, 226
, 229
removing, 161
<system-event-listener>, 361, 362
validator, 164
XML (Extensible Markup Language), 8
templates, 7
attributes, 32
Facelets, 9, 27–30
naming, 32
testing
client behaviors, 262–264
implicit navigation, 127
text, adding comments, 324
types
Ajax request error, 396
annotations, implementation, 188
@Size annotation, 166

U

UIComponent class, 2, 344
UIInputComponent class, 373
UIs (user interfaces), 1
UIViewParameter class, 206
unregistering listeners, 342
user interfaces. *See* UIs
using pages, formatting composite components, 86–89

V

validation, 4–5. *See also* enhanced validations
adding, 347
APIs (application programming interfaces), 197
applying, 212
beans, custom validators with, 185–191
classes, 188
classpaths, 155
constraint annotations, 164–173
directories, 157, 190
disabling, 168
empty fields, 185
error messages, 167, 169, 287, 371
errors, 161
grouping, 179
libraries, 155
managed beans, 156
messages, 171, 191
view parameters, 210–213
validators
adding, 211
configuration, 210
tags, 164
valueChange event, 64, 77, 81
values
empty, 181–185
input, 171
null, 181–185
validation messages, 166
VDL (View Declaration Language), 7, 84
ViewController project, 17
View Declaration Language. *See* VDL
ViewExpiredException, 386
viewing pages, JDeveloper, 89
view parameters, 6, 193–194
adding, 217
bookmarking, 216–221
component parameters, 221–222
data tables, rendering, 213
directories, 201
environment configuration, 194–195
forms, submitting, 210

view parameters (*Continued*)
GET request, 208
Java EE Web applications, 195–205
in JSF 2.0, 206–210
overriding, 226, 232–234
POST requests, 205–206
preemptive navigation, 216–221
preRenderView event, 214–216
redirects, 223–234
rendering, 214–216
validation, adding, 210–213
views
managed beans, 273
navigation, 215
scopes, 265–266
Source, component hierarchies, 105
@ViewScoped annotation, 267

W
WAR Deployment profiles, 35
webapp1, 134

Web Content root directory, 29
Web context root, specifying, 36
WEB-INF directory, 250
WebLogic Servers
configuration, 11–14
deployment, 40
options, 68
redeployment, 110
web.xml deployment descriptors, 21, 22
wizards
Create Deployment Profile, 103
Create Java EE Web Application, 49
Deploy webapp1, 128

X
XHTML (Extensible HTML), 118
XML (Extensible Markup Language)
documents, formatting, 250
tags, 8